SATSVARUPA DASA GOSWAMI

POEMS

VOLUME 9

WITH INTRODUCTORY ESSAYS
BY REV. JOHN F. ENDLER

ALSO BY SATSVARUPA DASA GOSWAMI

Srila Prabhupada Lilamrita (vols.)

Handbook for Krishna Consciousness

Readings in Vedic Literature: The Tradition Speaks for Itself

Your Ever Well Wisher

Prabhupada Nectar (vols.)

Srila Prabhupada Smaranam

Japa Reform Notebook

Qualities of Sri Krishna

Vaisnava Behavior/ The Twenty-Six Qualities of a Devotee

Japa Walks/Japa Talks

Japa Transfomations

Story of My Life (vols.)

Looking Back (vols.)

Cover by Caitanya candrodaya das
Graphics by Antonina Zelenina

SATSVARUPA DASA GOSWAMI

POEMS

A RETROSPECTIVE

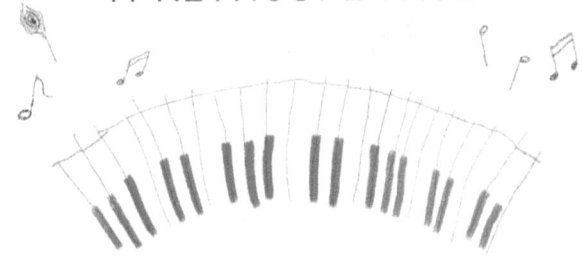

VOLUME 1

WITH INTRODUCTORY ESSAYS
BY REV. JOHN F. ENDLER

GNP 2019

ISBN-13: 978-1-942770-98-5

To His Divine Grace A.C. Bhaktivedanta Swami Prabhupada
who initiated me and thousands of young men and women into
spiritual life, and directed us into
devotional service to Lord Krishna.

Without his blessings, my life would have no meaning.

Retrospective: (from Latin *retrospectare*, "look back") When an artist is using the format of a retrospective, revisiting the entirety of his prolific, dense output over many years, displaying the evolution of his body of work.

CONTENTS

ACKNOWLEDGMENTS

Thank you all who helped.
Saci-suta (press manager and donation to print)
Caitanya Chandrodaya (layout, cover and profreading)
Antonina Zelenina (title graphics design)
Krishna Kripa (proofreading)
Guru dasa (proofreading, donation)
Nitai Gaurasundara (donation)

AUTHOR'S PREFACE

This book consists of poetry from the prose and poetry volumes of *Every Day, Just Write*. It was conceived by my friend and avid reader of my books, Rev. John Endler. He was reading the long series, *Every Day, Just Write* and he wished that the books could be more widely read and distributed. The volumes of *EJW* are available in e-book format but they don't have many readers. (So, John thought that if we just publish the poetry it would be more accessible than expecting readers to consume the entire volumes of *EJW*.) The *EJW* books were mostly written in the 1990's so they would appear new and fresh. (My poetry used to be the least popular of my writings. Readers couldn't understand them, and we sold fewer poetry books than the others. A new generation of devotees and seekers are more receptive to my poems.) John and I were excited at the prospect of publishing only the poems. He would write an introduction explaining the poems in the context of the volume of *EJW*, and I would write an introductory note. John typed the poems on a weekly basis, and we were off on a happy, new literary adventure.

Throughout a vast portion of my adult life, I have appreciated jazz, and much of my poetry has incorporated jazz style and has made references to jazz musicians. However, in the summer of 2018, I made a *vrata* (vow) that from this point on in my life I would listen only to Prabhupada *bhajans*, Vaisnava songs, and *kirtanas*. At one point I considered removing my jazz references from the poetry but my secretary, Baladeva Vidyabhusana encouraged me to keep these references because this would highlight the significance of my *vrata*.

I am seventy-nine years old, and I want to be prepared for my death. I would like to pass away hearing Prabhupada chanting "Hare Krishna" without John Coltrane at the back of my mind. That is the seriousness of my vow.

Satsvarupa dasa Goswami

INTRODUCTION

One hope animates my soul: To spend day and night singing Your holy names while living in Your divine abode. You servant Bhaktivinoda begs a place in the supremely cooling shade of Your lotus feet.

Srila Bhaktivinoda Thakura
Saranagati
Dainya
Song 6, verse 4

Beginning in 1996, Satsvarupa dasa Goswami embarked on a literary project that would encompass almost fifty volumes by the time of its completion in 1999. The series would be entitled, *Every Day, Just Write* and would yield an artistic work whose content would traverse both genre and media. From the poetic, to scriptural commentary, memoir, travel log, and illustrations, the author would reveal to the reader his expansive horizons. In these remarkable volumes, one discovers a man who is a devotee of Sri Krishna, a disciple of A.C. Bhaktivedanta Swami Prabhupada, one who is an initiating spiritual master himself, and who lives within and serves the movement founded by his spiritual master, the International Society for Krishna Consciousness (ISKCON).

Every Day, Just Write is a record of a remarkable individual who, at mid-life, seeks to discern his particular and distinctive vocation within a movement fundamentally shaped by its preaching mission. Satsvarupa Maharaja grants to the reader an intimate view upon his soul as he explores both a calling to solitude devoted to reading and chanting, and the tension that he experiences within himself, and with the broader institution to which he has devoted fifty years of his life. In a very prescient reference Satsvarupa Maharaja comments upon words of Henry David Thoreau, who once described himself as inspector of snowstorms, while he is an inspector of the heart.

This reference to Thoreau is not coincidental for I would place Satsvarupa dasa Goswami literarily within both the Transcendentalism of the nineteenth century as well as the literary modernism of the twentieth. With a keen eye toward the patterns of nature and its attendant rhythms that the careful observer discovers therein, Satsvarupa Maharaja's writing breathes the very atmosphere of the locales in which he finds himself. One is particularly struck by surprising features that he discovers in both Ireland and India. It is important to emphasize that this author's writing is fundamentally rooted in the land upon which he stands from the *tirthas* of India to the rugged coast of Ireland, and to the peaceful woods of Pennsylvania. In this regard, *Every Day, Just Write*, possesses a keen kinship with both Ralph Waldo Emerson's *Journals* and *The Maine Woods* of Thoreau.

At the same time, Satsvarupa dasa Goswami has come of age as a writer during the tumult of the twentieth century, and its diverse artistic streams course through his work. One will discover within this literary project daring and adventurous poetics that resonate with the rhythms of Thelonius Monk, John Coltrane, and Charles Mingus, musicians who stood at the forefront of an emerging and diverse movement that itself would challenge the received forms of musical composition. The startling appearance and flavors of the jazz scene would find a home within the work of Satsvarupa dasa Goswami. We move to poetics both daring and even riotous as the rhythms of these musicians so dear to this author, dazzlingly direct the cadence of this wide-ranging body of poetic achievement.

As the twentieth century gave rise to prophetic musical movements, so within literature and poetry would traditional forms and genres be challenged. In this regard, the poetry of *Every Day, Just Write* resonates with and innovates upon these new directions in the arts. From the syntactical boldness of E.E. Cummings, to the confessional work of John Berryman and Anne Sexton, and to the divergent trajectories pursued by writers such as William Carlos Williams and Joseph Brodsky, the unpredictable poetic pastiches found within Satsvarupa dasa Goswami's poetry yields what one could aptly describe as outsider art.

Artists who explore new frontiers and traverse commonly received boundaries inevitably occupy the position of the outsider. These individuals are voyagers who cross familiar lands to discover the unknown, giving to them the status of artistic, philosophical or theological outsider. This has undeniably been the experience of this writer and painter, and it is certainly the most difficult position of a religious leader. To thoroughly appreciate the poetry of *Every Day, Just Write*, the reader must keep in mind that this is the artistry of a religious leader, a devotee of Sri Krishna within the Gaudiya Vaisnava tradition. The outsider art of Satsvarupa dasa Goswami is indeed characterized by diverse currents of literature and poetry of the past two centuries. But there is a deeper and more profound stratum that finds expression in a myriad of ways, a foundation rooted in the writing and devotion of the great Vaisnava authors, delivered to the west by A.C. Bhaktivedanta Swami Prabhupada. Through his mission, the riches of this religious tradition have now been made available on a global scale.

Again and again, the reader of *Every Day, Just Write*, will meet Srila Prabhupada as both spiritual master and intimate friend and well-wisher. The reader will be introduced to the great texts and personalities of this tradition through Satsvarupa Maharaja's own reading of the magisterial *Srimad-Bhagavatam*. Ultimately, poetry will carry the reader to a transformative encounter with Sri Sri Radha-Krishna, the Supreme Personality of Godhead and His eternal consort, who is herself the reservoir of all Beauty. This writing may ultimately be considered a work of theological aesthetics in which Beauty, Truth, and Form are held as one.

This is writing delivered from the heart to the heart, a chronicle of a soul's journey through both the challenges and joys present across inner terrain as well as the world at large – in service to both *guru* and fallen souls, in that eternal quest for the love of God.

Rev. John F. Endler

CHAPTER ONE - OUR GROUP AT NILACALA

JAGANNATHA PURI, JANUARY 1–17, 1997

India's city of Puri has a long and rich tradition within the religious history of the nation. Puri is particularly significant for members of the Vaisnava tradition for here one finds the spectacular temple of Lord Jagannatha, which imparts to the city its particular character. Jagannatha is understood to be an incarnation of Sri Krishna, the Supreme Personality of Godhead. Puri's significance is further deepened for it was in this place that Sri Caitanya Mahaprabhu, himself an incarnation of Krishna, yet playing the role of a devotee, enacted a significant number of His earthly pastimes in His ecstatic devotion which drew many to Him.

It is to this place of pilgrimage that Satsvarupa dasa Goswami transports his reader in this, the fourth volume of his *Every Day, Just Write* series. In this volume we are introduced to the complexity of contemporary India. As we see in this volume Puri is a place, as Satsvarupa Maharaja describes, where both vacation goers engaged in frivolous activities and devotees on pilgrimage may be seen simultaneously.

Sitting with a small group of disciples in one of the city's hotels, Satsvarupa Maharaja will make good use of this time to read and discuss the brilliance of Krishnadasa Kaviraja's theological biography of Lord Caitanya, *Caitanya-caritamrta*. As he explores the depth of this text, Satsvarupa Maharaja will release his poetic voice to convey with an abundance of imagery, scripture, and confession his personal experience as a Vaisnava, who stands at the unique intersection between contemporary India and its devotional traditions and treasures. The author's 1987 volume, *A Visit to Jagannatha Puri* is an excellent companion to this volume of *Every Day, Just Write* because in the former volume one encounters as well a sustained meditation upon the *Caitanya-caritamrta*. The earlier volume, written in a more formal style, also offers to the reader a Puri *parikrama*, if you will, and thus provides wonderful descriptions to the significant locales of the city which form the backdrop to *Our Group at Nilacala*.

India's austerities become palpable in this writing as does the atmosphere, which breathes the presence of the merciful Lord Jagannatha, and Lord Caitanya, whose magnificent *sankirtana* movement creates a particular genealogy in whose lineage Satsvarupa Maharaja stands. Further this volume is particularly significant because within it a remarkable series of poems emerges in which the waves of Puri's seas themselves become the touchstone for meditation upon Sri Krishna and our lives before the Lord of the universe. These poems are ultimately gathered and published in a volume of their own, but here in these pages the reader is given an opportunity to witness their genesis from the heart and soul of Satsvarupa Maharaja.

As always in the work of Satsvarupa Maharaja, the practice of writing is rooted in a particular place and the characteristics of that place suffuse the language, syntax and form of the work. *Our Group at Nilacala* brings this sacred place to the reader, and it is a testament to both the spiritual depth and artistic authenticity of this author that reading itself becomes a pilgrimage for those who enter its pages.

Night notes, pink clouds, blue
clouds...
I'm only here tonight, snug night
it will be in Krishna's peaceful
harbor.
Lord Krishna, Krishna
He's the one. And then
the morning comes to take us
away.

Night notes under desk lamp
facing the lake island, I
see boats pushing off to cross
the strait. And a two-week-long guest,
a spiritual seeker, finally leaves, his
pack on his back. May he take
Krishna's names wherever he goes.

This night, facing the gingerbread-
trimmed boathouse where Abhaya
and her children live...

each day here I wrote something
except one or two days I missed.
Pinker, bluer, darker,
the water shimmering and moving, the black
Kerry cows munching in the green
until it turns all dark.

pp. 2-3

Night of the first day of year
ended,
I am here still,
still heart-beating
'tho everyone from long ago has
passed on,
gone from here but the souls leave,
the souls come back.
Hayagriva dasa gone and returned,
returned where? Are you *there*?
Are you with the Swami?
There in Goloka it is night and
day perpetually with no drag or fear
or death - all bliss in
varieties of play with Govinda.

Night notes on earth cold
first day of the year,
written down, London, 1997.
Oh, the time is arbitrarily
tracked on calendar,
Time is Krishna can't be changed,
Time is Krishna's form to
push you
every day.

Syama, Syamamayi,
Krishna and Radha's dance
beyond time – a night of *rasa*
dance is a day of
Brahma – just try to
figure it out.

You can't.
So, you say, "Night notes,"
you say prayers,

you say Hare Krishna *mantra*
while you go.
"It was nice."

pp. 16–17

Shelter

Shelter in Krishna is what I want and
to remember Him.
How? By chanting you
end the day and start the next,
long day's journey
to India. Again, I'm going
to end one life and start another.

p. 37

My Guru Maharaja

Guru Maharaja, mine and his,
you know who I mean.
Read and test and know,
understand your man.

My Guru Maharaja is
no ordinary man.
And yours?
How are you set for a leader
you can die for?
Ask me I'll tell you
about mine.
Read *sastra* and decide
and no one can tell you

Jesus Christ is yours,
or Mohammed or
Joe Blow Gurudeva.
You gotta know.

He's a devotee of Krishna, the genuine guru.
He's a dive guy. What?
He's awake but words
infringe, squeak in from the periphery. Let's hear
another few choruses from the dogs at Puri. Dovetail
their howls – Oooooooo. They wail like Lead Belly,
Blind Lemon Jefferson and company.
Oh, I gotta dog's life
he's sticking me with his thing.
Oh, I got a belly full
of puppies on the way
Ooooooo bitch
it's a dog's life,
and I don't mean in America
where I hear they pamper them.

pp. 69–70

Puri Beach
Puri beach sands and lifeguards wear
cone-shaped hats
understand they have come for fun
return to Godhead isn't so important.

In the square a new statue of
Caitanya Mahaprabhu,
He appears to have gray hair
but nice arms forward as if the
ocean is calling Him and He's running
Cataka-parvata

Each *lila* I'll speak, I'm not
important,

and they better stay awake.
Nilacala ocean filled with
Indian holidayers –
we're in this hotel room going over
His pastimes each day.

pp. 71-72

❈   ❈   ❈

Speaking
Speaking to devotees my brand
of humor and realization
Prabhupada taught me
I assimilated, I don't know
exactly what I give, but
I try
although this kid is still impure
Krishna lets His mercy
come through,
Now go on speaking, go on
speaking, Gambhira's not far away.
(Oh no?)

pp. 73-74

❈   ❈   ❈

Darker it grows
the soul is tight is eternal
can't die. Eating
evening bananas is another
chance to hear your master
lecture in '73 on surrender
to Krishna the soul is
eternal can't slay or
be slain, but his body
new he takes.

p. 74

Master, you've bound me
in a network of
lotus stems, I speak with
New York accent, you
too, in New York
you brought us
to truth – grapes you
gave me as a reward
for typing.

p. 77

The Waves at Puri
(frontispiece, The Waves at Jagannatha Puri)

The Puri waves, the Puri
    waves catch your metaphor in rise and fall of waves
on the beach. Don't go too far out. But what is the length of
each piece, chorus, stanza? It's shallow – five breaths and
two sonatas – no longer.... It's all here in trance and steno
pad. This age it's all computers, but I don't go for that....The
Puri stanzas. Roll in, in praise of Gauranga.

p. 80

(Poem 1, The Waves at Jagannatha Puri)

Of course, I'm just joshing,
the waves will sloshing bring it
all out, in the breaking wall
of water sea frothy dirty
amulets, true worth, clean...
come clean, come clean
come dirty...

I'm simply fooling,
my total seriousness
flows each wave crashes
relaxed and independent
at Puri.
Relax and brace yourself
for what's to come.

We have come here to expend pen cartridges and good karma, to spend all bad karma – all *karma*. The *nirvana* idea means cutting your throat when you're sick – cured but dead.

We live forever in Krishna. Sure hope it's so. We are here, a sample party of eleven gringos. Madhu has a green card. We have a wing to ourselves at the Birla Hotel, which is not a bad place – no smoking or meat-eating allowed, no alcohol in the rooms – and I am speaking *Caitanya-caritamrta*.

pp. 80–81

(*Poem 2, The Waves at Jagannatha Puri*)

Thunder dull caress
rumble...pauses and
hits the bosom of the earth.
The waves of Puri
the crows of Puri
Jagannatha's tongues fried
in oil or ghee,
the sugar grains, cool
A.M., and a meeting we
propose to hold each day.

Don't stop, mister. Tell of us sails at sea, of Indian lady and kid in sandy backyard of the Birla guest house, of Radha and Krishna on a swing. Permit us to read of Lord Caitanya's topmost heavenly sports. We aren't qualified to enter? Then tell us of His 48 years, the simple arithmetic – 24 years here, 24 years there, of which six are this and two are that and the last twelve.

at Gambhira – which is nearby – a small stout cell we can't enter nohow.

p. 83

✦   ✦   ✦

(*Poem 3, The Waves at Jagannatha Puri*)

> Waves at Puri. Gray sky and water
> meet. We're happy in this shelter.
> Devotee: "Amazing how we walked
> in the commotion of streets and then entered
> the peaceful atmosphere of Siddha-bakula."
> She says they will go to Tota-Gopinatha
> maybe tonight.
> Wash, wash, waves wash
> my heart. Wash, wash –
> I'll go to bed and pray for good
> dreams. But not anxiety.
> Not ready to face it as Radha
> and the *gopis* did?
> No, I want peace, he said,
> and rested his head on a too-narrow
> pillow surrounded by four walls
> of mosquito nets.
> I want *pax*.

He said, "No one can help me but those in our *sampradaya*. No one can sing to me."

"Here is a picture supposedly painted by Visakha,"

someone offered. He saw it – the portrait of Kana she showed to Radha. Charming and young, He snakebites their hearts...Waves, waves, never stop, even after I've left Puri for Vrindavana via taxi over speed bumps and to

the Indian Airlines waiting room, where I'm likely to wait through a three-hour delay for the Bhubaneswar-Delhi flight. At that time get out your violin. Let's see your inner reserve. Pace and chant the mantras and absolve. Write a hundred verses praising the Ganga?

pp. 86–87

Night
Night, our group all together
in Puri now go and rest and
God will protect you
never never forget
the Lord. I do I don't
I am a fool.
I am the *sisya*
never forget, never disobey
the rules, never go to
people who can't accept
those who love
Vishnu and Lord Caitanya
and Prabhupada.

p. 88

Jagannatha is Kind
"Jagannatha is kind to crippled devotees,"
I prayed and wrote it to Swamiji.
All right he replied, very nice.
God in *daru brahma* form –

always know He is full spirit,
not little. He comes to you
nayana-patha-gami bhavatu me
nayana-patha-gami – Srila Prabhupada told
Hayagriva to say it at the installation
in San Francisco '67.

Thanks to Jagannatha and
Swamiji for being kind.
Said Bhurijana, "There's an early Bob Dylan
song – 'Ten thousand dollars at the drop of a hat
I'd give it all gladly if I could get it back.'"
We loved those days, but these days
I seem to be too crotchety fault-finding.
And schisms! Whoever
thought it would turn out like this?
me an old feeble guy –
and so happy and more Krishna conscious than I
was and so free now to write and read
I was married and now I am free,
free as a bird
in a cage of my making.

p. 92

Compromise
Can you believe it?
Old-timer in Levis, bare chest
man, you wander by waterfront,
warehouses.
People you meet are ex-Hare Krishnas
or buried Hare Krishnas
really sad in me for Visnujana
old times of purity gone.

Man, I'm wandering, and I too am rotten and lost
I talk to a guy who vaguely remembers
me and asks, "Do you expect us
Sats, to be better? Is that

your trip?"
Hey, I'm half afraid he'll
beat me up if I tell the truth,
or the cops or Navy
or street goons,
someone bound to get you
so keep wandering as long as
you got this lucky streak
and your head isn't bashed in,
keep movin'
don't even sing,
don't chant until you
wake up from this
bad dream—you're compromised.

p. 105

Siddha-bakula going

Siddha-bakula going. I and my friends
deliver us from commotion
of streets
deliver us from notions
of our inferior status.
Ha! We are white and black
and not *brahmanas* or
Hindus of Puri.

Believe we will
go there, Prabhupada our guide
and if I can find a corner
quiet, Krishna will speak through
me and to me –
understand the holy names
learn them again
and chant, chant
chant.

pp. 106–7

(Poem 4, The Waves at Jagannatha Puri)

Waves at Puri break on shore
bathers don't go out far,
shout and jump as waves break waist high,
no bold swimmer,far-out
ladies in full bathing dress.
I watch it all from the distance of
my room, the waves come in
rows, in white splash,
thunder and shouts of feeble,
happy vacationers.
Waves of Puri break
on my head and heart –
I'm so foolish and demure
and timid (false too).
I hide from between
lines of this verse. Haridasa
Thakura was bathed here
after he died
(he reasons ill who thinks
he died).
The holy ocean,
the taxis waiting now as
we go to see
Haridasa's tomb and the ocean
never far away. I wait
for the time when I'll
return peacefully to this
room for a night's rest
and hear the soothing surf
and wake to it again.

pp. 107–8

Leaves

Leaves from Siddha-bakula, he said
it's easy to get them laminated, but
they can't last forever –
will they help you improve?
V-shaped ducks flying I miss them
at Geaglum. How many lives
can you live at once?
Either here or Geaglum or Wicklow
or some place I imagine in the
States.
Krishna. Krishna. Krishna.

p. 113

(*Poem 5, The Waves at Jagannatha Puri*)

I hear the waves at midnight when
I wake and remove earplugs. It's
music. I won't call it drums –
it thuds but reassures,
pacifies. I like it best when
no one is there shouting in
the surf. With first light
they gather and by morning they
are crowded on the winter
beach. Often, it's gray and too
cold to swim, and families or
students, in sweaters and
scarves and shawls and *cadars*
and pants and *saris* or long dresses
stand at the border beyond the wet
and watch, simply watch
the sea.

p. 115

(Poem 6, The Waves at Jagannatha Puri)

Do the waves make sense?
Do they have a message?
"If I want a message," Uncle Jim
used to say, "I'll go to Western Union."
Do the waves rhyme,
and are they on time? Yes!
And they don't come on the
shore more than they are allowed
by the Supreme.
Sometimes – rarely –
every one hundred years in some places –
He allows the waves to come up
and soak or dismantle
the beachside hotels.
Ha! Then the laugh
is on the capitalists, although poor people
also drown.

The waves pound and don't stop.
They could kill a man.
I hear them from a timid
distance. I praise their
drumming rolling qualities,
I sing of the hypnotic Supreme
the drunkenness of trance words,
the drum (admit it, it's
a sort of drum roll), a
roll call of names
of the living and the dead.
"From thence he shall judge
the living and the dead."
Just here happy with our
group in Nilacala...

pp. 115–16

Dreams

Dreams lead you nowhere
you want to go.
Really a maze, through these
buildings, lots of sex offers there.
Did you like it?
Eh? I'm a *sannyasi* not a
Senoi warrior, don't want
sex intercourse
let me tell you
my destination is Great Kills in
the dream
sex is distraction but when
I wake I ask,
"What's this Great Kills stuff? I want Krishna"
so, I go to Prabhupada and
bow down, he seems concerned and
he knows the answer.
One of these days...

p. 118

(Poem 7, *The Waves at Jagannatha Puri*)

By 4:30 A.M., long before sunrise, they
are out on the beach. A tea *walla* sets up a
bench, and they sit there facing the
ocean, twenty feet from the waves' edge,
sipping tea in glasses, huddled
in the cold, blankets, jackets
and later walking in larger groups
across the sands, not doing anything,
just walking, and when one sees a
crab they all gather around.
I like their innocent do-

nothingness, the no-ghetto-blaster mood,
the no fighting, no bikinis, no strutting,
and even though their visit is a *karmi's*
vacation, they go for a *darsana* of
Lord Jagannatha.

p.120

(Poem 8, *The Waves at Jagannatha Puri*)

Yeah, tune in, them poundin'
waves, and crows and *wallas*. "I'll have
one please," a straw basket woven and
in it Jagannatha tongues, pastries, old
sugar-crusted buns, nuts, balls with
salty sweets. You are
a rapacious one
to sing a song of ocean. Maybe
like Yeats you should lie on
a board and get your rhythms
tight and shut.

Tune in. Door shut to keep out slow-flying bugs and
mosquitoes that hide in room corners and in passport
pouches and book bags. Ah, my thoughts...the mosquitoes
warn like gentlemen, and I paw them away.

Passing on the street, a guy overheard Madhurya-
lila dasi speaking in Hindi. She was saying, "You say I
should live here, but they don't allow us to enter the
temple." At that moment, the guy passing, a perfect
stranger, says cheekily, "Maybe next time." And the man
walking beside her said that it might take three *yugas* of
rebirths before any of us can see Lord Jagannatha in the
mandira, but if Jagannatha wants, it could happen in three
days. Puffed-up Puri *pandas* and me.

pp. 120-21

(Poem 9, The Waves at Jagannatha Puri)

The waves thump and rump
and drum-roll on the beach sand
hard thigh.
Crows chorus picks at pus.
"We thank them," the ornithologist said,
"for clearing the roads of carrion."
And the drawing of happy faces
with crayons surrounding the form of
Lord Jagannatha. Ubiquitous – He's on the
motor scooters too.

I like to write and read and talk to myself (who else listens?). I feel like I am putting down another layer of clean lines and sentences whenever I write, like painting.

You know, I'm bored of the old presentations of Krishna consciousness. We saw we speak for newcomers, but I want to hear someone speak from the heart. Not something obnoxious or sentimental. It seems that when we open the floor, people immediately start complaining or talk politics or try to hurt someone with their outpouring of grief. I don't mind grief, but speak it in a way that it sounds like blues music. Speak everyone's sadness or make the Krishna conscious element so true and full of yearning and appreciation that we don't mind the pain. Don't be a twig that snaps off the Caitanya tree in the wind. Bend, be flexible, and keep going.

pp. 121–25

Indoors Man

Indoors I spend my time but
free to go out
never hardly do go out

dat's me he said, lookin'
in the mirror of
old lonely pasts when he
was a kid on sandlot baseball
field, Queens.
Oh, that's me indoors happy
when the energy flows
really. Ramesvara music,
see him free to write what comes.
Many's the time I checked
the mind
atma calls, please give us
peace. Take rest early tonight,
midnight rising
may not come,
but if I can I'll
toot my horn
in lines, poems and pictures
of brawny tan men holding
up a palanquin of
Jagannatha Swami.

p. 127

(Poem 10, *The Waves at Jagannatha Puri*)

Thud and wash. They'll
be getting up soon from their
beds, but I have a head start.
Immensity of sea is small
compared to light of Brahman
(*sastra* says, and *sastra* is all,
is mother telling us who is
father) – immensity of
sea and stars are tiny –
liquid in a cup.
Brahman is only partial

manifestation
of whole spirit
who is Krishna the inconceivable
Ashoka, Acyuta.

He is kind to the devotees revealing
Himself to you and me.
Here in Puri guest house
I tack a print of Srila Haridasa Thakura
looking at the *mandira* dome
and chanting holy names,
holy surf...

p.131

Dreams

Dreams are okay if you can use
them in a life of Krishna consciousness –
Rally around
a dream of bliss more
likely sadness –
each one has multilayers, and
you can never figure it all out they
say when you get a tingle you'll
actually know. But I want
my tingles Krishna-centered.
Dreams are far-out stories
I tell for readers
who see what I don't
and we all want.
Haribol.
Brood, man. Take rest. The waves are pounding on
the breast. You better be good. Your time runs out.

p. 132

(Poem 11, The Waves at Jagannatha Puri)

> High waves, Indian body surfers –
> afraid? Stand waist high, jump
> as it breaks, then recedes to knee high...
> The fishermen oblivious to playful pull
> on the hundreds-of-years-old ropes,
> on the boat bobbing, wildly buoyant
> the shouts reach me here.
> On my desk, assortment of Jagannatha, Subhadra,
and Baladeva cards with gold embossed decorations, ready
to be used, adored. He is ubiquitous...
> I see a Godbrother on rickshaw. I duck inside and
hide against the wall, then wash my master's clothes. We
heard of Sarvabhauma's great faith in Jagannatha *prasada*. I
don't like it much when they bring those standard hard
sweets, old and stiff. I'm such a nerd.

pp. 135–36

(Poem 12, The Waves at Jagannatha Puri)

> Vroom, room, no room
> to go – the surf rushes in.
> Die down noon coming
> shouts incomprehensible
> the splitty words the
> beach we could sit on a
> small portion of it, eleven of us
> and me in center to one side.
> I project a voice of ocean poems
> but where is Krishna in all of this?
> They have a right to know.

p. 136

(*Poem 13, The Waves at Jagannatha Puri*)

> He's in everything: Jagannatha's face,
> the jackass-neighing night,
> the Vrindavana reality,
> the criticism of the local GBC
> by the local *pandita*,
> by the paid Gambhira *panda*
> and the muscled tattoo-armed
> men, and me fleeing in a
> getaway to the rickshaw with Gambhira
> guards shouting after me, "Stand!
> Stand and fight!"
> Their voices are lost in the surf.
> The play of Indian vacationers is also lost,
> but even a little *bhakti* – never.

He gave me a wilting piece of marigold garlands from inside the Gambhira. "They were having *kirtana*. We went inside and it was all right." All right, I'll go tomorrow. Today the surf, the secular, the mundane, and remembrance of the Haridasa Thakura-bathed-in sea.

pp. 136–37

(*Poems 14, The Waves at Jagannatha Puri*)

> Wake up from dreamland and hear the
> surf of Jagannatha Puri.
> It's not the same as when I
> stayed ten years ago at the Samudra Hotel
> (when it wasn't a dump). I was
> nearest the sea, and it was romantic.
> I actually thought of Lord Caitanya
> (or is that just my imagination

making it rosy?)
I know from *Caitanya-caritamrta* on
a night of full silvery moon the
Lord dove into the sea when
Svarupa Damodara read of
Yamuna scenes in Krishna's sports.
The Lord went inward floating
to Konark in His spiritual body.
He was a *gopi-manjari* on
the Yamuna's banks watching Krishna
the blue lotus sport with the
white-lotus *gopis* laughing,
splashing water, hiding, embracing...
"Where have I been? Who brought
Me here? Did I say something humble?
I was with Krishna, but by your chanting
you took Me away."

Stop and hear, stop and
open ear. "Boom" it
goes, so heavy it could break
your bones and smash you
like a salamander on the hard beach. But
if you know the art, you can ride
the crest of a smooth wave.

pp. 148–49

(*Poem 15, The Waves at Jagannatha Puri*)

I know I'll be true.
the helicopter of night with light
flashing cruises down the coast ––
searching for Indira Gandhi's murderer
or Sikhs and intrigues
of politicos and Army men, drab

itchy wool platoon of
millions in tanks ready to go
over the border to China or
Pakistan if so ordered by the latest
created emergency.

Come on, man, bring your head
to sublime considerations,
like *Raga-vartma Candrika*
or the *prema-bhakti-marga,*
raga-marga-candrika prayers of the Six Goswamis.
Leave Ray Charles. Make your choice.
Hear waves and implant Lord Caitanya's
pastimes on your written page –
He bathed daily in this sea and said,
"From now on it's a *tirtha*."
Before anyone comes it's dark
and all-night pounding
"Krishna, Krishna, Krishna." The pounding
sound, our master said, is the *gopis'*
heartbeats in separation from Syama.

pp. 149–150

Rest doesn't always bring
ease I want. I wake up
foggy instead. Tag on
Sri Krishna's name, keep
going
toward afternoon, waves
wash on Sunday.

p. 154

Clothes hanging out on balconies
of Hotel Raj some hundreds
of yards from here and
frisbees have finally made it
to India.
Beep beep, Ambassador,
waves break standard anywhere,
but here you know it's
Ocean at Puri.

p. 155

Music Box
The words "music box"
drift into mind...
Jagannatha Swami calendar...
the nature of music.
You just write.

Sitting under the calendar,
seven days here
one week to go
"In case of fire, break glass."

Christ and Krishna, don't make a
fight between them.
Be yourself. I surrendered to
the guru thirty years ago.
"Oh, you must have been there
in the beginning."

pp. 156–57

✦   ✦   ✦

"Give me a little
peace," he said just when
he began hearing the *gopis*
had anything but peace and
Krishna told Arjuna, "If you don't

fight then I'd prefer you die."
"He was so dissatisfied
with Arjuna's decision,"
Prabhupada said,
strong in lecturing in
England, '73.

Master, where are you? I
ask rhetorically not expecting
an answer.
The wind rustles the page,
write while you can.

p. 157

(Poem 16, *The Waves at Jagannatha Puri*)

Night waves, blissful night waves
the frisbee-sun is down, it's dark, no boats
out there. Fishermen return to village where
they fry fish on earthen stoves and conceive
more children in pious low-caste
wives. Got to make a living, and they live
in Nilacala.

I'm a visitor here in a room all day,
but all around me on all sides I hear
wash of surf encircled in soothing
sounds. Talked with my dear old friends
Narayana K. and Bala of old times, washing
our sores, admitting our wrongs and the
wrongs of the system, forgiving,
seeing the good –
eternal in service wrought.

What do I want to say, to be? To rise at midnight and
read of Lord Caitanya dancing and chanting and preparing
myself to share it. A devotee tells me he wants to serve
Radha and Krishna, but I can't breathe a word of this to

others. I don't know. I just drink thin milk (from poor cows?) and squeeze some thin Indian honey (from poor bees?) into it. I'm on top of the ladder of species, a rich human being from America, but still I'm ignorant of the soul and find fault. I want to rocket somewhere, but have to crawl, be patient, so I look forward to dreams and writing and clues and waking to hear the surf.

It's all phony. I don't care about anything except getting something done, leaving something, and playing and wishing I could but knowing I can't enter genuine prayer. Ocean, ecstasy, steadiness, no rancor. I have to pass tests, not get left behind, not fall down or disappoint. Can you hear me, Ocean?

pp. 157-58

(Poem 17, *The Waves at Jagannatha Puri*)

I wake thinking, "Now hear the surf.
Open your ears to . . . " –
the thuds and boom remind
me of women slapping laundry
on the riverbank. This
is Nature's all-night work,
God behind it remotely.
Work of ocean you can't
understand. Why the ocean?

So big yet these oceans are just
full teacups floating
on planets in outer space.
Here I am on the shore of one.
My soul a tiny spark of God's
immensity. Scratch your pen,
connect. It's God
Himself and service to His
devotees headed by Radharani
whom we are urged to know –
beyond *aisvarya*. Remember?
Prabhupada is teaching you;

listen to the surf
and get up and chant.

pp. 164–65

Milk Worm

Milk worm I never
heard of but I like it
when
I, me, the servant
draws without caring how
it will
look
for observer.

Krishna Krishna, I love
to draw in His name and form
whenever I can, but
He's there anyway in
all energies...
My truth is yours –
we're all part and parcel,
one Supreme.
color and
form pour out
of hands like words,
"Krishna" is best of all
to cry out at death
with knowledge and pleading
for devotional service life after life.

pp. 167–68

Many Lives

Many lives both you and I
Arjuna, we've had, but

never can you remember them,
although I do.
Yes, Arjuna knew it too by
His grace.

Love to be there one day
but so far I struggle
for strength each day –
I want to be a devotee,
make a beeline to His lotus feet,
but ecstasies must be paid for,
samadhi is no joke.

p. 179

(*Poem 18, The Waves at Jagannatha Puri*)

Waves long rhythm
dithyramb, the shouts reached
a high peak at noon.
What's that? I look out,
some dark jokers in rubber tubes
a little further out and a line
of shouting timid surf riders.
I like it better at night and
overnight at 1:00, 2:00, 3:00 A.M.
they've got bright lights on
towers to keep the beach crime-free.
But it's a crime they
don't come here to remember Sri
Krishna Caitanya Mahaprabhu,
a crime the sellers and dogs litter
and they don't let us into the temple,
it's a crime
that I complain
and waste time.

Pinch me a little and I howl,
can't hear myself think,
sink. The surfers here don't
risk drowning and neither do I.
Nothing ventured...

I know it's eternal
the washing in tide,
waves
touch and withdraw undertow.
I dreamt of my master.
He was holding a special
class to teach pottery...
these things are my own...
but the ocean is everyone's –
everyone's Lord Caitanya,
I speak a salty drop
of ocean chanting.

pp. 179-80

❊   ❊   ❊

(Poem 19, *The Waves at Jagannatha Puri*)

Night at Puri is blessed, we're
in a sheltered place, can rest hearing
God's waves the soothing
nature ocean without
much interference of people
and their horns and voices straining.

The planet bends
around in a circle and all along
the ocean edge the water froths and
spills upon beaches beyond our sight.
At midnight where is the moon?
The air is blowing. A bird calls.

People quiet down,
I drift away in
sleep in my own room, sleep
under nets, and dream of devotees...

I am not yet
at the pure, advanced stage where
I see Krishna, but
I go to sleep happy to wake
and hear.

p. 185

(*Poem 20, The Waves at Jagannatha Puri*)

Geaglum's far away. Madhu pacing
outside the hotel rooms in an open
air space. Below in the dark gardens, Rama-raya
paces. I go out there awhile, pacing and fingering
beads as they do. Is any one of us praying?
Is a *bhakta* praying at Bhaktivedanta Manor
as he goes around the bend like a racing horse,
trampling over the creaking temple room boards
in *japa* circumambulation?

The waves' noise. When I woke
it seemed so loud I thought it was
a nearby dock and we'd better clear out
of here before the tide engulfs us.
I thought of the Staten Island Ferry, the way
they way they used to reverse engines and then slowly
crash into the wooden pilings and
everyone on board would be jolted forward.
Have they invented a smoother way to stop?

It was fun – the tall boards would
groan and the hold the huge ferry a moment,
then water
gush through the boards, green moss clinging,
and we would smell the salt air, hear the gulls
cry and circle.

The ocean sheets pound down in
dark in Puri.
It's not my home, but I come here
and always hear ocean and talk
about it like a broken record
wherever I go.
"Have you heard the waves?" Are
they coming up into our bedroom,
encroaching? Are we safe from
Nature? Oh sure, God won't
allow it to come
an inch closer than allowed. But if He
permits we will be washed away
Pralaya, destruction...
Wash, wash your heart and
soul, be washed
even while you sleep,
your dreams full
of ocean surf.

pp. 195–96

❋　　❋　　❋

Changing Mind

Change mind twice a day
hey which is it? You
are going to Vrindavana or Caribbean?
Go change – your diapers
change your mind, your seat, your
college major and girlfriend.

Each year you change your musical
tastes, but I got the same God
and guru.
My worshipable Lord is Krishna.
I believe. That's a fact.
Save me,
never mind if Narmada goes
to a *rasika* group,
deliver me back home please
I'm drunk but want to cooperate
and go to bed and rise
chanting peep! Peep! Hare Krishna.

pp. 201–2

Milk Energy
Milk is good for soul
and cow gives.
I offer it to Master

Listen, Lucretius doesn't know
Krishna does, and *He* says
"I accept."

Each cup of milk is your
chance to be or not.
Drink in the right mood.
Each day.

p. 202

Raghunatha reduced his eating
God was pleased and came
to eat the rotten rice
"But who can do this?"
At least behave and
try to reduce sense grat.

p. 204

(*Poem 21, The Waves at Jagannatha Puri*)

Waves covering, enveloping,
peaceful now the day's surf
foolishness is over and the fishermen's
work is over. The sea is
by itself, washing the beach more
completely, not threatening to
flood us (although you sense
it could happen).

Waves of Puri – I stay indoors,
don't see temple or Deities
or *sadhus* with elephantiasis.
Just stay indoors and while
surf roars I speak to our group about *japa* –
how to face our lackings.
Tough guy: "No pastry puffs in
the name of *japa* notes."

But now I'm silent,
relaxed, at peace,
the night surf is on the way,
motors die down,
dogs not visible – one stout
brown one grabbed the

skinny one by the neck
in his jaws
then let him go.
I watched from the balcony.
As sky darkens,
crows stop.
"Take rest early," he advised.
Hear, hear
japa and waves
go together.

pp. 204–5

Mercy

Mercy of God will come to me
as He desires, as Gadadhara knows.
Each one has a chance.
When it comes
choose to act
receive the mercy by standing
in the right place.

p.208

(Poem 22, *The Waves at Jagannatha Puri*)

Waves sometimes sound like
wind or rain. Then I focus
and hear and recall what they are
and where I am.
Krishna-Balaram Mandir has the bell

and parrots.
Each place has a certain sound. Here it's the surf.
I'll be sorry when I leave
and can't hear the engulfing
surrounding sea.

We're going to Gambhira. There's no way I will be able to capture Lord Caitanya's mood there. The Gambhira caretakers will prevent it, and the various external conditions, and the condition of my heart. It might help if I could approach alone the way I approach little bridges on my Ireland walks. I could look down at the water, be startled by a duck scared to flight, and make little advances, meditative pauses – but there's no chance. Just to touch that place will be purifying. It is inexplicably deep.

pp. 212–13, 215–16

(Poem 23, *The Waves at Jagannatha Puri*)

Good-bye waves of Puri.
Old friend, I'll see you, hear
you another year.
Or not. Is this good-bye forever?
Will I meet Lord Caitanya?
Will I come back to visit the
Gambhira as an outsider
again, in my next life?
Be kind, be kind, Raghunatha
Gosvami prayed to Radha and Krishna.
They're kind, he knows.
But he prays for more mercy.
Eternal good-bye and return...

A generator motor is drowning out
my last chance
to hear Puri's waves,

but they pound anyway
and the fishermen with practiced eyes
extract fish from the sea.
In my eye, I see the V-line of ducks
over Geaglum.

End this poem to waves.
Your literate nice sayings I don't
deny you, but they're no
surf. They're your expression
of what can't be said.
The waves say it.

pp. 224–25

CHAPTER TWO - ROOM 42

VRINDAVANA, JANUARY 17–FEBRUARY 9, 1997

Room 42 is the room in the Guest House of Krishna Balaram Mandir where SDG always stayed in his annual pilgrimage to Vrindavana. It had a large open space, and an adjoining screened-in porch. From the porch you could see the trees below, the parrots flying from the branches, the monkeys scampering on the buildings, and the devotees walking back and forth on the campus. For SDG it was a home away from home, and he mostly stayed there, not venturing out on parikrama.

From Puri, Satsvarupa dasa Goswami travels to the city of Vrindavana, the place where Sri Krishna performed his most intimate pastimes. It is here that *Every Day, Just Write - Room 42* will be written, and more specifically in the room that Satsvarupa Maharaja describes above. Though he will not venture far from Room 42, still the author will write:

> Vrindavana is out there and also
> in this room
> as much as I can comprehend.
>
> *p. 27*

The poetry of this volume is infused with the atmosphere of Vrindavana. *Room 42* contains a long series of "Vrinda Free-writes," addresses to Vrinda-devi, which in the dynamic poetics of Satsvarupa Maharaja's style, moves then to the horizon of the author's consciousness. These brief poems gather the author's thoughts and place them in the larger context of an appeal, exclamation, or conversation with Vrinda-devi, that wondrous gopi who arranges Radha and Krishna's pastimes. Addressing Vrinda-devi in this series of free-writes creates a mood of both immediacy and intimacy which becomes palpable to the reader.

The thematic content of this volume's poetry is seen as well with a series of poems dedicated to, or inspired by Vrindavana. These are often lyrical odes to this place and express Satsvarupa Maharaja's profound yearning to enter into the inner reality of the holy *dhama*. Further, a grouping of poems entitled, "Room 42" not only conveys the author's profound connection with Vrindavana but to this familiar room which becomes a window both upon the outer Vrindavana and the inner reality of Sri Sri Radha-Krishna.

Vrindavana is a particularly potent setting for the reading of the scriptures and the writings of the *acaryas*. Wherever Satsvarupa dasa Goswami travels, the *Srimad-Bhagavatam* will be his companion, and in this volume, the Tenth Canto is the perfect touchstone. A reference to Srila Bhaktivinoda Thakura's incomparable *Bhajana-rahasya* is another testament to the depths of this author's rootedness in the deep reservoir of texts that comprise the Gaudiya Vaisnava tradition.

For Satsvarupa Maharaja, time in Vrindavana is also marked by tension for one who is seeking to find his place within a changing religious institution. Demands upon his time tax the fragile health of the author who navigates expectations that he would fully participate in both programs and meetings, expectations, which put in stark relief his own discernment to now lead a more fully retired life. Such a life is beyond the glaring light of institutional management and leadership, and the attendant politics that shape the mood both within the Mandir and the Society at large.

Room 42 is a remarkable volume, replete with poetry that bears aloft the character of Vrindavana, both outer and inner. It is a record of one who seeks the inner life of the *dhama* through the pages of both *sastra* and the writings of the *acaryas*. As with *Our Group at Nilacala*, Satsvarupa dasa Goswami brings his reader on an intimate journey, recorded in Room 42 of the Guest House but with a horizon that extends beyond the confines of this material world. One may enter these pages and receive a glimpse of that realm where Radha and Krishna are eternally delighting in their shared pastimes.

Vrindavana Is

Vrindavana is known by the veterans who
refuse to leave, summer or winter,
I don't know
neither do I want to suffer in
body to stay here.
Don't love the lanes, residents, not
touched by particles of mercy of
attraction to Radharani's abode.
Ask me. I'll say, "Whatever is
best for headaches."

Ask me do you love
Radha's *seva*? I'll say,
No but I want to hear
Vidagdha-madhava.

p. 38

Pray: you close your eyes
and right now, what you have just read
ask Krishna to teach you
you need it.

p. 39

Vrinda Free-write #1

Vrinda's song I lay away
Radha's songs I pronounce
not allowed to speculate
damn the rockets I say
a free-write's got to
make sense.

p.47

Vrinda Free-write #2

Vrinda is Tulasi's favorite is
lore
Radha is yore and new always
not allowed to speak of Her
don't unless you are pure.
But She's *Mata-bhakti*.
Always follow your
Prabhupada even when
you're dull, dogmatic, blind,
eyesore, unclean –
clean up this place!
Clean up crude oil from Yamuna
and all will be well – you'll die entranced?
You'll die, period.
and British Airways runs on time.
It will be a rainy sad day
sun will shine despite your
death and new baby monkeys
frolic and lice pick at them and
pilgrims go to temples as usual

Into the sea,
into the Yamuna, ashes.
Don't bury me on the lone prairie
as if I was a *maha-bhag*.

pp. 47-48

I Could Do a Poem

I could do a poem on rice paper on
whatever paper was available in India.

I could get off the self-trip
the feel-sorry-for-yourself –
"I'm all alone." He dropped me saying,
"Are you going back up to your room now?"
What should I say instead?
Say, "I want to go with you,
I want to walk beside you and be
very happy as I used to be
with friends in my youth."

But it can't be.
I see from my window the eight-year-old
girls trying to be friends and play together
but they get bored with each other –
they try to invent games
to pass the time,
it doesn't work out,
they quarrel . . .

What I did last year may not
work this year. "Vrindavana is" –
you wrote and then each line came out.
But now Vrindavana is me eating pop-
corn in the brain? Just words like
porn and corn doesn't mean nonsense . . .

And when the *prema-nama* comes
when the *prema-lila* comes through
in *Vidagdha-madhava*, then you
know you're not eligible for it anyway.

Walk a few blocks around in corners in
Vrindavana, come to a one room flat of a
sadhu who's not following the *rasika sadhu*
and ask him what? Ask him
to show me the truth, press your nose
like Guru Maharaji used to do

show the gullible followers the light?
Divine Light Society.
Hit him on the head while his
eyes are closed and steal his money.

I could do a poem on rice paper he said.
I could do a poem if I were a pure devotee
or imitate Ginsberg and say
I have seen the best devotees
of my generation bloop
back into the strobe lights of *maya*.
I've seen the temple president
lock the *bhaktin* into a room,
and I have seen him run off in the snow
with the money of the temple in satchel,
I have heard the *rtviks* storm
the castle. I hear
the revolution is about to take place
they are waiting for the self-effulgent guru
he has already come here
he is this Maharaja and that one
in the holy *dhamas* . . .

I have seen the best minds of ISKCON
blooped and furry, *sannyasis* going back
into householder life,
who read *Bhagavatam* seriously
and yet fell down
but I have seen Carl Sandberg's poem –
"The women under the gas lamps
luring the farm boys"
seen the innocent ladies luring the *sannyasi*
seen the downfall, the uprise
heard the endless GBC meetings
resolving nothing really
because it's ongoing and can't be
finally resolved. Well at least for a year –

---

chalk it out and follow it,
Prabhupada said. And they
are doing their best.

But can't speak out –
"No one has a sense of humor anymore," said
the right-wing Negro radio talker
because if you make fun of a black he gets angry
it's the same with the Hare Krishna higher-ups
we all have thin skin.

pp. 56–59

❧   ❧   ❧

On the road, on the path
me and head and feet,
the feet that wore the shoes into the temple,
the head that dreamed the ramparts
spilling over with spaghetti and women, women
and your own mother attacking you
with colored pencils, they break against you
and you defend yourself
wearing Sir Lancelot armor.
And who else wants to attack you?
You defend against them all.

Yes sir it's me on the path the sandy
path being grave a little silent
walking and he's talking about how
he's gonna turn the place into heaven
have a pond in the backyard
called Radha-kunda Syama-kunda
and I can come here and write and
I'm feeling the oncoming sadness because
he has to go back to
the U.S.A. and those days are over,
so, I say, "We can meet again in U.S.A.

in Baltimore and Gita-nagari,"
but everything is changing, changing . . .
He's built a *japa-kutir* with a little
shelf like they do them, authentically
and you sit up there on thick grass mat
but no backrest and one swami said,
"Book me to use the *kutir*
on *Ekadasis* I'll do sixty-four rounds."
Boy, I thought I can't do that much
I've got no *prema-nama*, no *ruci-nama*,
got what? Offensive chanting?
I'll never live it down.

I could go there and write this
complaint, "Oh, oh, my aching ankle."
Oh, the distraction of the cricketeers
with white knee pads--I don't understand that game
oh, oh, I remember, Tommy Oakland and acorns on
Staten Island, through autumn leaves, and Edgar
Allen Poe poems and I fell out of
Tommy's car and ripped my new madras shirt
and was angry at him for being
so wild. It was a yellow car, and he
left the door open and I fell out
but lived to tell the tale in the Krishna
 consciousness Movement
where I live the retired life, I'll hurl
these accusations at me – "Why are you
not thinking constantly of Radha and
 Krishna in Vrindavana?"
You don't deserve to.

pp. 62–63

Short Lines

Reach rich widows
serve hot hannas
believe tall *sastras*
revel rascal misleaders
miss Radha and Krishna
japa your rounds.
Refuse entry to misfits
"Don't listen to helpless."
All glories to Camp Pendelton
and the recovery of my senses
sweet almond oil to you.
May Krishna give me a little
hint which way to go.

✤   ✤   ✤

Vrinda #3

Vrinda's secrets are kept from
reprobates like me unredeemed
nerds and ne'er do-wells. But
don't forget I may be better than
what actually meets the eye.
Or worse.

p. 71

Vrindavana is out there in the
temples and Govardhana Hill and
Radha-kunda in winter in
poverty and Indian language and
esoteric to me, the secrets
of Radha and Krishna – all these
are obstacles and reasons why
I'm not permitted.

p. 72

Vrinda #4
Vrinda is the *tulasi* plant?
Realize who you are. See the twig
Of Tulasi
Nevermind your foolishness
Don't ask me – I lost a shoe
outside the temple.
Ask my mother, ask Madhu
ask *sastra*, "Who is Vrinda?"

p.72

Vrinda #5
Vrinda is the way the *sadhus*
were sitting around a slow smothering fire, and
one invited my Madhu over he
sat with them but they spoke only in Hindi
he thanked them while ISKCON
sannyasis and gurus went by
with entourages and said, "What
are you doing here?" He said, "I am sitting
waiting for Satsvarupa Maharaja to
come back from his meeting with Navadvipa dasa."

pp.74-75

Vrinda #6
Vrinda this jerk is your
maidservant? No, not yet.
Really, he said you've
really got to slow down. Tell
that rickshaw *walla*, "Nyet. Nyet. Bas."
No. Ouch! Pressure points hurt
loud pain is good for you –
"Your organs are responding."
Dhanudhara Swami is here. Vrinda,
America, you grow there
too, O beloved of Krishna.

p.83

Surrender
Surrender to what happens,
Lao Tzu said, "Flow."
Unless Krishna's in the center . . .

Rasa dasa wrote me his seventeen-year-
old son was killed by train
Rasa wrote me *Litany* brought
him back.

End the day in surrender.
Never forget you're not a
special guru or Kafka
fan anymore you're
cela, sisya,
dasa
Dee Dee Dee surrendered to Prabhupada
Each one. I met Laksmimoni at
the entrance gate, said, "Hello, hello"
smiling, fadeout
like a film
fadeout,
we are all vanishing...
Bring us to master's lotus feet
or is it too late?
No! I surrender my love.

pp. 86–87

O Lord, don't let
them drop it, don't let
them drop that atom
bomb on me.
Stop it, bee bop it,
O Lord...

p. 89

Tribe Dream

Tribe sends out dreamers –
"Don't come back until you get a good one."
Recent results? They sit around
campfire and discuss them. Look for peace –
Indians, Americans, rich and poor
share their dreams. Look for wisdom.
"But it's already in the *sastras*."
Yes, but it must come through me.
Each one holds their post,
deploy, report, seek the good
of the whole.

Dreamer! We scorn them, we
practical people:
"Religious folks don't dream unless
they are pure devotees."
Each night, each sleep
another chance.
Ask your dream-self. Help me find
the deep inspirations.
May I commit myself to dreaming
even when awake –
See the dream of a Krishna conscious
world and me working for it,
dream you're serving your master,
you are with him,
he accepts you in his entourage.
Dream and act your way
back to Godhead.

pp. 94–95

55

Sublime Theater

Actors gather and
choose to work.
This group is beyond my control,
over the false-ego...
Hare Krishna, Hare Rama...
See the birth of theater,
despite the splayed out and frivolous actions,
they come together and work.
Commit themselves to art.

Oh, make it true
make it art for Krishna
make it pleasing to His Vaisnavas –
in verse, like Rupa Gosvami.
He's the best playwright,
his actors and stage of Vrindavana
may I read it again!
Oh, act it in love,
to the best audience...
Each moment in Vrindavana is precious:
I give it to you
here is the golden chance –

Theater for Krishna,
the Radha-Krishna *lila*
in the universe of Goloka –
never mind the dirt and hogs
and your own wretched surmises –
Banish it, bathe it in His perfect words,
dirty mind released.

pp. 95–96

Vrinda #7

Sitting on the porch, you're in Vrindavana.
Vrnda, save me, my head gets –
you know.
Repeat messages of Prabhupada
never tire, please bless me with that –
don't let me stray from his feet.
Prabhupada is "good enough" –
let my words help others.

p. 106

❈   ❈   ❈

Vrinda #8

Vrindavana *dhama*, damn my
hard dull *et cetera*.
Rama Rama Ramana
the words of the sense-
enjoyer can never know peace
nor soothe the hearing of
aspirant devotees.
Down we go
another one.

p. 109

❈   ❈   ❈

Vrinda #9

Vrinda I'm rising
recently at midnight
"Never fear," the Lord says.
Don't you know, I fear,
and I'm seeking solace
in Your names –
O Krishna, Lord of Vrinda.

p. 112

Vrinda #10

Vrinda, I'm so low-powered –
railroads don't know me
never make sense,
don't look behind
always wasting time.

p. 124

❀   ❀   ❀

Vrinda #11

Vrinda, there's a nice *tulasi*
house in Wicklow
really, you'd like it, kept
by Hare Krishna dasi – names
of *tulasis* like "dear to Krishna"
written on each pot.
Never missing care, the
plants thrive.
Dear Lord, please make
me a maidservant.
Always pray like
that? You don't?

p. 124

❀   ❀   ❀

In Vrindavana

Oh, the parrots are singing or
is that the crows? Yes, it's caws.
How could you mistake it?
Because you were not listening.
You are baptizing, you are
crawling low-powered,
you confess that. Oh, I am not
a harmless loser...
I don't care. Great straight now.

58

This is Vrindavana where saints live –
go out and see them carrying
just the right staff for
walking down Bhaktivedanta Marg.
Go check them out.
Bhakti-rasa dasa wandered
off the *parikrama* trail to what
looked like an ideal
little thatched roof mud-walled
village, but the young boys gathered
and stoned him! He ran away
in his bright orange Western
winter coat, and they
pursued and he felt purified.

p. 125

I looked out and saw
one *sannyasi* from South Africa
with scarf wrapped over neck and mouth
and the other eccentric one,
his eyes rolled up and
when I looked again he was asleep.
And someone asked me after the speech.
"Why did Bhaktisiddhanta Sarasvati
chastise his disciples when they didn't
give the beggar some *paisa*?"
Because they were hard-hearted.

p. 126

In Vrindavana today it's cold and
dark-skied, yesterday it was sunny –
I like the sunny days
when heart lightens, and I think okay
I'm going to make it through this one.

But I can't chant in love
or remorse, or anything.
Lord, Lord, please help me.

p.127

❧   ❧   ❧

In Vrindavana

Quiet, the bell is ringing for
noon. You just have to listen
and all Vrindavana is chiming in
even in this room.
The heater is humming quietly
sometimes the electricity cuts off –
it does it at 6 A.M. Dark breakfast
and I light the tea lamp,
and go on eating papayas
(offered of course).
And the heater cuts on,
and you remember you were dreaming,
and you awake in Vrindavana.

Oh, you wake in Vrindavana.
While I was lecturing
I noticed there was Aindra
wrapped up in woolen robes
just like the ones that Bhagavata Purana
dasa is wearing – the uniform of the
twenty-four hour *kirtaners*
My uniform is knit cap from New York,
sweatshirt from London,
wrist watch from Hong Kong.
Glider slip-on shoes from Puri
and Fix-O-dent pasted in
teeth.
from Brescia, (John Franco

put them in),
and all this paraphernalia
I'm carrying from state to state.
For me Vrindavana is just a place
in Uttar Pradesh, but if I think
that way it is one of the ten
offenses against the holy *dhama*.
I don't think that way.

pp. 128–29

I believe in the holy ghost
I believe in the forgiveness of sins
I believe in Akrura *ghat* and Tattha *ghat*
and gutty get
and the old mother who wears
saffron and plays the flute
during "Jaya Radha-Madhava."
I believe in Laksmimoni's right to be
disappointed in me for not going up to her
and saying hello.
I believe in the sands of Raman Reti.
I believe I will get out there and see it.
I believe in Abhirama's house and the reddish
flowers that grow there on the metal frame.
I believe Bhagat-ji lived there and
gave me an orange once.
I believe in Prabhupada
Who makes it all possible.

p. 129

Walk

Walking, your ankle says
okay me too in Vrinda
ban.
Always look around for

sights to treasure –
laugh while you can
stumble your mantras
you too, add to footprints,
Krishna's calling you.

p.130

* * *

Vrindavana
Vrindavana, I'm on the surface,
scratch my skin.
Rest and read and write and work in
room 42.
Never go out? I do...Walked to
within sight of Madan-mohan Mandir and turned
back with sore feet, fogged head.
Don't tell us. I will. Vrindavana is
my spiritual home. We aspire to die here.
And that will be the end of
another chapter of ISKCON when
Brahmananda, Satsvarupa, etc. finish up
the class of '66 one by one goes
(we hope) to join with Swamiji.
And Vrindavana? Oh, go there, go to Krishna
and His friends. But you
need *laulyam* and that comes after
many lives of sincere practice
with His full mercy.

p. 139

Vrindavana Is
Vrindavana is always reminding me
you'll have to die,
you bow down in his *samadhi*,
"Prabhupada," and suddenly remember
he's here, his body is buried

---

here. What does that mean?
Why do we forget it in a
haze of vague Prabhupada-isms?
Prabhupada and the temple Deities, dark
mangala-aratis in the cold,
an electrical brown-out.

In Vrindavana yesterday there was a
monkey fight – the devotees on
the ground were calling up to
the monkeys – excitement
between the species.
In the morning announcements he said,
"Beware of monkeys who steal eyeglasses
and cameras."

In Vrindavana Radha and Krishna play and
pure devotees can partake but
don't imitate. Prabhupada said
come here and then, surcharged,
go out and preach again.

Vrindavana is the place more
than any other where you can
contact Radha and Krishna.
And here I go sleepy
lie under heavy quilt and
dream – not of the perfection.
May Krishna bless me with
a drop of *hari-nama* nectar.

pp. 157-58

Vrinda #12

Vrinda, Tulasi, I saw you
one moment in the temple
in dim light your delicate
branches and leaves I didn't
have time or presence to
bow down...
release me from feeling
nowhere in Vrindavana.

I love you, Vrindavana.
When I
die, it's here I hope
and remembering Srila Prabhupada
and be born again in Vrindavana
in this world or *that*.

p. 158

Vrinda #13

Vrinda, Vrinda I can't direct this
one to you, I'm just a fellow who
met the Swami back then.
Really Vrinda, I could have
spent this day better, watered
Tulasi-devi and walked around her.
No, I didn't go to my Swami's
rooms and sit there and write.
Don't know if I'll take a pill
on that long journey...
And night is coming,
the parrots,
days running out
for another stay.

pp. 161--62

Vrindavana

Vrindavana, you are the summit
reserved for best
not allowed am I –
Don't believe you'll
be born in Krishnaloka when
you die here?
Ah, ach!
Believe it you fool. Don't
come back a monkey.
Austere I am not but hope for
a special ticket to get to
head of line.
"Not allowed – loafers
and shnobs."
Her dirt, her secrets.

p. 180

❋   ❋   ❋

Vrinda #14

Vrinda is the plant –
Tulasi and a *gopi* – she's the one
who recreates Vrindavana in pleasant
kunjas and bowers for Radha and
Krishna.
Now you know? Oh, I don't,
that ain't easy. I prefer
to eat marshes and mellows,
Wind in the Willows I saw
that book on shelf in temple president's
private home in Delhi –
intended for his kid.
Vrinda – you are all things –
but you exclude, kick out
all that falls short

of pure devotion to
Radha-Syama.

p. 181

Caw, caw
awful how you
fail to tune into Vraja
Vrinda poems calling
out from back seat of
old Studebaker and
Plymouth times and memories
crying out
Prabodhananda Sarasvati,
I know the names too...

p. 199

✧   ✧   ✧

Room 42
Room 42 is where I stay because
of headaches I get here.
Open...I'm free of them for five days
in a row. I press a button, and a bell
rings in room 41 and a lady's voice says,
"Open the door, please!" –
a source of endless jokes.

Madhu comes in, and I say I don't
like this guy, I don't care for this trip.
The fourth floor where
monkeys come down from roof.
Two monkeys, me and one at
top of stairs – in imagination I run
forward to him and he stands his ground
snarling and baring his teeth until he sees
the brick in my hand.
Land of Radha and Krishna, next
year I won't come to 42,
but I tell you

this is also a good place for
chanting
and reading *Srimad-Bhagavatam.*

pp. 205-6

Vrinda #15

Vrinda, land of trees
the forest of Vrindavana –
Ramacandra is in Ayodhya
Narayana in Vaikuntha
does and bucks hear the flute,
and here I am
dwelling in down
original mind covered.

p. 216

❊   ❊   ❊

Prabhupada Appreciation

Prabhupada, I'll tell them,
refused to compromise.
Always love him – work for it
because he saved us and we
are in debt to Hari forever.
Unless you try you'll never know.
People who daydream only
always fall back –
don't, darn it, don't
because you love to love him
serve him – he just
wants your love for Govinda.

p. 217

❊   ❊   ❊

Vrinda #16

Vrinda, I need to know more about
right tales of your glories so
I can sing these irregulars,
not leave them so empty.
Don't abandon us, dear Tulasi
you grow even in North,
asked to stay there by your devotees
who wanted
what Prabhupada said.

p. 231

Vrnda #17

He was pleased when
tulasis appeared first in Hawaii then
in a St. Louis, Missouri, attic
with fluorescent bulb through snowy winters,
even Boston, even Sweden,
barometer of devotion –
now, the twigs are dry,
don't cut, take care, let her
bloom –
Devotee's plant
connected to Radha and Krishna.

p.231

Room 42

Room 42 is where I do
open to Lord Krishna
open your heart
Madhu knocks, I unbolt the door

to 42 - a magic number?
Two is Radha and Krishna –
mind and heart
beads and hand
books and brain.

p. 232

Tulasi

Tulasi-devi, plant of Krishna
under your leaves the dirt
let's touch with our fingers
and then to our head
she's the beloved of Vraja
in service of Radha-Syama.

p. 249

Vrinda #18

Vrinda, I'm in my master's
residence room, sitting
near him. He's the master
of us devotees
ask him for direction and service.

p. 250

Krishna-nama

Krishna-nama, You're the way
realize it. I ask. I say
Krishna, Hare Krishna, words
never stop. Ask Him
actually pray, "Please help."

No, I can't do it alone

ask Gurudeva, ask Nama
may I improve? May I persist?
And when you die...
Krishna-nama.

p. 250

Be on guard for monkeys
of spit and obscene polish
get rid of all influence and
bring yourself back to *tapasya*
of digging for gems in
Bhaktivedanta Purports.
Use (I'm tellin' ya) all your
clerical tricks, study aids,
index cards, notes and whatever
to get a daily reading program
underway.
Oh, yeah.

pp. 252–53

Room 42

Room 42 is rich, but
open the door sometimes
out there beyond the screen
is the world yeah
my headaches don't allow me
to venture
forth past this door
inside plenty is here
to listen, to chant
to read of Krishna stealing
butter and the *gopis* worrying, "Is He all right?"

p. 254

Mangala-arati

Mangala, auspicious
and all I can think and feel is who is
near me, pushing me, and can I fit my
body between these two devotees?
God is here, but I'm worried
how I look before the others.
Stop pushing, all stand still,
Satsvarupa is here!
Love, *prema* escapes me.

Arati is heaven on earth
realize, spit on
your bad manners, good manners
open your mind and rise above
the petty concerns, you are
all alone, auspicious
in *darsana* of the Lord.

pp. 277–78

Room 42

Room 42 contains me.
Open the door for *prasadam*
open your eyes after sleep
my heavens...
four days, two nights
six left...
42 is 24 backwards
and 14 is a number I used
when gambling with dimes
at the wheel of fortune
in St. Clare's Church.
Did you win the Eucharist?

Naw. I won the prize for
sad
boob.
Anyway, forget all that –
from room 42 I go out
surmising
that next year
I may return to Vrindavana in
a new location.
But this one is ever dear.

p. 278

Room 42

Room alone before 9 A.M., sounds
distant. Open your mouth, shut it, *saumya*.
Open-shut case. He's a nervous
wreck. A lazy piece. Too many pies
and creams
make him burning in gut.
Four, four. Two, two, his
room number. Give up the key when
you leave in
two days plus one and a half.
Then where do you go?
When do you return?

p. 296

Vrinda #19

Vrinda I'm plumb out
realize I love Krishna
somehow
now go bathe
don't forget *tulasi*
and chant.

p.297

The Bell at Krishna-Balarama Mandir

Bell ringing 12:30, caw caw
elephant hand? No, little hand
of me
little life
little bell, moment gone
Swami, Prabhupada is in
his rooms, and I'm with him
dying – got a long (a little)
way to go. Not long now.
Hang on to the rail.
I forgive you for not braving
it to Carib this time. Go
rest and come out better for
remaining days.

p. 298

Books

Books, writing, it's okay
I go this way
open gates and write with picture
of Krishnadasa Kaviraja Gosvami on desk
and Rupa Gosvami, Krishna's
very dear devotee
sitting under Ter Kadamba
with feathered pen writing.

p. 299

Room 42

Room 42 lease up,
I signed my name in Register
O. Stephen. O Statsfer
Oh, time is up, "Time is
flying!" Madhu said.
I asked him, "*Which* time?"
Today you mean?
Or – he meant for our
stay in Vrindavana '97.

42, 42, get it?
24 backward
no more coming back
go to Vraja-loka with
Srila Prabhupada.

p. 309

Prabhupada

Phony Prabhupada lover
real one I want to be
as reader and follower
Brahmananda, Satsvarupa, '66
Hayagriva, yeah well now
Vrindavana means die and go
Prabhupada is waiting. I
always make sense but not
in this one.
Done poem done
always his *sisya*.

p. 310

Forget it Mac
he never entered
son a devotee,
father a captain dead.
Herman Melville Queg queeg.
The fourteen-year-old boy aspires to be a professional
writer. I told him about reality, hack-writing, etc.
He asked for a list of literature.
Give him this:
Sax Fifth Avenue, Joplin Gray
Zane Gray Mysterious
Ox- Bow Incident
Never-Never-Land
Sex Among the Indies
or give him the list of spiritual books, *Bible*,
Upanisads...
This will all confuse him. He could live on the dole
that change too.

You mean they will have to earn a living or turn to thievery?

You can't expect in this world that your writing will get published and earn you a living. Learn to chant and read Srila Prabhupada's books like your Dad does in his trailer-*kutir*.

pp. 323–24

CHAPTER THREE - A WRITER OF PIECES

USA, FEBRUARY 10 — MARCH 12, 1997

I discovered yesterday that I am a writer of pieces. Don't worry how the pieces will connect. Trust that they will, especially if you write often and deeply. Don't worry how this practice of "piece writing" will be published pieces. Trust that if you write some "hot" ones (and you will) they can be juxtaposed for a collection. Or some books of pieces can be published just as they are.

This discovery is a closer look at what I'm doing, seeing it on the focus of the basic element. I work in this genre, and I ought to accept myself as a writer of pieces. They run in length from one to five (or sometimes nine) pages and then stop. I rest and breathe and break in between pieces, and the reader may do so also.

Satsvarupa dasa Goswami
Part One "A Writer of Pieces"
USA, February 10–23, 1997, p. 152

The New Oxford American Dictionary provides numerous definitions of the word "piece," revealing its complexity and the broad net, which this word casts. A piece may be:

(a) a portion of an object or material produced by cutting, tearing, or breaking the whole.

(b) a written musical, artistic creation or composition.

(c) as a verb, "piece" suggests to assemble something from individual parts or to slowly make sense of something from separate facts and items of evidence.

In this sixth volume of *Every Day, Just Write, A Writer of Pieces*, one may discern the scope of this word and its varying shades of meaning. For indeed, Satsvarupa Maharaja himself understands his writing to be portions of a whole, fragments which individually point to something larger. This is inherent to the free-write medium of composition. Such writing will indeed be fragmentary for this style possesses no agenda and subsequently no planned conclusion. Rather, in free-writing, the author moves in multiple directions as he or she feels inspired or even compelled in moments of artistic urgency. This stands in stark contrast to formal styles of composition which are linear in nature.

In addition to being a portion of a larger whole, this writing is also characterized by the verbal sense of the word "piece," that is to assemble something new out of individual parts. The free-writing process precludes foreknowledge of that identity of that creation, but indeed both the author and reader come to see that something new is emerging. Literally, I would suggest that the *Every Day, Just Write* project as a whole is an assemblage of pieces, which is yielding something unique in a most dramatic fashion. The piecing together of these disparate parts is rooted in many places, from Ireland to India, to Pennsylvania, Europe, and the Caribbean. This writing is also an assemblage of the close readings of both *sastra* and the works of the Gaudiya Vaisnava *acaryas*, as well as events that are unfolding around the author. Ultimately, *A Writer of Pieces* is the assembly of a life.

The character of this life that is in this process of unfolding before the reader is that of a man pursuing the knowledge and love of God in the footsteps of his spiritual master. This is the deeper "piecing together" or assembly that the reader witnesses. This writer of pieces expresses with candor and authenticity the composition of a soul in the process of transformation by Sri Krishna, to whom Satsvarupa Maharaja has devoted himself. Our author clarifies for both himself and his reader the transcendental yearning of the eternal soul to be placed once more within the cooling shade of Sri Sri Radha-Krishna and the loving shelter which They offer. *A Writer of Pieces* expresses both the human predicament and the truth of our eternal identity, souls whom delight in the loving service of and joyful relationships with Radha and Krishna, in the beauty of Their heavenly Vrindavana.

Cain and Abel, where is the water? I need a drink.
My Lord Krishna requests
me I mean rescue me from
the jargon ocean of birth and death the real *svabhava*
the water drink willow wassal
when you can't talk straight
the brain deficient can't remember
where it left its dreams and
anyway too many, too many
better be a snowflake
capturer
and all right under the quilt-covered comforter
your life out West has a toot-toot
　　　　　while you can blow it up
I mean your life vest when the ship alights on water
747 blowing out the stomach
in time for a
less than hearty lunch but
something
something.

p. 56

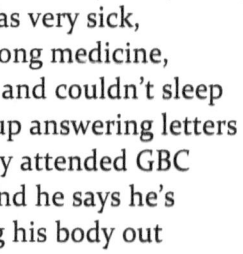

Her guru was very sick,
Dr. gave wrong medicine,
he vomited and couldn't sleep
but stayed up answering letters
and next day attended GBC
meetings, and he says he's
just wearing his body out
so he can die and meet
our master soon.
Teresa too said she wanted to die to be with Him.

p. 57

Ah you have left
provisionally
keep warm in this habit
Mayadevi, please don't
trip me up just for a little while
indulgences in my quiet
life. A man's got to...
answer his letters,
light votive candles
and chant in grief –
he is nowhere, played
out non-sorrow
non-joy, non-plus
no, no, yes...

p. 64

Krishna Krishna Krishna Hare Krishna mantra
Krishna will kill the duck
and deliver his soul into
sayujya or other *muktis*
I believe
I believe. It's true whether or not...

p. 70

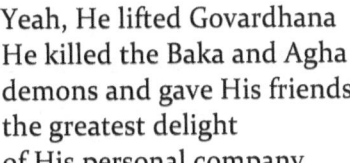

Yeah, He lifted Govardhana
He killed the Baka and Agha
demons and gave His friends
the greatest delight
of His personal company.

p. 76

Getting ready to spin the top
to smile and grin and be there
answering. "This I know –
Prabhupada said..."

p. 83

Tell us sir how you felt
tell us how to get along with
each other, to have faith in
flawed ISKCON and how to
drive a car when you are
feeling bad. And tell us,
if you don't mind,
how to believe you are
someone vital for each
one of us?

p. 83

"Have you been on a ranch or farm in the last two
weeks?"
No sir.
"Are you carrying more than 10,000 dollars in cash or
checks?
No sir.
Are you...
No sir. I am a resident of Ireland.
Are you an *avatara*?
No sir, although I have come down from the spiritual
world.

What is your view on the origin of the *jiva*?
That is not important.
And did you get a warning dream this morning?
Yes, and I will watch out for women and slugs.
What about Monk?
Which?
Which?
Thelonious.
Oh, he's okay. I guess. Fast and slow. Balliett called him, "an avant-garde Duke Ellington."
Remember Air India had *krishna-lila* as interior decor?
Yeah, that was about twenty years ago. Why mention it?
Because your brain should be like that?
You mean with pictures of Krishna sitting in the tree with *gopis'* clothing and holding
Govardhana Hill and so on?
Universal form they didn't have. (Come to kill you all.) I can't manage it all the time. But I serve Him regularly. In twenty minutes I'll do the worship of Srila Prabhupada. He is worshiper-Krishna.

pp. 102–3

Hey thanks young man
I dig you too.
Krishna should be known
in everything
but not as the god of the Hindus
or as Hare Krishna kids hustlers without
knowing depth and sweetness
infinite kindness and power
of my sweet Lord.

p. 132

Here's a riddle –
if you can't eat the tea
and spill it into the sink
then where do the rashes
come from? What's the
origin of his headaches –
and don't say liver-kidney
pancreas block – I want to
know the truth.
"You mean like he's suffering
 from disciples' sins?"
(lowercase "f")
Harry, Ned, Jim, Johnny
Nazi Swatsticker, he's suffering
the all-suffering lot
no living entities
medicine for that is
hari-nama, if not
in public (the best)
at least alone cry out for
your soul and everyone's –
huh? Possible.

pp. 132–33

(While listening to "My Favorite Things")
　　　Give your life brother and sis, it's not going to get
better, your chronic pain, but take those sun shiny days and
those musicians who quell your down-dums,
　　　　　whose chords you like to hear. Listen, bring your
best girl or friend to hear it at the Five Spot or in the hick
town Tottenville.
　　　　　He said, "I liked it." When you hear WCW it's like
a delicate ordinary voice talking seriously to his mother or
best friend and it's not "poetry" but talking, talking – yet
extraordinary.

Happy sing
they can joy jump, I don't mean the rock 'n' roll or watered down jazz I hear on airplanes.
The McCoy Tyner
Coltrane on soprano sax, Elvin in ¾ time, "My Favorite Things."
My favorite black man
my favorite leaves
squirrels
pain in subtle and gross. Don't fast or gross out or cleanse again and again. Be happy eating Anartha Ma's cooking.
I've had enough, give me some *capatis* and let me die happy in soul, jelly roll
he ain't just practicing
(Trane) he's blowing blues –
God is in all this
Love Supreme things
I know like an Indian
on that horn they play
forget it
you're in America
blow it long
wavy trill wrills
and Mrs. Leon Wilder may
not like it but I do.
Going back to that time and finding Krishna in all things. I'll find Him yet.
Now get ready to hear your Swami. That's your way too.
Sliced noodles
no salami
drew pics of fruit on walls when I was hungry. I'm not so attached to what I eat. Just go along with it.
I wanna ride with him to skies and back good old days, good days with us now – I'll take a *capati* too if you don't mind.

Play, play
play, play
gimme gimme
the way to go is here.
He keeps going, and we hope he'll make it, take us
home before too long, we had a good time Daddy.
Daddy – lead us to death and be speaking God's
Name.

pp. 140–41

My be-loved pieces
my snatches of hair I mean
of truth. My calm
old boy drawings and
walks a little longer
discover gradually your new
truth in writings keep ahead
and pray to read and chant –
and write, the big three.

p. 172

I am the pippest squeak or at least a pip squeaking through
this first movement, feeling a little redeemed to have
written my way clear of the *karmis*,
let it be said
I died a devotee-aspiring
don't know where I'll go
but stand with the theists
and scorn nasty words of
atheists. God is all.
Kyrie Eleison
Krishna is God is sweet is
known only to His pure devotees.

p. 178

(from Part Two "A Writer of Pieces" USA, February 24–
March 12, 1997)

I may want to talk with a few friends in the apartment in
Queens.
      And now fair reason,
      guts and intestines, and burps
      and reasons (again) and soul
      of wit, pit, I ask you –
      go into the other room and chant
      on your beads. It won't be
      heard on Manhattan streets, but
      if you pray nicely God
      will hear and be present and
      you can ask Him:
      please bless all sufferers,
      please inform the members
      of the Hare Krishna Movement
      of their duty.
      "Unity in chanting" advocates one
      letter-writing campaigner who says
      if we all went out chanting it would
      solve all problems. Yes but.
      Anyway
      beads count too, and
      it's what I can do. Pray
      as Prahlada Maharaja prayed, and get
      ready for your lecture stint.

p. 58

      Oh, he's an ordinary bloke
      who says he's Gurudeva, but
      we know one who's the
      real thing –
      a *maha-bhagavata,*

the prince of peace
the Lord of hosts
the everlasting Father Wonderful! Marvelous!
Yeah, he admits he's an ordinary bloke, so why is he eating so fancy?
But Prabhus, disciples, you cook and offer it to me.
Yeah, but we did it thinking you were the direct rep of God. As *sastra* says. Now we see differently. We changed our minds. You get off that fancy seat now. We no longer accept you like that.

O *brut art*, O *Srimad-Bhagavatam*, O time to pursue that study and life.
(Again) we worked for you, honored your child-like drawings, and published your poems, but what about our own poems and drawings? We too could use some encouragement and cash like that. How you squandered and took advantage of us, and lay around all day with a headache.

But –

we only gave to you because we thought you were perfect. You are not. You are human like us. Why, then, did you agree to receive such ultra honor? Why? Your books are raw art, ego too, pokey shoo.

So it goes.
I wanted to write
here it is, pokey
shoo, dreams and all, in bedroom slippers, he roams around in the room we gave him
and writes and reads and
we could too
if given the facility,
act as guru. When he –
He hardly knows much, and

what does he realize?
Even his guru said of him
"Our Satsvarupa is a
perfect gentlemen, but he
cannot manage."
He said that?
And Sats admits he sometimes doubts, dislikes what
his guru says, wants special attention, was a water rat, sulks
and pukes. He admits he can't chant *japa* worth a plugged
nickel.
So why serve him?
He's not the prince of glory
he's not the Lord of hosts
or the prince of peace. He's a scaredy-cat. A luster for
women, a weird-o poet, and we could use the dough
to print our own books
and peddle our own sonnets and live in
a house, and travel with a spouse to
India once a year.
I fear we have been misled
instead.
Let's push him into the drink
or off a cliff or at least
throw him out to chant with his dreams (with titles)
into the streets.
Ha, ha, ha, ha.

He wrote about me and said I was not steady, and
that hurt when I saw it in print. He told me
not to listen to the Beatles, but he listens to Bach and
Johnny Griffin. He spends money like water, ordered an art
shed and canceled it.
Oh, he's not the prince of peace
he heard Vivaldi
he drew crayons like a
spoiled kid and what's more –
he dreamt of a whore

---

he (censored) like a rabbit
and now just look at him,
he's trying to bury his prose.
Look at his big red nose,
toothless!
Haggard! So weak his head
aches and maybe that's from sin –
let's do him in as the *rtviks*
say. Let's go straight to Prabhupada.

Better end this now
sorrow ape,
the day is long,
is short and soon it's five
when I've got to jive behind
the low desk telling
them like a disc jockey
by impromptu words
as I play tapes of the master.

pp. 91–94

CHAPTER FOUR - SIMPLICITY IN IRISH SPRING

NORTHERN IRELAND, MARCH 12—APRIL 29, 1997

A return to Geaglum, Northern Ireland, is a homecoming of sorts for Satsvarupa dasa Goswami for this will become a setting that is both a home and place of retreat, as he seeks to fulfill his distinctive vocation of reading, chanting, and writing. Such an oasis is vitally important for one pursuing this particular path of the spiritual life while at the same team navigating the challenging roles as an initiating spiritual master and institutional leader. Geaglum will be the setting for a vast amount of the poetry that is written during the years of the *Every Day, Just Write* project, and it will provide an atmosphere conducive to the inner exploration discovered within these volumes.

The title of this volume, *Simplicity in Irish Spring,* embodies the themes and lines of flight described above. As Satsvarupa Maharaja himself writes:

> So far I am calling this volume, "Simplicity in Irish Spring." But it's more like wanna be simple but not actually able to do it. I have to be patient to overcome the jet-lag and get into an early routine again. I hope I can rise at midnight and read *Srimad-Bhagavatam.*
>
> I don't have to ask for things, they'll come my way...But try to keep cutting these things down, jettison. Aspiring for a simpler life where I concentrate on the most important things.
>
> *p. 27*

The quiet atmosphere of Satsvarupa Maharaja's living arrangement, a small house and shed, allows him to reflect on matters of heart and soul: meditation upon *Srimad-Bhagavatam*, reflections upon dreams, exploring the need of individual expression within a religious institution, and his relationship with both A. C. Bhaktivedanta Swami Prabhupada, his spiritual master, and Their Lordships, Sri Sri Radha-Govinda. This volume leads the reader inward, and the author's own explorations create a window for the reader to traverse his/her own inner terrain.

As is often characteristic of the poetry of *Every Day, Just Write*, Satsvarupa Maharaja draws upon topics and themes initially expressed in prose, which are then profoundly transformed into poetic form. Within the poetry one encounters the author's inner challenges and aspirations, devotional verse, and reflections upon his immediate surroundings and the events of the day. This verse is permeated with praise of and calls to Sri Sri Radha-Krishna. Further, his poetry is wonderfully populated with characters as diverse as the Gaudiya Vaisnava *acaryas*, writers, musicians, Godbrothers, even family members. This entire gallery of persons is ultimately gathered within the shelter offered by Srila Prabhupada, who has made this entire life possible.

How, you may ask, does of all this fit together? Often times, Satsvarupa Maharaja asks this question of himself. His wrestling with this profound issue is inherently connected to one of the underlying themes of *Every Day, Just Write*, as a whole, the struggle for individual expression within an institution that is not always understanding. Where might one find relief in this process? Again, and again, our author leads the reader to the *Srimad-Bhagavatam*, to both texts and purports which serve as a balm to the devotee. We discover in this volume that for Satsvarupa Maharaja, writing emerges from reading and chanting; this *sadhana* is the wellspring from which his writing will emerge.

O tell us sage, what's the best remedy?
I told you, man, now do it.
But sometimes we get drowsy.
Write your way out of it.
But sage, sage...
You are on your own."

p.141

Reading, chanting, writing. In the solitude of a simple
house, an even simpler shed.
Welcome to Geaglum.
Lord, make me simple
allow me to face the trials
thinking of You always
like residents of the spiritual sky.

p. 9

He writes himself, a
sure sign of false
ego. So how can he be a
pure devotee?
Who's talking?
Are *you* one?

p. 20

Be not proud
a hairy squirrel crouched in
a tree
doing the dance
St. Paddy's, St. Vitus', Vat 89 in
Trinidad, Port of Spain, Carnival time and

yearly Guinness Stout brown in the glass
I saw last night in Aer Lingus lounge,
            and now I better
get back to bed because I
feel a little twinge
behind the earnest
physical eye
and aye
Ginsburg is gone,
    his money and advice to early ISKCON with him.

p. 21

Don't disturb this man
monk, don't disturb
Susan Sontag at work
AIDS I don't know why
TB I don't know yet
Who is Vice-President of
U.S.A. in Premier
Mitterrand
of France? De Gaulle?
War? Peace, Pax
Nobel Pax winner who?
You don't even know if your
own Momma is?
You are pretty sure your Dad is
in Italy, where? In Naples?
Don't bother me I don't need
his birth town, parents' names,
twenty books on shelf
lace stuff,
need lunch plenty but
no more eating until
next morn.

p. 35

To simplify my life I seek regulation
and no more snow to shovel.
I mean it . "I'll stop thinking about dreams
even though I have given something to them
and I'll pray mantras while awake."
O Radha-ramana of Vrindavana
it won't be easy to simplify my life.

O Krishna, sometimes Your words
are stern, and I
can't change that but
Your pure devotee too is
as soft as a rose, hard as a thunderbolt. But not
with shame or dogma,
I approach You.

p. 41

Krishna is all
Krishna is God
Rama too
see silence that way
never abandon service
and you'll reach *param gati*.

p. 45

I Too Can Praise the Swami

Swami Bhaktivedanta's 1966 New York
world *sankirtana* journal has been published.
Always I want to remember
I was there and he, he was
in charge and surrendered
utterly to Krishna.

p. 57

I had a dream that I was hanging out with
          Allen Ginsberg and then
William Carlos Williams. They had me
copying out their poems. At first
I did it on a chalkboard, but then a large scroll.
Hayagriva tried it for Allen, but Hayagriva
said it couldn't be done. I did it.
Allen was getting a long poem off
I don't remember what about.
Then I was working for WCW.
I said I preferred him. "Yes," he
said, "I'm good," or something like that.
Maybe it wasn't WCW, but one of his disciples.
I said, "Everyone loves you."
Then he let me go into
a bar in Great Kills, and
I realized that I had been *cheated*.
My own writing opportunities had been lost.
By serving them, I'd gotten
nothing in return.

I have to laugh now, awake,
how the dream source made it a joke.

But it's serious too. Serve the Swami,
and don't hire yourself out
to celebrated poets.
They can't give you Krishna,
which is all I want – to serve the Swami
so that Prabhupada will give me
a tooth like he gave to Hari Sauri.
He earned that by hard endeavors late at night
massaging Prabhupada until 1 or 2 A.M.
I too can praise the Swami.

I am mentioned in Volume IV in two places
in the BBT book report sent by
Ramesvara Swami that, "*Readings in Vedic Literature*
is being published." Prabhupada made
no comment. And I'm mentioned by Harikesa
Swami who says, "Satsvarupa has written in his
Vyasa-puja homage this year some highlights
of the life of Srila Prabhupada." So
          they ask Prabhupada
to tell more.
I too...

pp. 58-60

Aches
Henry
Aiks
AIDS
Rescue the swimmer in the sea.
     Despite the lack of grateful response, the rescuer does
it anyway.
     God was kind to send His son. I dream of a balloon
with eight lights and an art studio, and me not free of
headache. Simplify your life – here comes direct sunlight
glancing too brightly into your window, hitting your
delicate eyes on March 18, *pax*, center, avert disaster, steer

this little ship.

pp. 61-62

Swami Bhaktivedanta
was the man, one, *guru*
pure devotee who came to
America the beautiful, America
the trashy, the nation divided over
Vietnam.
'Merica, my tears of thee
 I too surrender to the guru
to our shore by Sri Krishna.

p. 70

Swami is the name we called him, the title
when he appeared in our midst and we said we accept
and decide to follow you, *guru*.
At that time he accepted
me and Keith, Howard and Paul,
Joy and Judy, and Bruce Kirwan
came much later, the '70s or '80s
then was gone from sight. Hari Sauri
mined his diary and said here is the Swami again
tough, decisive, manager guru breaking the hearts
and will, hitting the opposition with
hard logic. He draws lines between
in and out and we
chose in, with him.
We didn't want to miss Krishna's heaven
or lose this valuable human form
of life. We agreed that Vyasa was true, Krishna
was truth, and allowed
Prabhupada to capture us. Simple,
a life surrendered to the master.

p. 73

O Hare is the address of the Lord
and then Rama means pleasure you don't
have to spell it out just go on chanting
and when the tape stops you can go on your own
and you eat for sense gratification that's okay
but offer it to Krishna.

Hare is the address to the Lord's Energy
and Rama is pleasure and then every
time ever fresh and Rama and Krishna
you don't have to follow any pattern,
but it's ingrained in you the mantras
scientific arrangement goes on in your
sleep you were chanting and singing with a group.
I like that too.

Don't stop for theme or method.
It is spring and very windy all night.
I didn't use earplugs
It was a bit cold so I put on more clothes
and you know the rest.
This cipher...

pp. 74–75

"Swami is the name," he said and we said, "Okay,
Swamiji too."
and Judy became his student and painted
and Paul Sherbo and Umapati and me
instead of the Swami
we called him Swamiji and bought him
turtleneck shirts on Mott Street
with stretching necks.

pp. 75–76

Maintain the body, and the
act of *vaidhi* duty, don't
invite falldown. Keep it up -
the daily *sadhana*
toward perfection you'll never
reach.
Ah, maybe...if He wills.

p. 95

Instead of *darsana* I get
doo-shan. Huh?
Never mind, you can't understand – I'm just fooling
with words.

p. 95

Had a dream
I ascended to the spiritual world by
giving up the world's
temporality?
No, but read it awake.
Bali Maharaja attaining the Lord's
eternal company. I'm on His side,
and He helps me not to commit
suicidal blunders
if I'm tempted by Satan
the Evil One. Screw it!
I mean, "Get away, Satan!"
Could say it stronger...

p. 97

Oh, chant a *lakh*
a lackaday, alas
I chant a peck and a bushel
but no amount may earn
you *krishna-prema* automatically.
"You are too restless to
chant absolutely."

p. 99

Pain, pain go away
you've got it easy I know
ugh a dug
rub-a-dub, merry Merc of May.
March winds.
Daffodils!

p. 99

Go lie down now and breathe
easy,
blankets heavy on legs.
Can't fall asleep? Anyway, rest and time passes, you'll
get up at least by 1:00 A.M. I hope and chant
your rounds with strength.
Pray for that.
This ink flows to the Don
the river, the ocean of *bhakti*. My master is there. In
gopi dress, I don't imagine.
I will get back into bed.

p. 101

Prayer

Prayer escapes me, must be for
advanced mystics and pure simple folk.
Religion is the thing they study
at the University of Vermont's Religion Department.
Remember?

Add to that prayer is the
missal book, the thoughts
for the wild horses-filled mind cannot
concentrate on prayer, St. Teresa
of Avila knew that and taught her
own conversations with God that seem to
demand you already have devotion
and you follow in her Church.

Why is prayer so hard for me?
I don't even recall that Prabhupada
wanted me to pray. But he does.
He said chant Hare Krishna, the name of God
the best prayer.
It means please let me serve You
and be active. Work hard
for the spiritual master, and
your whole life becomes prayer.

No loafing or bluffing. Arjuna
didn't sit down on the chariot long
before Krishna told him to get up
and listen to the truth.
Arjuna got the point and worked.

Prayer, prayer
where?
Every birth that you can't think of God in your mind
I don't know...

pp. 106-7

102

Dear Moony dasi,
I gotcha letter. You sure wrote a long one. It took
     time too
take it all in. Now here's what I got to say:
You be a good girl, d'ya hear?
Don't drink beer.
You got to listen to the Mick,
I mean, the Master of all.
Don't lessen your hopes,
don't prepare a hangman's noose,
just goose a juice and don't
watch old TV.
You'll be free maybe
before me
and waltz your way
into the arena
in three-quarter time.

Gee, that's no kind of responsible advice, father.
Okay. Frown. Furrow brow.
Look here, little sis or bro,
always be on time and chant and
pant and want no evil in
your short life. Do as told
by higher
authorities.
Do and don't. I like you
as you are with some
 improvements
I only hint at –
knowing you can't change your
leopard's spots
so live with it and take
this offer as sincere.

pp. 110–11

You get what you want. Want a tiger's body? Want a jiver's
body born in human life but living without Krishna
consciousness? Suffer as you choose.

> Oh, if that's the stakes
> then give me a Bengali
> right-on *bhajana*
> Hare Krishna Hare Krishna, Krishna Krishna
> Bhaktivinoda Thakura
> and all that.

p. 112

Oh, oh, open that mouth for the dentist, to put in
bread and *sabjis* and cream puffs if I could get them,
cram in a large dessert (with butter and sugar-honey),
Open that craw to say
Lord
ache
rotten mouth, he's dreaming his life remainder away.

p. 119

This, this, this
apricot
wants open mouth and
say silent top-notch
you'll be all right if
you just behave and die
in right grave. No women
or men scandals. No
Watergate Whitewater
Abscam Contra Iraqs

Jazz Bach we discovered
in his pocket a ticket
to the opera, and
false dreams and
dirty peeps
at sexy dolls
of night sleepers?

pp. 120–21

O tell us sage, what's the best remedy?
I told you, man, now do it.
But sometimes we get drowsy.
Write your way out of it.
But sage, sage...
You are on your own.

p. 141

Geaglum is gay
and also glum. They say it's a
claustrophobic community.
He doesn't want to move from one to another.
He said some people left that
tight community and improved themselves.
I don't want to judge or comment,
but since he asked me, I will say
chant Hare Krishna and if you want to
move to Dublin and stay on the dole
go ahead you're a free
man. But consider your wife and children
and somehow be part of the society of devotees
because ultimately, we're social souls.
Don't be alone

that's illusion,
and don't go with anyone else
under the apple tree
except Krishna and His devotees.

p. 153

Vrinda, you grow in
communities all over the world.
I'm your small devotee here
just spewing words
of self-interest, self-aggrandizement.
The *tulasi* leaves I don't eat,
don't like their taste, bow down
before her, and take the brass spoon and
 acamana water and put three drops
and touch her earth.
Protect this little plant.

Suzanne enters the unheated greenhouse
to care for her and pick out the bugs
and the mites and the chiggers
the delicate fragrance of
manjaris. Manjaris,
that word again. Please make me
a maidservant of the *gopis*
of Vrindavana.

pp. 154–55

Writer

Writer is funny, he works
right-on for Krishna in essays.
I tell you poems and pieces too
tell Krishna Krishna the robot speaks
sends us poems his speech end
his sweater is holey, his pipe he smoke

he has no mustache or beard or beer
or women in bed (in head?) in dreams
he is pretending to be, I mean he is
presenting himself as ideal *sannyasi* or
at least legitimate one.
"No illicit sex," he tells the householders
and *brahmacaris*. That's a heavy order.
Is he following it himself?
Writer, tell all. Never.

pp. 166–67

Dreams are for everyone but
rarely does a devotee see
Krishna face-to-face,
eh? Then shut up and don't
allow them to appear
in print.
Merrily, merrily.

Working with dreams when
oh, oh, you could be
really into Six Gosvamis
Krishna too. I hang my head
in pugnacious shame. Found
out. Scrabbled over. Got
nothing to say. Keep your
dreams to yourself.

p. 169

I was saying
the gift of the Magi
the gift of Christ,

the suffering of the stations of the Cross.
You're excluded, this is their day
for mournful repentance.
Don't imitate or deride it. They have their devotion.

You make my own act of confession,
I don't want to,
but I do love the Lord, His holy names
are one. My fault is I do not preach
with total dedication. I don't
meditate the way I should.
Of course, I'm in there trying.

pp. 192–93

Then blue ink,
believe. Going down
your page. Krishna is talking
to Brahma all the answers
in *Bhagavatam*, ten subjects
in twelve *cantos*, and this *canto*
rounding out that Krishna is
source even of Vishnu and
I believe.
I want to serve, I
want to be counted among them.
I want to lose the false self –
so many "I's." I know, all
servants of the Supreme,
servants of His servants.

pp. 199–200

Now it's time to stop if you are to start your *japa* at
1:00 A.M. And let us see if you can come back more times
today, not just to add words, yet the purpose is sometimes
not much more than spreading ink
        seeing face and hands
        not a Narcissus, so don't throw tomatoes at me.
        Krishna, I smile,
        Br'er Rabbit outfoxes the fox
        and he can go elsewhere for a meal
        while I chant Hare Krishna in my habitat,
        a writer.

p. 200

Swami

Swami, controller of the senses.
Want to be one? Can you imagine?
One guy visited our storefront in '66 and said
(he was from Canada), "I'm a swami."
We laughed, "You! A *swami*?" To us
there was only one.
Now many. You, a *swami*?

p. 222

Swami, how they love you
said the *New York Daily News*. Pictures
with him beaming and Henry Street
devotees surrounding him at JFK.
All those smiles "Kirtiraja, Bhav"
"Mr. Swami, please tell us – "
...I was in Boston.

p. 226

Sing a song the only song you know.
Patrick Ball is dedicated to
playing the Celtic harp and
you to writing the smoothest
easy flow in an
invalid life – it's not
invalid it's valid but
headachy
prone to Krishna.
This I know.

p. 229

Writing as art, as alone, as showpiece.
Brodsky with big nose
in frizzly hair and baseball jacket
is a poet of wry wit,
a formalist but confessional, a
civilized voice, they say. Very well. And me? I am a
morsel to be eaten by the demigods?
A stardust? A soul proper and soul encased.
Woolly mammoth may not have existed, have to ask
Srimad-Bhagavatam reader or Sadaputa may know. Oh, tell
me pleez
where to send my money.
Right here in my pocket will do.
Krishna and the *gopis*
Krishna and my Prabhupada. Print the essay by SDG
showing him the quiet champion, quiet for our cause, he
can lead us, so leave him alone and send fudge in the mail,
and apologies, and gather around, he can put the world at
peace and in order if we will only listen.
He didn't survive a hundred years' war, except to die
and come back.
Tinsel, tinsel, too many letters, I'm going confused.

Go ahead, man, tell it again.

This Agrani Prabhu said he will not object if I
reinitiate the lady. So, do it. I wrote to the
  disciple in England. Told him he don't love and
protect me. He said a former disciple of mine burned my
books. Burned? Not just gave away or sold? His is
inflammatory speech?

  Whereas I am quiet. I grip the pen tightly, squeeze it.
The wind howls.

  Love moment: when I pet Tilaka's long, skinny
muzzle. He looked so light and clean
  today,
  his fine white and tan fur, classic collie in North
Ireland. Barks! You walk on.

  O water of lake, heal wounds.

pp. 242–43

Swami

Surface, rats and mice not
in my kitchen.
Which or witch, he's not
afraid, Narayana *para*
devotee
makes heaven of hell.

p. 255

Prabhupada

Prabhupada! They claim allegiance
Rah! rah! Who's best?
Ask me. I'll make a fist
beat down some and
house no strangers
unless they say "Prabhupada *ki jaya*"
Please make sincere acts within and without.
Ask no one, ask yourself
do I love and serve him
always? Sometimes?
Don't indulge in breaking
those four rules!
You made your promise
 to *him*.

p. 255

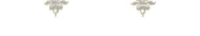

Two Holy Names

Krishna quickest *Nama*
Rama is fine
Siva too
non-name is void
alas they say it. Krishna!

Hare addresses Hara
and that's
right,
eh?

p. 256

Blow your horn

I will play a sweet pipe for Him. How do you know
it's for Him and not your own
atma? Your own daddy-
begotten ego? How do you
ever know? The guru approves
the Lord smiles,
it feels right, some Vaisnavas approve.

"You get away with
murder, you'll be chastised
for this. You will be
left behind on judgment day."
Don't play no flute around
here, they say.
But I'm reading in the shed,
got new curtains in there to
keep out bright sunlight as I
hope to play horn and keep
my eye out for intruders.

pp. 256–57

❧   ❧   ❧

Don't bother me, don't roast
me, I told you I'm reading
Vidura. Yeah? Well
let's hear somethin',
wholeness ain't a closed
circuit. Give.

p. 258

❧   ❧   ❧

Swami

Swami is a super-title, I
don't deserve it. Swimming in
ghee, you ate your Ekadasi
meal, *swami,* control
your senses and your temper,
swami,
dream,
sit up,
be a nice *swami* and now deliver
your lecture. Or are you
just a *baba-ji?*
O *swami,*
your necktie is showing and your
brahmana thread is awry.

"You're not a real *swami.*"
I'm talking about a real
swami, a devotee of Krishna
who doesn't flinch.
Where can we find such
a preceptor today?

Swami, how they love you.

p. 262

Swami, how I love you
I don't behave wrong,
Aunt Jemima sings, "Swanee"
how we love your pancakes
and Uncle Ben's rice, and
Genny warfare
and you had a rich ethnic upbringing
you are telling it as it is. The names and Studebakers

look like backwards cars in 1949 on the old highway
to Queens and Long
    Island and Brooklyn and we went
our way in our '53 Dodge, dodging
    me and sister in back seat
each looking out our own window.
Oh, sex in loins
in the night in the hair and follicles
and little kids like angels cut out
and pasted on the windows of the stores at Christmas
and days and nights
and Mommy and Daddy I didn't know
    what they did in their bedroom.
So help me God.
So help me Krishna.
Don't talk of God, Prabhupada says
"Okay, then Krishna."
No! he says. Not Krishna. Krishna is far, far away
we are just talking common sense.
You are subordinate, you have to bow
    down to someone.
Why?
Because that's your nature.
I don't agree. I think we're all spiritually equal.
That is your disease. You are thinking wrongly.
I'm thinking wrongly?
Yes.
Then how should I think?
    You are subordinate always. You have to bow down to
death, disease and old age. The thing is to find out, since
you have to bow down anyway, whom you will bow down
to, who will make you happy.

pp. 271-72

❦   ❦   ❦

Lord Krishna appeared 5,000 years ago. Go ahead, write it as an exam paper.

My sweet Lord. A fragment of your thoughts, a penny each. Peach. It's just the surface.

Words go deeper, slow down, and finally stop.

pp. 272-73

❋   ❋   ❋

The old-faced lady with
blond hair and curls
was tending to something
outside when Satsfer,
gripping blackthorn cane, ambled
by, suffering
a little in the foot and
"praying" his head
(in his own world)
would be clear enough for
an early Saturday morning speech.

p. 273

❋   ❋   ❋

Kirtana magic bliss
Did you see how Krishna acted
to convince that guy to take a
book? Did you see Radha smile
this morning during Deity greeting?
O Vrindavana, you are covered
to me because I don't try to
see under the Kali-yuga crust.
The thorn stops me, and
I never reach the rose.
Ah ugh, Aghasura,
I stub my toe and curse all
demons and temple proprietors and

beggars and rocks and too-hot
suns,
I curse the world
and wind up cursed among
the atheists.

pp. 275–76

Sarge (Bilko, Phil Silvers)
I see the miracle in a
good joke,
a 1950's TV screen lit
up black and white and
free of snow,
the Dodgers winning again,
the Nuke and
the miracle of me getting free
of illicit sex in '66,
of loaves and fishes,
of Christ risen.
Risen.

p. 276

Controversies down on us,
I want world peace and
quiet. Sit for a concert
by Madhu and some children
innocent and a book by me
bound well so it doesn't
fall apart.
The miracle of seventy-two poems
in two weeks,
of spring,
of writing coming out just
right the first time.
What more do you want?

I want
freedom from my petty desires.

Lord may demand of me,
"Now play a more active role" –
fighting for ISKCON in ISKCON.
I replied to Him even,
"I can't, Lord, I get headaches.
If you make me Superman Junior
then I could do something
for you."
He could reply, "You stay as
Tiny Tim, but still do something
wonderful, limp to the bat
and hit the home-run."
"How about a single?"
Stand up, Anu.
Gotta get down
your act
is stinkin'
in the Line.

Is writhing in the Ball.
O maiden, Maidan
Pandal. Give us your
poor broken blokes.
Stop
O Lord, I'm straight.
I'll do as You order.
So said Arjuna and
me too.

Then?
Then I am waiting to better
understand. Or I *am*
doing His will right now.

pp. 277-78

Our God is better than Walsch's God.
He is Govinda, He is the Navadvipa Lord
they've never met.
We can bathe in the Ganga and Yamuna
know Narottama dasa Thakura
and all the saints. We can lead them toward that path
but as Prabhupada says (Seattle 1968)
     see how few people
come to hear from us because
it takes a rare soul
intelligent enough to know
that Krishna is God.

Krishna on Kaliya
me free of order
and forgetting my cold feet for awhile
as I write with
new primroses in sight.
Collie, I touch his head for good luck.
O Krishna, I just read of Uddhava's lamentation I
     don't have to be afraid.
But yes be harnessed,
you horses of the unconscious
you opposite, *anima*
shadow, don't revolt even
in dreams and say you want
a piece of the action!

I pray in silence, but I should pray out
loud, sing mightily on St. Patrick's
Day before half a million people
who line the streets and inch their way
toward the *kirtana*. But I was silent here
at Manu's house in Co. Fermanagh, and

couldn't fall asleep while thinking someone
might come and invade.
I would've bluffed them that I had no money
because I'm only a guest. Would I die
before giving them my money and
 much-stamped passport?
They might kill me anyway.
Sometimes they want you to beg for your life,
and then they shoot you.
Better to beg Krishna for life
then see what happens.

CHAPTER FIVE - THE PRIMROSE PATH

NORTHERN IRELAND,   , 1997

Do not, as some ungracious pastors do,
Show me the steep and thorny way to heaven,
Wiles, like a puff'd and reckless libertine,
Himself the primrose path of dalliance treads,
And recks not his rod.

> William Shakespeare's *Hamlet*
> *(quotation, p.63)*

Lead me – lead you, yes
I lead you down the
primrose path where the flowers of the
      genus *pimula* bloom –
bearing tubular yellow five-
lobe flowers and a rough leaf
shaped like a spoon,
growing close to the earth.

Wildflower emblem. I don't
want to mislead you or me.
"Primrose path" a cliché means
I'm leading optimistically
and naively saying, "Come along, it's
nice and sweet and good," and
you gullibly follow, but it
turns out to be not at
all so gay and light but

I mislead you.

Why choose a misleading
way for a volume title?
I want to contradict it,
disprove the cliché,
celebrate the actual wildflowers
that grow on the path
I walk in weak feet
weak head
but me in April
in Geaglum.
What I say and feel –
but be on guard too that
it's not a mislead "primrose" path.
Aye, and neither a
too prim, affectedly
precise and proper way –
the abandoned, the delight
of the little flowers skirted
on our walk as if they were
meditated there by Nrsimhananda
brahmacari who made a
mental path for Lord Caitanya.

pp. 4-6

The spring season continues in Northern Ireland, and for Satsvarupa dasa Goswami, as he continues to pursue his distinctive vocation, chronicled both in prose and poetry. Shared above is an extended poem found at the opening of this eighth volume of *Every Day, Just Write – The Primrose Path* preceded by a citation from Shakespeare's *Hamlet*, which appears considerably later in this volume. The title of this volume evokes a central concern for the author in his life and service and artistry: an absolute commitment to authenticity.

William Shakespeare is credited with the phrase, "the primrose path," which is spoken by his iconic tragic figure, Ophelia. The phrase connotes the duplicity that is all too common among religious leaders, to whom Shakespeare alludes. These are ones who lead lives of comfort and privilege while exhorting their flocks to the very opposite. Satsvarupa Maharaja employs all of his poetic sophistication to evoke the meaning of this phrase in the poem which I have quoted above.

> Why choose a misleading
> way for a volume title?
> I want to contradict it,
> disprove the cliché,
> celebrate the actual wild-
> flowers
> that grow on the path

In this poem Satsvarupa Maharaja stares unflinchingly at himself as he considers the spiritual life to be fraught with pitfalls for one who lives complacently without the disciplines of prayer, self-examination, and repentance. The task which the author places before himself in this volume is the practice of those three disciplines. For Satsvarupa Maharaja, we are all works in progress, and his candid and honest portrayal of his own life is what has endeared him to the many who appreciate his books.

During the unfolding of the *Every Day, Just Write* series, the reader increasingly sees the ways in which Geaglum is home to the author. Geaglum provides Satsvarupa Maharaja with that sense of peace that serves as a catalyst for both his spiritual growth and artistic development. In this volume, there are numerous reflections, like those of the nineteenth century New England Transcendentalists, upon the beauty of the setting which but mirrors the beauty of the Supreme Person, Sri

Krishna, who is the creator of all things. Paired with meditations upon the beauty of his surroundings, Satsvarupa Maharaja provides enthusiastic descriptions of his painting process, descriptions which are themselves colorful and lively.

There are two additional features within this volume that are of particular note. To begin, Satsvarupa Maharaja shares with the reader his own internal dialogue as he is simultaneously preparing *A Poor Man Reads the Bhagavatam* for publication. This series which would ultimately total four volumes offers a commentary upon selected texts of the *Srimad-Bhagavatam* and purports written by A. C. Bhaktivedanta Swami Prabhupada, Satsvarupa Maharaja's spiritual master. The author notes both the similarities and contrasts within the respective forms of *A Poor Man Reads the Bhagavatam* and *Every Day, Just Write*. Under consideration are the often more formal style of the former series, and the open-ended free write style of the latter series. In this the reader encounters examples of the fluidity of Satsvarupa Maharaja's artistic forms wholly united in a relentless commitment to authenticity and the avoidance of Shakespeare's primrose path.

Additionally, in this volume, Satsvarupa Maharaja reproduces a collection of note cards that he has called, "Short Note Files." While perhaps not poetry in the customary sense, these creations bear the features that make the author's poetic work so distinctive: a breaking open of traditional forms, and an exploration of the frontier where prose and poetry intersect, only to have that frontier fearlessly erased. These note cards, included herein, give to the reader an additional window upon the world of the author, cards which Satsvarupa Maharaja describes as being scattered upon his desk and taped to his walls. With this image, we are certainly given a visual representation of the free-write process.

Finally, I would direct the reader to "Dog Violet

Poem." In this expansive poem, Satsvarupa Maharaja addresses in one place the collection of themes described above. The author deftly heeds Ophelia's exhortation to reject the primrose path, and instead he directs his readers to the ever challenging and ultimately redemptive path of spiritual and artistic integrity.

Lead me down the primrose path.
Path me down the toothless
lower plate.
Down to the hellish planets not –
 unless you need it, did even
Jesus have to go there on a
visit? Did Yudhisthira have to
see? We know Narada goes
there to preach.
Spare me!

p. 3

❋   ❋   ❋

Lead me – lead you, yes
I lead you down the
primrose path where the flowers of the genus
                                        pimula bloom –
bearing tubular yellow five-
lobe flowers and a rough leaf
shaped like a spoon,
growing close to the earth.

Wildflower emblem. I don't
want to mislead you or me.
"Primrose path" a cliché means
I'm leading optimistically
and naively saying, "Come along, it's
nice and sweet and good," and
you gullibly follow, but it
turns out to be not at
all so gay and light but
I mislead you.

Why choose a misleading
way for a volume title?
I want to contradict it,

disprove the cliché,
celebrate the actual wildflowers
that grow on the path
I walk in weak feet
weak head
but me in April
in Geaglum.
What I say and feel –
but be on guard too that
it's not a misled "primrose" path.
Aye, and neither a
too prim, affectedly
precise and proper way –
the abandoned, the delight
of the little flowers skirted
on our walk as if they were
meditated there by Nrsimhananda
 Brahmacari, who made a
mental path for Lord Caitanya.

The little flowers way.
Fioretti, Saint Thérèse,
little Stevie's little life.
Little strife,
he avoids the worst,
"I get headaches,"
dear primrose path
and Nature
spring
is temporary.

They won't last long but
at least this season while
I write.
Flow gently, sweet Afton
while I write this refrain,

flow gently motorboat –
disturbed Lake Erne,
flow empty of that noise in
morning at midnight, all dark
while I write
grow the roses yellow
Éire passing time.

pp. 4–6

✳   ✳   ✳

Poem for Swan
transfer to poem for Krishna
my Beloved.
"My Sweet Lord" first heard
if only a snatch at an
outdoor cafeteria on my
way in Brazil from farm
to city. The second time I heard it,
a few bars only during a radio
announcer's interviewing
me in Port of Spain, Trinidad.
Never heard of it otherwise,
Hare Krishna pop song.

To Swan, graceful
Krishna. To Krishna the Names
I recite,
to me self off-centered,
off-color
and off and on like the
light that flickers behind my
right eye. Krishna
is all, all energies,
yet one. He's Swami
alone on 76th Street,
and my thumb aching to

write this down.
Swan is Krishna and ducks
its head under lake
to simply eat
and I watch. Krishna Krishna
I "can't wait" 'til 1:00 A.M.
when I chant and
fail you know failure
in chanting with love, but
sometimes do it in 6 minutes 20 seconds
stopwatched per round,
sixteen at one sitting –
including walking back and forth
in the room
they give me
Krishna swan lake
Krishna Holy Name.

pp. 18–20

❀   ❀   ❀

Krishna on Kaliya
me free of order
forget cold feet awhile
as you write this new primrose sighted

p. 27

❀   ❀   ❀

O Krishna,
always some letters in your drawer,
crayons and colored pencils in
the second drawer and micro-cassettes
and Dictaphones in the top drawer,
reach in with right hand
as long as He lets you,
but know He has power to
take it all away.

p. 30

Scratch scratch, in the shed
notice it's too hot in here so
I push open the window, then
hear the birds' chip-chip, see in
my mind words and form
"grass...green." Give up
artifice. Krishna
Krishna Krishna the Morse code
clicking rapidly,
Hare Krishna, Hare Krishna.
Who am I asking when
I ask, "Is this a poem? Is
this acceptable to offer
the Lord?" I am
asking myself and them,
Lord and guru,
I am asking.

p. 44

Sitting in this room
I don't like the chair, and
I need fresh air,
but it seems too much to suit up
and go out there, the boots
the coat and then I might meet
a mama and her kids or the dying cows.

"Is Bach a nondevotee?" someone might ask.
Yes, definitely. Anyone who doesn't know
Lord Caitanya or cry "*He* Gauranga!" can't
help me. And you, are you a nondevotee?
That's a good question.

We say I'm aspiring. It's
a quaint ISKCON word, as in
"I'm aspiring to take initiation from

so-and-so Maharaja." I am aspiring.
It means I can't do anything I like
such as play the recorder and
claim this is for Krishna unless it actually is.
It means my private life is private
and protected,
just me and the Lord in my heart.
Then why do you tell us all this
stuff? Why do you bend our ears so?
We have given you so much time,
do you think it is right?
I don't know. That's up to you.
I just have to write it,
right it, Krishna Krishna Krishna.

pp. 50–51

❊   ❊   ❊

Swami 42

Swami some Swami
women at distance
attracts no one but God
means he's kind not cruel
I am not one yet.

p. 63

❊   ❊   ❊

Krishna Krishna leave your writings
for the future. Put them on
CD before it's too late,
etch them on the rocks, and
go as light as you can,
carrying little because you are
only one ten-thousandth of the hair tip –
to next life
San's books San's publisher

San's not everything but
San's sins, O karma
catch me at the last.
But I'll chant Hare Krishna
and skip rope home free –
you think it'll
be easy?

p. 64

❉   ❉   ❉

O Beauty but
Beauty but, Prabhupada
used to say, pointing out
the deficiency in English.
But he wrote in English.
Sanskrit is perfect,
English barbaric.
Modern is worse, one line two miles
and next two feet.
But Krishna, Krishna my broken
tongue speaks only my mother tongue
which has become my father's English
mixed with Prabhupada's mixed with
my own jargon from America
and the jargon of ISKCON –

Anyway, hesitant but
proud
jolly feisty Beauty
put
Beauty but Delhi
laddu, a Bengali saying.
Punar musiko bhava
and 20-20 vision
and Now.

He's gone to Goloka or
to a pure devotee place,
and I'm talking in this shed
to You. He could
understand me pretty well
without a translator
or interlocutor.

"What is the word
for being in chains?"
He asked me, and I supplied
"Shackles."
Yes. He took it and went
back to his work, dictating
in Bombay flat, low desk and
I exited downstairs to
bathe from the big barrels.
Remember, Prabhupada?

pp. 65–66

But I may be phony
and weary and not at all
strong to face diminishing body
ah...death...

Ah work, and the constant
pressure (as if eyes on me)
of my peers.
You poor pampered babe.
You could use a stint in
U.S. Marine boot camp.
No, don't say that.
Be sensitive with me,
I get headaches.

p.77

The "art" is shmart
you like to do it, a
red man with black
stained eyes, like leaky
currants, and a foot loose
into depths of your
unconscious. As last-minute
thought you attach *tilaka*
there, the devotees want
to know what you're up to
and you can't give a good answer.
If self-expression is so attractive
why can't they do it too?

Repression is not *always* bad
said Father Groeschel
in his pointy white beard
and Capuchin robes.
Are you to listening to him?
Yes, because knowledge is free
and from God so he might have
some too. For conclusions I
go to Krishna conscious people.

pp. 95–96

❊ ❊ ❊

And every step
primroses
my promise
to Lord Krishna...

To be a devotee
in springtime.

p. 110

❊ ❊ ❊

Sleep is another thing
worth controlling
although you need some,
make it a rule not to
fall asleep in the
pit of hell where you
can't come out for
hours at a time.

Krishna, Lord,
Rama, His brother,
Sons of Nanda and Yasoda.
Even if I don't go to Vrindavana this year
keep trying
arrange your life in that way.

p. 113

❀   ❀   ❀

You are wearing down we
heard the swans are
mute and fly three together
low over water but you
heard them squawk
something, reported
red berries and holly leaves,
new buttercups,
primroses steady amid their
green leaves
and stems, dandelions, the wave holds
keep walking until the end
of the path where
Kuveri is dying
lying down and facing
her nose out the
open pen, waiting.
I stand with her

and then come back here
to read *Navadvipa*
Bhava Taranga, alert
to the descriptions of the *dhama*,
the Lord's garden.

pp. 120–21

* * *

I'm not a bad guy.
As the cows sit in pasture
and as the Irish devotees,
mostly *grhastha* men and women and
children but some *brahmacaris*
too (embarrassing me) get
into their boats,
so, I sit here and read and write.
Don't fault me. It's a way.

pp. 121–122

* * *

Rama-navami Blues

1
Listening to my own *Hare Krishna Man* songs,
those were good old days. Did you know?
Fueled by and springboarded
off with such an unsavory
pair, JK and AG, who was reading him with
the devotion of a friend years after
his alcoholic death.
I am alone it is
Best that way. I'm just a little itchy today
because so many are going across the lake to
the island, and I'm afraid they may want me
or criticize me...No, it's okay, I've

got my medical pass.
It's as if they're forcing you somehow to behave.
If you don't go down into the temple room
and sit down while someone reads
an hour and a half from the *Ramayana*,
then what are you going to do instead?
I'll read Third Canto, Uddhava is
telling how he was ordered by the Lord to
tell His last pastimes to sages and even to
the Deity Nara-Narayana at Badarikasrama.

That's not a poem, but I wouldn't mind
having another long one.
You can make this *Every Day, Just Write* anything
it can turn into a legend
can become a hundred and fifty-two esoteric verses.
Or what's more likely is that you'll keep as close as
possible to the bone each day. Maybe more of it
like the good bread Mother Isani makes and I
offer to Prabhupada and eat with my *dal*,
and so on. I mean everyday fare,
guilt, shyness, little fierce;
inner flame, getting ready to tell someone who
may ask why I'm still ill – tell him
I'm always this way. Then grab your
bead bag and...

pp. 123–24

2

Those early mornings are good for a long
poem like Olsen's, but I don't care for it.
And "Paterson". My own squatter's rights,
 Geaglum burst out, tell something like
dandelion's rights, cow's rights,
squatter's short odes.

If you agree that you are
a writer, and you're not going to
give up reading *Bhagavatam* to *be* a writer,
if you settle on all that, then
maybe you could get beyond bankruptcy
to the inner source of
imagination
Krishna's
full manifestation,

you mean an elf fable?
No. A ranting against water-skiers
or fishermen? No. Long poem to a
death of
a cow? No but all of these things.
If I could just sneak away and be free
of guilt and embarrassment and
feelings of unworthiness (the material kind)
and finally free of self even
then praising Krishna in my own words.
No, no it's not to be,
it's just what is.

This declaration of independence
while they row the boat to and fro
and I walk and sit and read by
fading light. You never loved me,
I wrote the right book
it's all going down and devotees
know best. It's a shame we're not better
not more together socially, and me more willing
to meet and shake hands.
But it's better as it is.
Better and better
every day say the optimists.

pp. 124-25

3

I can drink so much water "eighteen ounces"
from 12 midnight to 3:30 A.M.
You drink that much?
We want to know if you were to
drop the little life of water drinking
and such, leave the author's private life behind
what would you have?
You'd have to think about that a long time,
would you?
I would have my basic needs.
I need to read a lot and then lean over
and use the legal pad. They go
side-by-side, like two rails of a
train track. The *Srimad-Bhagavatam* propped up
at an angle so I can read okay and
beside it the open legal pad. With right hand
I write, and I read tracing down the page with
a pencil. That's all.

You mean you would tell the history
of some town? Or some other metaphor?
No, I would probably stick to
actual life. The life of Hare Krishna.
I don't have time for anything else,
I don't have the imagination,
it doesn't seem right.

My spiritual master told me to preach.
I am avoiding that in some way
but trying to pass this off as preaching.
I really can't do much else.
And so I say again and again and again,
Why don't you just throw off all these misgivings
and be who you are and sing only the song
you've got? " If the fool would persist

in his folly, he'd become wise."
Remember that, under the George
        Washington Bridge?
I say don't go back to those memories,
your own hand, the bathroom floor wet,
the particulars, two more weeks here,
not even that. Tell these days,
a little at a time,
Rama-navami blues.

pp. 126–27

Dog Violet Poem Continued

Okay I'll talk with Madhu about
how I felt yesterday. I think what I should have
done is gone over to the temple
at 4 P.M. and watched the *arati*,
then returned. People would have seen me and
yet I would not have overdone it for a headache.
Now I feel like a Catholic who missed Sunday Mass.
You used to be condemned to eternal hell for
that mortal sin, but now they've changed
the rules. We are different, and no one
is criticizing me that I know of.
My internal critics did a job on me.

Here I am on lower Lough Erne,
or between lower and upper.
When Anandamaya and Prahlada arrive
they will grow roses. "We want it
to be just like Vaikuntha." They will use
        Geaglum for vegetables.
The householders need social development.
Build a roof for the *gurukula*, "But

where are the teachers?"
He asked me, "Does Prabhupada want
social development and how much
does he want it?" I said it's important,
but I didn't care so much about it.
You mean because you care more for Rupa Gosvami's
intimate thoughts as Rupa-manjari?
No, not that, I'm just not
into it. As a teacher I can teach
that ox plowing is good even though I don't
plow. And I can say *Krishna-prema* is good
even though I don't taste it.

What kind of teacher is that?
A general practitioner
can recommend enthusiasm in *bhakti*
for all *rasas*.
But then what is your specialty, sir?
My specialty used to be history, but then
when I heard from Dr. A., her fire of
love in quoting Shelley, I told
Dr. Pessen as we walked from the ferry terminal
toward the office building that housed
Staten Island Community College,
"I'm switching to ___English Lit because
        English Lit is more actual life,
you get to read novels." He defended
History and told me
how just that day Nehru and other Eastern leaders
were meeting and this life too, this is the shaping.

But what is your major *now?*
My major is walks in the woods
and words that come
writing freely. And that the *Poor Man's
Bhagavatam* is my pass into the spiritual world.

My theme, my specialty is
to be a fellow. I will teach the masses not.
I will write for Krishna's pleasure. But you
see, I have to be honest and say I don't
know Him. But I *do* know Him!
Krishna, save me!
Give me the privilege of saying
Your Names.
The mind gets in and pushes around, but
still I shall chant on my master's
order.

Who is this master?
I won't tell you, you blasphemer.
I will keep silent. I will only talk
of external things. I will be a teacher in
no way. I am actually just the routine
deliverer. But then I go to speak
and it comes out:
Krishna consciousness is the way of life a
group of us have chosen, and we need
social development, that's a fact.

But I'm in the room typing this
Writing this with my pencil and pen.
Krishna consciousness is the general course
and the special subjects are assigned to
various qualified teachers.
I could be one, but I say I can't teach
every day. So, they let me
go to pasture, here at Geaglum.

But I have to walk past the active preacher
and the younger men who gather around him,
and I feel silly alone, but this is what I want.
I could even be more alone and that might be
better as long as they don't come fishing

for me like those men I saw with a net –
they caught something and threw it back it in.
Leave me to play in my natural
environ, and I will write
you nice books like *Poor Man Reads the Bhagavatam*
and *Every Day, Just Write.*
I can do it, just give me porridge.
I'll offer it to my *guru.*
As for lecturing, I'll do it once a week
for an hour. That's enough, don't you think?
Let's continue this.

pp. 131–36

O Lord, I kick off in
my boat, not to sea but
a few-minutes crossing to
the temple island where
you can see Radha-Govinda
through the window before
you enter the building.

You can also see maroon flowers
blooming on trees, and daffodils,
the boot rack,
the peacock droppings near
the entrance, Syamananda dasa
welcoming you.

I didn't go yesterday, but
I've made peace.
I am an aspiring devotee
of the Supreme Lord and
want to please and entertain
His people.
Krishna Krishna, I am Yours.
Let me go now and walk

the primrose path and
see Kuveri dying and
think
and be there at eleven
to worship my master –
I'm his personal servant again.

pp. 138–39

Cool off, don't write
a note in anger or
sarcasm. Be yourself
poet. Live your own
headaches. If you don't
want an electric machine to test
you for allergies,
then say so.

Live and eat as you like.
Don't complain when it
comes. Don't harm or hurt
a brother – even an
enemy. If you had strength
you could paint those
delicious black stretch figures.

Go walk past death-stalked cow.
Go back and lie down
on your bed in quiet
as if it will always come
but then go away leaving you
clear for tomorrow.

So, chant Hare Krishna,
keep to your own, don't

be a critic, not of his,
or yours.

I'll let you eat what
you want,
breathe what you want and
suffer your eye ache
as time ticks away...

Words, words, words.
What is the matter,
my Lord? Oh, nothing.
Just a Hare Krishna
with a few body pains
growing old before his time.

pp. 155–57

Oh damn the occasion, the Freudian unconscious
and to hell with the Jungian bag of tricks.
We have our own way and to hell
with that too? No, no to hell with
you, you rebel young man. I am a
devotee, but the pain comes anyway.
I am the dick arresting the snot-nosed, bloodied.
I am the thief-catcher, he said. I won't
tell who because you will attack him
in your prose. But he said I am the policeman
to catch the thief. And Dr. Patel was outraged
and said if you blaspheme India's saints
we won't walk with you anymore.
Srila Prabhupada said so be it
then we shall read *Krishna* book out loud
and not enter into controversy.
We did it, wet sands, happy days.

No matter what else, if you
could walk with him and hear the teachings
you liked that walking school
like a student of Socrates. Now it's harder.
But sometimes I come alive as in the
bathroom, the tape recorder on the floor,
Wow! He said Krishna is to be remembered,
that's the whole thing. It doesn't matter if you can't
argue or read books, just remember Krishna
in one way or another, love Him and
you attain the essence.

p. 158

Oh, tra-la-la-la it won't
be long before May
enters, and you can look at
more flowers. It won't be
long.

p. 175

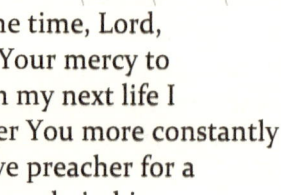

Please give me time, Lord,
and give me Your mercy to
improve so in my next life I
can remember You more constantly
and be a brave preacher for a
whole life through, in his
care, in his cause.

p. 175

I do want to see You
in some small way I
do feel You are already here.

It's not wrong to "cash in"
on this. Practice the presence
of God, nothing convoluted,
not a mere method –
but He's here or else
there's nothing.
Do this as soon as possible
before it's too late,
Hare Krishnas, even empty ones
fill the "void."

pp. 192–93

Prabhupada is here,
and a vise has
turned in my head, but
not so bad yet.
But it stops me from
getting into reading or
              extended writing.

p. 194

Swami, we love you
when you tell us of Krishna
and when you control the senses
that means we have to do it too.
I think we are all *sannyasis*
but not in the spiritual world.

p. 203

This Krishnaite boy senses
the little first flicker of the
daily pain he lives with.

It's not so great;
it's all he's got.
It keeps him out of the military.
He's heard that people become ill
this just to avoid the serious
work of finding themselves.
They feel a personal failure at
becoming a pure devotee.
Maybe that's true. Or
it's just a vein or
vaso gone spastic as it
might happen to any old car.

I live with it as it lives with
me. It signals, "to
shut down," and I quickly
write a few lines which
could be my last.

Say Krishna, Krishna
if you don't mean it
say Caitanya, then listen
again to the signal call.
Okay, call it quits it's
9:30, go back, lie
down, walk past Kuveri –
she's much bigger than me,
dumber,
but she's got her own
dying and death, and it's
not psychosomatic.
We chant to hear hearing,
Hare Krishna, Hare Krishna
and her black face looks
back a little pleading?
No, that's your imagination.
She's dying, dying, and

I'm still walking the
primrose path.

pp. 205–6

✤   ✤   ✤

This room is filling up with pictures
I've drawn. The latest a man with stout
arms and a skinny torso fingering his
brahmana thread and saying the sannyasa mantra.
I wrote the words in color, gopi-bhava.
Another shows a bird man with three legs.
He's ready to fight or to
flap his wings as he walks to the left.
He's a powerful fighter-ally,
poet-duck-man-devotee,
he distracts the eye from looking to
the Vrajavasi painting of Radha and Krishna
and that's not good. But on the duck-
        man's page there's
the word "Krishna" carefully lettered. There is time
to look at him and time to look
at the calendar print of Radha and Krishna.

Another drawing is of the skinny man chanting
on red beads. All these are up and more to come.
But I'll start to take them down because we are
leaving this room. We are leaving for the
South of Ireland where we will
stay five weeks.
But you never know.

April was good, sunny, mild
it could have been cold and rain-swept.
Hare Krishna, I didn't go to the temple on
Ramacandra's Day but went other times
and read Caitanya-caritamtra.

149

This is not a very interesting poem?
It has been a quiet time.
I like the silences here and the view
of the lake and how they leave me alone.
I get headaches every day, that's all right
if that's the way. You're in the right place
for that. Even if you venture out to Europe
and hack it
you know you can come back here
to your Geaglum room.

pp. 213-14

Develop art
always again a rookie
old times are there but
no need to plug in for new
karma. Beg release from
ghosts. Got to confess question
not necessarily outward.
Be true. Face it.

pp. 251-52

You can improvise he said
rising from his bed.
I saw you doing your *Poor Man's* stint.
What was it you wanted into print?
Something about born *brahmanas* today
and holy wars and the price to pay.
You preach straight first then go for it,
but sometimes there's nothing but wit
and not much of that either, just grinding
the way cows eat hay. The day is gray
in county North Ireland this Yank
is worried that he might mussed

by some Brit or Catholic when he goes
to travel. He'll have to
write it down although
blood and tears are rare.

Now as for the scripture and the soul,
he knows about it but in theory.
He grows weary and his poems
are not great. He can speak in American
toads, foods he longs for...
making sense, no sense, the hope
of lenient treatment from his master but
maybe he will get the boot to the head.
I'm not in bed too long
now three days in a row without headaches
so you can expect one soon,
but I'll not let it ruin my day,
just take it along, look at it and pray
when you get clear be here
chanting Hare Krishna, the canon tacked on,
songs in the air, the quiet I love
here, the song and no turf,
my master
the canon
I live by
it seems,
never leave that. Pray for that.

pp. 255–56

He was going to say
Krishna, Krishna, I'll get to know Him
in *Srimad-Bhagavatam* and
Caitanya-caritamrta, that book of

intimate pastimes, exceptional.
Maya, be at bay
and serving the Lord as
in my best days better
than ever, paying attention
to *hari-nama* and hearing the Lord's
lila, maybe accepting new
austerity, new duties, new
humility, non envy,
becoming dear to Krishna and
His *Bhagavad-gita*, my master...
calls me.

p. 268

CHAPTER SIX - SOMETHING READING OR WRITING, SOMETHING READING OR WRITING

IRELAND, APRIL 30 – MAY 19, 1997

"I tell you this my practical experience. I am here always working – something reading or writing, something reading or writing, twenty-four hours. Simply when I feel hungry I take some food, and simply when I feel asleep I go to bed. Otherwise, always, I don't feel fatigue. You can ask Mr. Paul whether I'm not doing. I tell you, I take pleasure in doing that, I don't feel fatigue."

A. C. Bhaktivedanta Swami Prabhupada on
the Bowery, Spring 1966

"Pen cuts, leaves ink trace, a miracle discovered long ago by man."

Satsvarupa dasa Goswami
Every Day, Just Write, Volume Nine,
"Something Reading or Writing, Something Reading or Writing,
p. 180

The ninth volume of *Every Day, Just Write* receives its inspiration from the wonderful words above shared by Srila Prabhupada in an early lecture. This is a volume in which Satsvarupa dasa Goswami carries the reader through the breadth of his own reading and study as he continues to live in the quiet setting of Geaglum, Northern Ireland, as well as in the suburbs of the city of Belfast. In this volume which consists mostly of prose, Satsvarupa Maharaja reflects upon his own different styles of reading and writing. Let us consider these in turn.

Lectio divina, as a form of reading, is a contemplative practice characteristic of Christian monastics and is a hallmark of monastic spirituality. In this manner of reading, one engages the text prayerfully, not seeking information through critical analysis. Rather it is a listening for the Lord to address the reader through the medium of the sacred text. It is often said that in this manner of reading, one rests in the text in an anticipation of a moment of *darsana*, an encounter or audience with the Supreme Person. This a seemingly simple but deeply challenging style of reading in which a verse or even a word is relished in a moment of prayerful engagement. In this volume, Satsvarupa Maharaja invites the reader to join him in his meditation upon the breadth of the Vaisnava scriptural tradition, with a particular attentiveness to the words of his spiritual master, A. C. Bhaktivedanta Swami Prabhupada.

In a shift of mood, no less significant, is reading as theological study, as Satsvarupa Maharaja describes as the pages of the *Srimad-Bhagavatam* lay open before him. Often, theological study is characterized as solely an academic discipline in distinction from devotional reading. However, Satsvarupa Maharaja demonstrates that nothing could be further from the truth. While study does represent a shift in mood from *lectio divina*, the discipline of theological study has always been intended to integrate heart and mind. In this way, this discipline of study becomes an act of adoration and surrender before the Supreme Person. Nowhere is this more wonderfully conveyed to the reader than in this volume's poetry in which contemplation, reflection and study transfigure poetic forms with devotion's radiance.

The first page of *Volume Nine* begins with the simple yet utterly demanding exhortation that Satsvarupa Maharaja asks of himself: "Just write." One should not let the brevity of this command to lead the reader to underestimate the depth of this challenge. These two words fundamentally define the vocation of this author and his response to this challenge is his unique offering of love and devotion to those who open his books. How does one reply to this vocational imperative to write? Is writing itself a form of devotional service? How does this vocation fit within the broader institution to which Satsvarupa Maharaja has devoted himself for over fifty years? These are the questions that this author asks of himself and his relentless pursuit of answers shapes the writing itself. The reader will encounter extended free-write passages, sastric commentary, poetic expression, as well the author's reflections upon preparation for public lectures.

In this particular volume in which remarkable prose comes to the fore, I would encourage the reader, as always, to visit *sdglegacy.com* to engage the full text. Prose and poetry seamlessly flow between one another in this writing of Satsvarupa Maharaja, and nowhere is that more evident than in this volume of *Every Day, Just Write*.

Krishna is on the Sesa bed,
I am not He
He is lifting the Govardhana,
I lift the blanket. I try to understand something, a
little bit is all I can do.
O Krishna
he said I can empty drawers out of the desk if I want.
But since he didn't do it I won't ask him. If the drawers
were empty I would put my crayons in there. Why not go
ahead and put them out on the desk? Invite yourself to
draw,

one drawing again and again
one hymn, one God in
ananta-rupam, there is
no end to varieties of material
pains and joys too
all dries up unless
you know Krishna. Rascal scientists,
sing Hare Krishna
in your sweat
or without it.

pp. 7–8

Truth is the song
Rama is the holy name I am
not always true
under all circumstances, but
to be like that I'd be a saint
to tell the truth
have a heart and forgive me
as I keep on serving,
increasing.

p. 18

Care and feeding of delicate
plant should be learned
by those who care –
too much water or too little
is dangerous for his health.
Same with sunshine. Don't
expose him to louts'
shouts or bleats of sheep
about to be slaughtered.
When you drive him over
bumpy roads in a cheap car,
do you know what it does
to his system? He gets
constipated. Think over
how to keep mites off him.

Put him in a pot and worship him
by many names, "One who is
dear to Krishna." And preserve all he
writes because you never
know, he could be another Shakespeare,
a Rupa Gosvami for us,
and it will all be lost if
you don't care.

Please care for my
drooping leaves.
Don't break me or burn me
prematurely. Give me hope to
write in piece. All I'll
give you blooming *manjari*,
eggs and chicks,
somnambulant poems . . .
the unconscious,
the conscious – he among his
Godbrothers who ought to be left alone
to tell a story of

what it's like to be a
converted shmerk.
the rose fading
the pebble in the brook of
ISKCON warbling his meters
uneven
ought to be given a foot brace
and cane and let to pasture.

In his brain are memories
and mystic scholarship.
It's true he's struggling in
basic ways to surrender to his
master. That too we may
appreciate. But this message should
by kept by only those who
love him. If others read of
my asking you to protect
him, they will laugh and
scorn
and what if he hears of that?
So, keep it quiet.

pp. 37-38

Swami, they love you in New York airport.
The reporter persisted, "At what age did you
have your first enlightenment?"
            He said at four or five.
The devotees cheered.

Swami, they love you,
you made us *swamis* too, junior to you
and gave us *danda* and order to preach.
Swami, I'm afraid.

I am not a lover of the Name,
but you don't reject me but give me service,
"Something reading or writing,
something reading or writing
and when I get hungry I eat some food
and when I get tired I go to bed.
I don't get tired, 24 hours serving Krishna."

He didn't go out at all some days
from the Bowery loft.
"I don't get fatigued. You can ask Mr. Paul
if this is not true."
Thank you for that class, it was very
nice hearing you talk about the Swami.
But what about you? Are you a real
swami or fake?
Oh, I am real. Are you a *vaidhi-bhakta*?
And how come...how come?
I am doing what he said to do,
doing what comes naturally.

pp. 43–44

   ❋   ❋   ❋

The two ton car fell on the
boy and injured his rumpus plus he
went on
until the bottom of the page
fell out in the drive,
felt a relapse,
escaped from the prison theater,
and they came after him,
and he ran into the city streets. Let's say he was
chanting holy names of God all the time.

pp. 45–46

Admittedly I am timid,
I am retired, colonel
...hieroglyphics scholar
dead tomb scholar book
worm, skinny old face
of old guy, a goofer
ridiculous clown painted
in sad smile.
Helicopter over the town
of Belfast – O little town
of Bethlehem, IRA,
smooth roads. "No use
fixing the front gate," said the
Hare Krishna chap, "They'll just
break it down again."
Low-class Catholics from
nearby estate do it.

p. 50

Say I'd rather be home
writing but I've come out
here to lecture – folks, do
follow these practices. My
master wants you to do it,
and he wants me to tell you.

p. 51

Krishna song is the best song by *gopas*
on behalf of self spirit desiring
real praises for green pastures the
soul is joyful, Krishna protects them,
satvatam patih.

p. 67

Never mind mundane, Krishna is all that is
blissful, and great souls
always praise Him.
Do people
know? Krishna can protect us always.

Saul Bellow's book I refer to
to make a point
oh, in Krishnaloka they would
not need that.
No, they just sing what He did
to Baka and how beautiful He looked.
Good to know that highest
standard.

p. 68

❋ ❋ ❋

Goloka is the planet of cows.
Oh, there they please Krishna
and love Him as He is
love Him as cowherd boy, the
original Krishna but he's happy.
Oh, don't tell us if you are
not pure. But Goloka is where
we want to go,
Krishna's pastimes so I mentioned it
in my lecture at Dublin's Hare Krishna center.

p. 70

❋ ❋ ❋

Calling to Him

"My dear Lord Krishna"
and Hare Krishna, Hare Krishna
the chanting by me is
also chanting instead of
Dublin roaming or

hearing "great music." O
Krishna I do so many foolish
things. And still you think
you are worth listening to?

❋   ❋   ❋

Want real, real, I don't
say Truth – although I aspire
for it, but real who you
are now
and make it Krishna conscious.
Writing will help.

Write.
Swami I know
you are my master,
and I serve you.
You teach me
of Krishna and want me
to tell others
about Krishna.

❋   ❋   ❋

Swami is the name, No salami
They think Swami is swarthy, wears scarves,
ensconced in salubrious scarves and
Swami means lying down on a bed of nails
or a cheater from India like so many.
Harper's magazine had the cover story, "What
happened to Swami Bodhi Maya Scait Bruti Padi Boomi
Nerthwalla?"
I said hold on, you blasphemer, but he got away.

O day of awakening
O poem of reckoning.
It took a while to get here
now sing free of Marlboro
cigarettes. Freedom from
pain, besides your spiritual master's
form...abide awhile.
Got nothing much to say.
The stuff...Lord
Lord You were here
before anything else.
Give me this day,
the right to serve You.

p. 112

Vidur, Vidur,
Vidura
got a shock.
Vidura dasa in Africa
serving bravely, demandingly
got a taste of Lord Caitanya's
mercy there.
Me in rainy meadow
and the hills of Wicklow to
write and read.

p. 113

Quiver quiver,
my head is like a vise.
The ink of a page of
cheap quality sinks
through to the next page and
blots and blurs on the page

where I write.
I quiver in doubt
and fear. Be steady, tell
yourself. Sixteen-year old
Pradyumna dasa says he has chanted
Hare Krishna all his life so doesn't
see it's a problem to vow, "I shall always chant 16
rounds a day." But it's hard
he says, to control the mind.
"You have written books on
this and my parents are a
source of inspiration so I'll
continue with hope."
That's good. I may have
good news for him about myself and
paying attention to the
 Names. But more or
less we are all
quivering.

p. 132

"Eternal vigilance is the price of liberty," they say in
America. Never rest complacent. You are
always trying to reach the goal of
no doubts and good taste
for teachings of that Personality of Godhead,
Vasudeva and transcendental
bhakti.

p. 133

Institutionalized confessors
are okay, but if your
ISKCON temple doesn't
have such designated
brahmana counselors –
then find one on your own.
A friend whose guidance
you can trust.

p. 133

Yes, I've done it, in Boston days. I did it, work hard
for Krishna. But you're always there, the self.
You want to please yourself.
Is it wrong?
Can you be transformed so you act just for Krishna?
To be madly in love with yourself is wrong they all say.
Narcissus is the guy who
thought he was beautiful.
It's possible even for an old
man.
Another foolish evil is
solipsism.
All these errors are put
down by literary critics.

p. 135

I woke up thinking Homer, the blind poet. The school
where we learned his epics. Don't need them now.
Your epic is day to day struggle with the same ups
and downs.
Oh, to be a steady *rancora*
not running from

the fray,
to be serving with senses
as I did in days
gone by...

p. 135

＊　　＊　　＊

Solip Narcus
was quivering in *maya*
a reflection of his self
in the water of a
puerile poem.
He got smacked
by the critics and seers
and woke up, got
off Maya's lap and
reported for duty with
a new name,
Krishnadasa-anudasa
anudasa.

p.135

＊　　＊　　＊

Wiper of tables,
washer of pots,
he heard we should Go Out
and preach, but he quivers at
that assignment
and does the next best
thing,
washing pots in
Krishna's kitchen and
obeying the bosses.

p. 136

#1

It's raining slanting rightward.
The *guru* –
a mere child in spiritual
knowledge and frail in head –
is in his sleeping bag
dreaming but wakes to faint
sounds of bouzouki and gets
up and asks if he can be less
loud while the goat beds
down on the cement ledge by
back glass door sometimes
bunking his head against it –
he sees his reflection
or imagines he can get through
to inside the house
and eat the upholstery of the chairs

Meanwhile the book is
waiting to be read. After
he's slept and he's
clear, get on
into the Third Canto,
More inquiries about Vidura.

p. 137

#2

To tell of the great steel-gray hulk
Saratoga moored in the harbor
of Naples and us approaching her in
a sailor-packed whale boat and
thinking *this is my home.*

Resuscitated
forty years later a sailor
on *Bhagavatam* seas.
Retired Admiral,
sea legs shaking
and my head like a vise.

"Don't," she said, "write
poems to sell your pain
and gain attention for
your merely sincere
confessions. You've got
to do something for all of us."
What if I don't
have it in me?

Then write as a little
Suka follower,
a peahen of Vraja,
peck at each day of *sadhana*.
I tell you we are all
more or less quivering
in illusion.

#3

Back window of his car is gone,
instead black garbage-pail-paper
taped, and rack carrier on top
for selling paintings,
Praghosa dropped by to talk
with Madhu. I heard his
voice and opened the window
to my hideout, looked down
at his car, the sunshine in
and out in Ireland,
goat at back door...

I'm preparing to tell them
on Sunday how we should
read carefully and inquire like
Vidura or at least as we are
able. I'm sick now,
don't want your pity
but won't deny. I was
not in the war.

I know mostly only ISKCON
and was one time one of
the eleven-only gurus and
before that
I sold Spiritual Sky incense in Dallas
or at least
I worried about it and talked
with Narayana dasa convincing him to
please manage it so Prabhupada's
gurukula could run on.

Astrand on land
a little while longer.
Write pages of what it
is like.

pp. 139–40

Swami, the upholstery is
worn-out, machines don't
work well because the
family doesn't have much money.
This country never enjoyed great
wealth like Holland and Portugal, what to speak of
the present super-powers.
I don't live here but
notice a few things and

my body, the flowers –
tiny daisies closed up in
cold and rain, the yellow
gorse passes as a flower,
a bush it is, despised by
farmers.
Now let's go. It's
May 10, and you have to get
this on record and let it
go.

p. 146

#4

Onboard this freight car
poem, the radiator grinds
comfortably, my shower was as
hot and cold as I could bear,
the goat is covered from us by
a curtain so we don't have to see
his arrogance wanting to come inside
and take over this house and make
us his slaves. It will never happen.

Daruka suggested they tie him up and
make him a scapegoat.
Drop him off
in Baltinglass or Tallaght.
I've a mind to return to the desk
to read some more
Bhagavatam at risk of nodding
asleep.

pp. 147–48

#5

The pines' arms move
in breeze.
I walked down the logging road
alone.

The daisies are crumpled by
cold and rain. I'm a warm human
who can think of God.

p. 155

#6

He came into my office and
like a businessman, I pushed back
my chair
put down the *Bhagavatam* where I was at –
beginning to appreciate how vast Maha-Vishnu
could actually *be*.

I took out my calendar
and went over with him our June-
planned trip to Spain
in the white Ford van,
roaring engine, hope it doesn't
 break down, or me. God save us.
We go for transcendental lectures and
hope to help people saddened
by loss of guru.

p. 160

Swami, I'm a poor excuse
picking at my cuticles.
But I love you
today is Mother's Day.

p. 163

You taught us the Mother is
the *Vedas*. Gargamuni
and Brahmananda you controlled.
I'm recalling '66 again.

Swami, that's you. Now
me too, you gave me the
name so I can't disown it.
Satsvarupa dasa. Now add
Goswami, you said.

But no regrets that I've
renounced women and wealth.
Have I? They seem to return
in a subtle form.
I'm okay in your shelter. We
are yours, sons and daughters.
Some personal aspects of your being
fade in memory, but you as
book writer are strong for me.
You will send me messages
in my heart when I am
ready.

p. 164

172

Trade noises: turn off the electric
heater which blankets out everything – a good
feature if you're parked at a gas station
but here when I turn it off I get
the rain beating on the skylight window.
I trade that for the typewriter
to get my immortal thoughts down.
I could trade that for the relatively silent
scratching of the pen which would enable me to
 tune in to the rain beating down at the same time
and drive out thoughts of the filthy goat.

The goat walked into the house yesterday when
Praghosa left the door open for a minute.
They got him out by opening the back door and
Madhu walked indifferently at an angle
        toward the goat,
not looking at him
until the goat saw he had enough space,
and he bolted out the open door.
That's a noise too, in the mind
in the brain...

p. 169

* * *

Noises means stuff that's
bothering you so you can't love
Krishna in your heart
in your *atma* soul.
I'm afraid sometimes to think
what it means to surrender.
My mind will scream.
I can't do it I say.
I want quiet and peace.
But then you'll get the wailing next life.
The sound of blood in your own ears,

your own next body, no end of
sirens and bombs falling,
falling short.

p. 170

❋   ❋   ❋

#7

I spoke on Vidura
the ladies on one side,
few men on left
children four in yellow
as in Vrindavana *gurukula* and
one boy pre-school in white
was crying, red face, red-haired...

Vidura is a "person"
I said, stumbling for word
choices and explaining myself...
"There are levels of reading and hearing..."

Questions? A few.
You didn't say, "I'm
reading privately, I want to get
back to it."

p. 172

#8

"They gave you a beautiful
garland of wildflowers," he said.
I thought he meant my
Wild Garden or that the *Bhagavatam slokas*

I read were a garland, but
he meant the actual woods-
flowers picked by a devotee
and worn on my chest as I read.

It's over and I'm back alone,
Chapter Nine, Third Canto.

p. 172

Lord, the books,
tell true life worth
torn out, perforated
from the quiet life,
much of it your own self
because you can't tell
other people's lives.

p. 177

#9

Love is – I don't know,
hladini, never-ending service.
You can't really say if you don't know it.
But I believe in love
of brothers and sisters, children
and spiritual fathers all centered in
love of God and Krishna is the
best friend, more intimate
than that.

p. 199

#10

This is
the exact time when you could
you could be reading of Brahma and
Maitreya or *gopis* and Krishna
you could be chanting on your beads,
could be ascending Heaven
or hearing a priest's confession
you could be at the eighty-first meeting
of a brahminical council with
the accountant giving an alarming report
but still you fall asleep.

p. 200

Hey it's real,
come and get it
Softee ice cream
ring the bells –
Sats is writing day and night
to be the one
the...dum de dum
a sonnet for friars
of ISKCON and its congre-
gation.

p. 202

#11

Now the yellow cool sun is
measuring time over the atoms,
beef cows lowing in pastures far off,
breakfast of fruits
on the way up here.

p. 209

Like the man with brush and glue
putting up new strips to the
billboard, replacing Guinness
with latest Michael Jackson world tour,
so is my holy name campaign
advertised in my brain.

p. 210

❖   ❖   ❖

On very tiptop of tall pine
a fat bird sits. Can't see who.
But I wish peace today
in serving Krishna in my way.
It's up to Him, and He says
Yes, it's up to you –
will you surrender?
Will you earn your spiritual name?
Répondez vous.

p. 210

❖   ❖   ❖

Swami means master
I have mine. Use time well –
You can't get it back.

Swami is rhythm and blues.
He's yours, master.
You're his, servant.
Beat it out against the force
of your rebellion.

Rebellion is caused by *maya*
on the bewildered soul.
Swami, Swami Bhaktivedanta
looked at me and saw my
hopeless, self-consciousness and

he looked sad, said Poet
Ginsberg.

Swami, the time has come.
I'm with you in separation.
My time is rushing to you.
You have connected me to you.
There's a time for a poem or
two. Then go to the chanting
room. Time to face the
truth. To face the opposition.
Face it and preach.

p. 215

＊　　＊　　＊

Your old boy complained
to you in Hawaii, I have too many
things to do – cook, write your letters,
etc., etc. Give me a break.
You said Pradyumna can help with
the cooking, but he didn't help
much. Yes, he did the *capatis*.
I'm grateful.

p. 216

＊　　＊　　＊

Here we go Swami. You are
watching from your place.
May we all somehow make
it, to where we are going
with you in our separate
ways. But on sort of one train
to Goloka.

p. 216

#12

Healing the Body Betrayed says
no one wants to be with someone who's
miserable. So be cheerful.
"I hope my wheelchair doesn't
make everyone uptight."

p. 237

✣ ✣ ✣

What's your chronic disease?
Do you live with it well? Its
intrusion on your life now
indistinguishable from your life itself.
It's who you are.

Jagannatha gets no headache.
His devotees have spiritual bodies.
Saints take pains to spread
His glories, help fallen...

"How are you doing?"
Okay as long as I don't go out
anywhere or feel sorry.
I can sneak in writing and
reading while no one notices.

p. 238

✣ ✣ ✣

#13

The woolen bright saffron cap
your master wears was
made in Vrindavana.

Soul is eternal, break loose.
Writing this in Wicklow
nearing June it's still cold.

p. 238

My father
was 76 almost ten years ago
and mother is 86 alive
or dead, such a small woman
we called her "Midge" with
love.
Now whether they are alive
or dead, our love is dead.
We don't even know each
other.

p. 239

⁕   ⁕   ⁕

Light dim in this room,
his Irish mandolin is twanging,
and I'm waiting. It's time for
a plate of kiwi fruit
and figs, apples, cashews,
a tin cup of apple juice.
Be strong and silent.

p. 239

⁕   ⁕   ⁕

Swami teaches us, I keep
going back to first days because
he formed us then, and I was
on the beam.
Swami, the controlled teacher in
saffron *khadi*.
Don't abandon the dress, the
shaved head, the way.
When you taught us it was
your mercy.
We "forgive" you any little
apparent discrepancies we see with
our faulty eyes. Please

forgive us our kicking and
rude ways.

pp. 252–53

❋   ❋   ❋

Swami, when you were
among us many took shelter
of your lotus feet.
Whammy Swami, Sammy Davis,
Swami Krishna, "Sami Krishna"
as the *New York Post* put it –
these words swim out of me
crazily not like Brahma's
emitting forms at creation.
You took us to the U.N. Plaza
on a summer day to
pray for peace and you said
on the way back to the Lower East Side,
"There will never be peace"
(unless they take to Krishna consciousness)
Hayagriva recalled it, recorded it
or was it Brahmananda?
Please gather us Swami,
your summer flowers,
your stinking hippies who
want to reform.

p. 253

Swami, the hermit walks alone
rubs out the bad thoughts in his brain
that one he thinks of and criticizes,
calls him an empire building, opportunist,
a rascal for criticizing me and writings.
You'd do better to let him get his reward,
in your mind wish him well and then release it.

p. 257

Now the day is dawning. It's good
you are left alone. The birds are crying out.
You'll see the snails and maybe a deer
and maybe another recently killed animal.
You'll chant one extra round with some hope
and then the 18th round will grind to a stop.
I tell you. The days are going to get
worse before better. I tell you I don't
know the future at all.

pp. 257–58

#14

Sitting before Prabhupada,
no one else. I acknowledge all the
others better than me, sturdier,
taking on burdens to please him.

Looking up to Prabhupada,
sitting here after a bath, fresh and rested,
he and I. The warm water I poured
on him while he spoke. I'm his *cela*.
They say it will be thunderstorms
over weekend and that's good;
at least it's not hail.

p. 264

If I want to be alone it's not
wrong. They overwhelm me.
I'm delicate. Shouldn't even say it –
but want to clear myself of the
charge, "He doesn't like Vaisnavas."
I'm reading of Lord
Brahma and his sons and the
creatures he creates.
Prabhupada's finger sticks out

from his bead bag. He can count
on me in this solitary way and
sometimes in meetings. But I can't
do much more. I need him
in the forms I'm receiving.

p. 265

Oh, whimsical brother,
you think you'll get an honorary
degree simply by sitting
under the light of the window and
reading? Yes, why not?
This is no ordinary book.
Whoever touches it, touches
Krishna, the Supreme Lord.

p. 269

#15

"This *ananda*, that *ananda*,
do your own work in your
own hand," he said to his disciple,
meaning you needn't depend
on a questionable Godbrother
but memorize 30 *Gita* verses as
all you need to equip yourself
to preach in South India.

p. 284

In Wicklow, Southern Ireland,
the grass is green deep
green pines, blue pale
dawn sky.
I'm here too, descended

from Irishmen?
No, an individual soul,
I knew it. Told my father and
mother, "I have my own life.
I'm not just an investment
you created."

p. 285

Swami's *Easy Journey to
Other Planets* affected me
when reading it in 1966.
Best change I ever made.

p. 285

The body can't
be well. It dies. Whatever
he says we try to accept.
Five *rasas* and seven, pick one.
Nine *bhakti* methods,
pick at least one.
How about hearing and chanting?

p. 285

Krishna and Balarama killed the
duck demon today.
He was as big as a hill
but Krishna broke his beak
as if it were a blade of grass.

p. 295

The poet priest
Gensei
gone is Datta to me
divorced his guru
and then his wife.

Walden trees cleared
now preserved in
Concord Inn I
said to NK I
am writing and they
said we will help you, we thank you very much.

p. 296

#17

You saw Prabhupada in Vrindavana.
Wise they were who took the film
of him in 1970, walking, walking
the young men and women beside
him, behind him. One took some
rupees out of his wallet and gave to
Prabhupada who gave to the *walla*.

p. 296

Walking in the narrow lanes. A
child passed them with a brass
pot on her head, I didn't see
the monkeys. The films are just
snippets...walking and chanting
and lecture...you can speed them
up but better just watch it all.

And then you are here, 1997.
Sunshine outside, daisies, go
upstairs, in your world. Hold
the book at sixty-degree angle –
"It is very much regrettable that unfortunate people
do not discuss the description of
                the Vaikuntha planets

but engage in topics which are unworthy to hear
and which bewilder one's intelligence."
Those who have good qualities go –
but not in one human lifetime.
Brahma says, "I too
desire human life for this."

p. 297

Anger's red eyes
the frustrated sage curses.
My anger at not being adored,
not being allowed,
not attaining my goal –
Vaikuntha for my own satisfaction.
I see my anger as an ego trip.

p. 303

#18

That cold in chest makes me
not want to read more,
disables me from being patient
to hear the Kumaras and gatekeepers –
clashing and the steady, descending
purports.
The involuntary cough and fogging
head prevents me from interest
in writing – even forget what
it is I might write and why.

Despite it I pluck
courage or habit and nibble at
this: Krishna is in all things.
I at least don't like the
nondevotees' ways.
I like Krishna things, *prasadam*.

I'm so whimsical, changeable,
not steady, durable. But
that's the way of this
world. Cough, cough.

p. 313

If I get better
I could sneak in a look
at a marvelous *sloka*
translated eloquently,
in devotional prose
Vaikuntha topics, better than
anything I or they
could do. When I get better...

p. 314

Swami, the broadcast is on.
When you were here it was wonderful seeing you
so many places where you were loved and
            where you loved to go –
saw the old film of you entering Bury Place temple
and then you went to Los Angeles, San Francisco
and then Dallas.

Swami, you sit on the *vyasasanas*,
you looked very grave in face and composed.
They honor you in Jaipur on a "float"
pulled by oxen
then again at LA airport
the way you taught and led us and we loved you.
The nondevotees didn't know what was going on.
We didn't care for them.
So many mistakes, but our love is not in vain.
Hare Krishna. The truth is still here
as long as we live and then

we have to take another body.
Even Lord Brahma doesn't live forever.

These words can't last either
after the floods, how long is it? –
36,000 years of flood and the same of fire
and you can't expect a special incarnation
to save your works
then write for the present
for people who can benefit
by hearing the absolute truth from
a corny carney guy.

pp. 329-330

#19

I've recovered and back remembering the
purpose of reading *Srimad-Bhagavatam*,
carefully allowing it
and bringing yourself to appreciate the
pure bhakti nowhere else
found. Thank you. Then
writing on it or after it and
another round of reading and
writing.

p. 330

#20

Since May is ending I notice
beautiful green swards, folded
fields, water, sheep and cows

at middle distance, farm house
nestled in land, gorse wild
yellow, white Queen Anne's
lace in narrow South Ireland
lanes.

Jaya
and Vijaya
didn't fall from Vaikuntha,
it was something special.

This morning
is special, and whatever he gives for
breakfast I'll accept. Put the key
under the door, and let yourself in
at night. I'll be out dancing
by the light of cold June moon.

I'll be in *Srimad-Bhagavatam*
don't bother me, I'll walk
where hundreds of blossoms
of some flowery trees are on the
ground. See no one, receive
mail at front door.

p. 341

CHAPTER SEVEN - CHOOSING TO BE ALONE

IRELAND, MAY 19 – JUNE 10, 1997

As for staying in this house or another house and not attending the ISKCON morning program, and not giving many lectures, go ahead and do the thing you most want to do. Trust yourself a little. I don't trust myself utterly and blindly, obviously. I'm always questioning. Can't get through a single day without it. But I am nevertheless hanging in there and liking it. This quiet life. And it is no empty life but full of writing and reading projects, and preaching also by writing letters in answers to what they write me...It's a hardly a complete exile or isolation.

Satsvarupa dasa Goswami
Every Day, Just Write, Volume Ten
Part One, "Choosing to be Alone", p.130

In Volume Ten *of Every Day, Just Write*, the reader is given window to a decisive moment in the journey of Satsvarupa dasa Goswami, reflected in its very title, "Choosing to be Alone." The process of vocational discernment that began in earlier volumes of this series is now to be embraced and acted upon. As Satsvarupa Maharaja writes in the passage quoted above, this decision is made with a personal imperative to trust, which he understands is both difficult and challenging. The leap of faith to trust oneself is combined with the author's ongoing concern for his commitment to the society of devotees established by his spiritual master, A. C. Bhaktivedanta Swami Prabhupada. This volume with its focus upon a life of solitude is set in the familiar environs of Ireland, a setting which has played a significant role in Satsvarupa Maharaja's sustained journey to clarify his particular life as a devotee of Sri Krishna, the Supreme Personality of Godhead.

Within these pages, the author consistently distinguishes his vision of solitude from that of the hermit or babaji. The character of the devotional life which he pursues is neither solipsistic nor self-indulgent, which would simply be another form of sense gratification. This cannot be emphasized enough for the most common understanding of the religious life of solitude is that it is a life solely with an inward focus, the life of one who has fled the world in pursuit of personal salvation. As Satsvarupa Maharaja makes evident in both his prose and poetry, the life that he pursues is markedly different. For him, a life of solitude is one in which he may develop his particular form of preaching, expressed through prose, poetry, and correspondence. His writings range broadly over a vast number of topics, as readers of previously volumes of Every Day, Just Write will quickly recognize. The confessional chronicling of one's man journey serves as a touchstone for the readers who might see themselves in the struggles and successes, the dreams and hopes that Satsvarupa Maharaja shares with candor and intimacy.

Further, this writing imparts deep readings of the Vaisnava scriptures and devotional texts, naturally bearing witness to the profound spiritual and theological legacy of Srila Prabhupada. The reader encounters Satsvarupa Maharaja in a most personal way as he reflects not only upon Prabhupada's writings but upon his personal memories of this one who has delivered the treasures of Gaudiya Vaisnavism to the West and beyond. This is preaching in a different key, in a different genre. The reader discovers Satsvarupa Maharaja's unfailing appreciation of the beauty of Srimati Radharani and Sri Krsna, the elegance of this philosophy and its absolute power to deliver fallen souls.

Within this volume, Satsvarupa Maharaja intersperses a series of twenty-four numbered poems, accessible in their simplicity and rich in their treatment of a wide range of subject matter. Like the poetically inspired writings of past Vaisnava *acaryas* and with the style of the great Impressionist masters, this series of poems begins with a devotional piece, simply entitled "Krishna" which includes this sublime stanza:

> Krishna Krishna Krishna
> the favorite word
> the saving direction

Part One, p. 2

With such an economy of words, Satsvarupa dasa Goswami expresses not only his personal artistic trajectory but the heart of the bhakti tradition which he claims as his own. Krishna, "the favorite word" of every devotee, points in "the saving direction" of the soul's true home, Goloka Vrindavana, that place of eternal devotional service in love.

The beauty of this volume arises from the intersection of its setting in Ireland and the distinctive style of life, in which Satsvarupa Maharaja clarifies the true character of his choice to be alone: this is a fruitful solitude which inspires the reader to grow in devotion and surrender, thereby moving the reader closer to home, back to Godhead.

#1. (*Krishna*)

Raining down, thunder
in Wicklow.
The beginning of another go
at writing a book.

Krishna Krishna Krishna
the favorite word
the saving direction.

p. 2

As cummings writes
    paris
    paris
    paris
in his 1920s poems and cannot
find words pretty and feeling enough
to express his love,
I do write Krishna Krishna
as I'm able
His inconceivable yet personal form
is *tribhanga* in the hearts
of pure devotees.

p. 3

The thunder makes you wonder
what's going on? Is it drums
of the sky? Guns?
Rain. Krishna. A new book's
gift...from KRISHNA.

p. 3

194

To dust, he died in his spit,
in a fit, in old age after he
couldn't play anymore. In the
two years while his case was on
trial, before he went to jail,
Chuck Berry made a batch
of good songs.

pp. 3-4

Be careful on high diving
springboard don't break
your neck in half-gainer
can't you just sing
Hare Krishna, Hare Krishna?
No, we've got to do it this way.

p. 4

#2. (*Coloring*)

Got a new paint set, the
child makes a cow and a
littler one, two men, Krishna
"The guru must sanction."

But he's gone from the earth
like all of us must.
He'll tell us now through
deliberating on his teachings.

You are focused on Krishna
and how to serve this Movement –
tubs of blue and forest green,
yellow, red, white...
pens scratch, "I want to

be a devotee."
Keep on staining and stroking
those blank pages
KRISHNA
will appear.

But whatever He
wants – that is the
service of the pure devotee.
I've got ink stains on fingers
to prove it –

p. 12

When I let go it occurs to me
"I don't care if it's
Krishna conscious" then I
say He's in everything and finally
print words thick and soft
like Japanese calligraphy:
KRISHNA
JAPA
Beware,
be mine, O Krishna.
It is fun coloring.

p. 13

Swami, you are the best.
When you speak it's great
and let me say this little song
means I love you in the
interest of myself and everyone else,
I'll preach for you.

p. 26

#3. (*To Vrindavana*)

Raining a gray bird lights
on pine bough, moves. Rain
tinkles on the skylight
I want to tell you.

I keep digging for
Prabhupada and
Krishna in me in
remembrance, straight
from the latest book-reading.

He's everywhere
but dancing in His own
world where He's the
center for those who
love Him and join Him
where He is more and
better even than God.

p. 33

Krishna in Goloka. And
Vrindavana, India, our temple
is reorganized. You can go
there: the sand and the *babas*
and the dogs, hogs, monkeys,
parrots, peacocks, mice, flies,
the temple towers, politics,
gundas, tourists, money,
wasted time, body ills,
"Here's a book" – sit and read.
Bow down 'n' worship.

p. 34

Radha-Krishna
everyone knows,
but only a few
actually know
Radha and Krishna.

Writing this in
Ireland. Where you
are, that is Vrindavana
or – what?

p.34

#4. (*For Lord Nrsimhadeva*)

You can't go to the same moment twice.
It's dangerous looking deeper.
Under the welcome mat I
found wet mold slime and
a juicy worm curling. Ugh.
I put it back the way it was.

p. 35

Under the earth the worms –
for magpies, ravens and crows.

"We want to know
why you are writing of
birds and rain tinkles?"
'Cause it's my world.
"Yeah, so how come?"
Whaddya want?
A dished-out feast at

dusk to break the fast

on Lord Nrsimha's Appearance.
I did hear Prabhupada's
book where Lord
Nrsimha is prayed to by Indra –
"This demon took the demigods' shares,
but actually they belong to You.
Long were our hearts
oppressed, but You killed Him."

p. 36

Lord who kills demons –
we routinely "pray" –
please kill mine, make me strong.

That's the prayer of a
brave soldier. I say Lord
protect my *sannyasa*.
May You reign and be prayed
to by all devotees.
Rain, rain
this day at dusk
the Lord killed the demon
in the archway hall
and later sat
on his blood-spattered throne
and heard prayers of Prahlada.

Please bless us.
We keep asking
You for help.
May devotees get
better and me
remember You and serve You,
Lord Nrsimhadeva.

p. 37

#5. (*A Sunlight Lights the Day*)

Prabhupada's hat and scarf are a
bit askew. Soon I'll come to
set out new clothing, towels, etc.,
for today's worship. But I
undressed with my back to him.
Regret and say you won't again.

M. singing playing bouzouki,
"But you can't find solace
in the words of other men..."
He turns to the Lord within.
Peace?
I hope so.

Hear wind, wait for pack-
ages, assure yourself as light
lights the day. When you
speed up the video, Tribhuvanatha
waves his left and right arms,
switching microphone from hand to hand and
stage workers behind him drop
chairs, everyone runs, and it's
over faster that way with
no quality – a complete distortion.

Even at the pace of Lord Brahma
it ends. There are only a few
themes and we repeat. "My dear
Lord, please help me find the way."

p. 52

#6. (*Seeking Center*)

All these things together don't
add up to a center. I keep
adding more trinkets, "Send
one dozen Ticonderoga pencils please
and pills for digestion." But even if
you fill up the rooms and suitcases
and keep adding inventory,
where is the center?

A simple heart is grateful
to God. Don't get stumped
by atheist arguments. Thank
God for water and sun, doesn't
want liberation but loving
service to Krishna. See others as
equal and offer obeisances to
life in all creatures.
I believe all that and read
it and like it. Sigh and re-
gather for another effort,
several times a day at
comprehension of the
center, goal.

"And you can't find solace
in the words of other men."
And you can't find center when
you yawn. I'll be okay,
just dwindling and dying. Ask
for old disciples by name –
how is so and so doing? Still
living on a Canary Island?
Who is the new regional adviser?
When is "it" gonna happen. Again.
And other queries and yearnings.

When He allows, you
may center, enlightened
and go on working.

pp. 53–54

#7. (*My Day So Far*)

Seven. My head and yours.
How is that with you?
The red hard hat, I'd recognize
the driver of the scooper,
followed by the white truck
that carries rocks.

Heard a goat croak,
sure enough they lassoed
and hugged and lifted him up
threw him into the car trunk
and off to Baltinglass where they'll
release him to his chances
in some new wild. If he's
as domestically inclined as he
was here, he'll seek out a
new house but no one
will love him.

And I wait in vain for
complete clear. Dark cold skies
could be nice indoors if you
read comfy and your soul was
eager for it.

He may come back to Éire
that aggressive *sannyasi*,
where the people are so submissive

and take care of you. Just give
me my piece of my private land and
don't ask me to meet him.

Kadarma. Waiting. Watching the
clock. It took nine minutes to walk
down the hill.

pp. 77–78

#8. (*Roundelay*)

This wonder choice of being
alone "with *Srimad-Bhagavatam*" he keeps
saying to convince himself
with wonder say God
as sweet or *aisvarya*
keeps saying
   alone
   quiet
above and in and out. He
says "Prabhupada" as if
saying is...

Don't mock him as if saying
is itself good
is saying Hare Krishna
mantras like any violin –
but I like finding
new ways home.

He dreams not *sphurti* vision.
He dreams the worst scenario
and exits by "EXIT" sign –
wake up in time before
you get sliced to pieces
in love with her.

p. 93

As if saying the
roundelay will
save you. We're not after
liberation it's just this
trying/shy/willing/

Open the book
and read/student passes
exam happy.
June is coming he'll
read on his vacation
*Srimad-
Bhagavatam.*

p.95

Get tired of their faces,
don't love
get tired of my solitude,
to walk into the reading
room I have no taste,
nor for their rhyming
doggerel
propa-ganda for
Krishna.
Just give me a mo'
I'm sure to recover.
Just put me in range
of *vacasamrtena*
by discipline force.

p. 101

#9. (*Nine Title*)

No hat, I guessed he doesn't need it,
my Prabhupada. "Is he just sitting
there?" Don't ask like that, "Does
he eat? How sleep sitting up?"
You might as well ask,
"How does the sun?"

And make a self-defense here
against charges of taking it easy,
not preaching.
You've gotten into the habit
of passing off quiet life
as enough, even say, "I take
a risk by turning a page, I
preach by reading with
my eyeglasses, instead of
mere travel."

Yes. There is time...
Faith in yourself. When the
Lord tells me, I don't feel
it yet. What can he tell
them that they don't already
know? That Krishna is God,
that I believe it, that I
worship the *grantha* and
give myself to that because
my master said three hours a day
and it is fine and more, do
nothing else if you can
actually do it. Read
or else how can you
preach? *Sannyasi's* shame.

pp. 104–5

❧   ❧   ❧

#10. (*Take It*)

Gravel crunch, someone is coming
to the front door. Is it the Garda?
They would knock, "Where is
Stephen Guarino? We don't wear
guns." Huns, he's upstairs
reading his preparation for
advocating his case in
tomorrow's court.

We heard he eluded an e-
mail from a GBC and claimed
he's got no computer. We want to
search him for a few questions.
"Yes, but he may have a few for
you too, officers."

Question: Why does a transcendentalist
spend his life in these topics of
theology? Reply: Life is not
meant otherwise for humans.
But a tree lives a long time,
a bellow snorts and breathes,
a pig has sex, in the village.
Even a moment of full
consciousness – is better than a dead
old life.
But where is the proof
you have attained it?

Don't say I have. Need more
lives. You Garda guys...
I'm reading in this attic because...
"We know, we know, you want
to meet with Krishna and bow down
but you have to risk for that."

In my mind they go away
with *prasadam*. I recall
my master or wish I could.
Now M. treads to the door says
he's going to practice singing and
playing bouzouki,
I approve!
So why not approve your own
attic study? I do.
I give you permission. Now take it
until they take it away.

pp. 106–7

I may look like death
fried over, a lean and
hungry look, such men
are dangerous. Behold he
hath a gleam and clamps
down on the right side. He's
wearing baggy orange sweatpants
up to 9 A.M. and hiking boots.
Goes into the woods daydreaming
in anxiety. I beheld him
gazing out a skylight window.
He didn't know we saw him
slink back and play his
piano. As for his "art" work
in poems, the less said
the better.

p. 124

#11. (*Fly to Him*)

He's resolved again. Leave him
there mildly satisfied, awaiting his
lunch. Fly with us to
Bindu-sarovara or even better
Vrindavana. Fly with us to *Srimad-
Bhagavatam*, texts dissolving before our
eyes into their inner-outer
meaning we've previously failed.
Now we get the mercy riding
through Sanskrit letters and Prabhupada's
translation in our own American English.

Dear Supreme Lord, dear
devotees all. Devotional service.
That's it and leave way down
on earth diatribes and flung debates.
Fly with Him to His place. Peace,
you and me.

p. 126

Down on your knees.
Whatever I write makes
sense in some heaven or
other. Not in hell, please.
Don't put me there, says
the Salvationist in me.
And I strive to serve Him
today.

p. 128

"A saturnine place is Gita-
nagari," said the astrologer.
That can mean ignorant but
a *dhama* is not so. It's
also detached and can mean
quiet and even sleepy – a place
with no grand tourist attraction
plans. Just plow and plant and
milk whatever cows are left
and worship the Deity in
relative peace while the
Tuscarora rolls, and summer
trickles and slows down.
And honeysuckle and phlox and the
Baltimore Oriole (flown in from
the city three hours away).
But why think of there?
I'm here in Éire
at a desk and Svayambhuva Manu
is talking to the sage: "Please listen
to the prayer of my humble self
for my mind is troubled
by affection for my daughter."

pp. 138–39

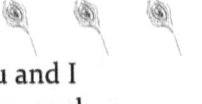

Swami, swim you and I
in the forest in the pool
with your other disciples. You say, "This
is the Yamuna, let us stop here."
This is where Krishna had His pastimes, let us
hear it from the Krishna *book*, yourself
telling us,
and then we can have a snack.

p. 147

209

Look
I don't wanna hear all this,
you hear?
I want to just read the sublime
and *bhakti-vaibhava*
notes. Pass exams, learn
slokas.

p. 151

Imagine an old sheep
hobbling, doing a leaping old
dance. He's laughable to watch
crippled, can't go uphill
yet he dances at summer
onset while daisies bloom
on the lawn and buttercups
I mean he can't do it nicely
but...
Hooray. Here's drinking
to (apple juice) your health
in Krishna consciousness
the antiseptic to miseries.

p. 153

#12. (*Like, That*)

Bleat, bleat Prabhupada's juice
cup sits golden, his chanting beads
I'm before him dull rascal
words like that
free us – mindset-cliché
but clichés are the well-
worn best only words
you can think of sometimes.
Effervescent, spirit soul
is servant of God. Like

that. Same words. So now
it's almost June, six days in
a row no headache. I'm
gonna get whapped soon.

Lord, Lord Visnu,
krsna-katha is *hari-katha*
and emperor Svayambhuva lived
in style, going to sleep to *shenai*
music of *hari-katha*, he
dreams of praising Hari.

And now hear from me.
Bright green almost a little yellow
in it from sunshine, the pines
erect spines stand up. A red
car leaves from this house.

Hear the latest news –
no, don't. Just quiet down
and thank God even if you
don't live (at some point).
Service never lost.

pp. 154–55

See the blessed
chant the holy
live the quiet.

p. 162

#13. (*Choosing to Be Alone*)

I am waiting and just sitting
looking out into a sloped yard
of uncut grass, tassel-
headed weeds that reach to
a pine forest and sheep bleating
somewhere.
I'm waiting and sitting, is it
lazy? Just don't want to get
riled before my meeting
with a brother.

Caw caw. You can worship
your master. This poem is defeated
but doesn't give up. Crick in back
of neck, dredged up memories –

Your brown lunch bag, sandwiches
inside, wrapped in cellophane,
made by mother, always one
of peanut butter and jelly. I liked
"Monk's Bread" not knowing in
those days it was Merton's
Cistercians or that I'd become
a Hare Krishna monk. Monk?
I didn't know even know Thelonius
yet. Or anything. But Monk's Bread
was (made in New York State), pliant
better than Bond or Tip Top soggy.

The lunchroom was a terror
yet I had my social niche as
long as I kept it. Punk,
good boy, scared, coping. At
home. A Staten Island boy who
actually loved to listen

to Allen Freed play rhythm
and blues discs.
That's all there was to me.
The rest was buried
under cars,
and Daddy kept me locked up.
Simply didn't know I was
something more than Stevie Guarino
with shirt collar turned up.

Now I know.
I'm waiting. Restrained. Playing
it alone. "Choosing to be
Alone," my hit song for
the month.

pp. 166–67

(From Part Two "Choosing to be Alone" Ireland, May 30 –
June 10, 1997)

#14. (*Hang in There*)

Hang in there if He or it wants
to give you a headache it
will and no Pachelbel's Canon
synthesizing but the Relaxation Company
can make it go away – although
they say the brain can choose
not to feel hurt. I dunno.

If He wills. I just wish I
could go on hearing of Krishna,
Uddhava and Krishna and *gopis* from
my master exclusively and just
be stoned, happy on that,

studious, occupied,
satisfied and not need to
roam around in
munis' books.

p. 13

#15. (*At His Feet*)

Prabhupada looks at me.
I was massaging him to zither
music by a Carmelite nun of
Luçon and thought No this will
mix into a Prabhupada, that's
not what I want.

So, I massage in silence and afraid
a lecture would
be too hard for me to take.
Get through this day you are
so concerned with bodily
pain.

Sing of God in glory and
sweetness. He's known by
Uddhava and gopis. He appears.
I just want to get it right,
parampara but in
my own self truly.

Is that permissible? Turn off the
zither. Hear.

pp. 13–14

#16. (*Pledge of Allegiance*)
Back again
avoiding sin.

Back to looking out window at green
and the yellow buttercups.

The urge to create
He'll accept it it's devotion
don't have to rhyme.

Love is what counts for
God, but how do you
get it? From Him, His
pure devotee. I serve him always
call it what you will
(*vaidhi* or *prema*, etc.).

He can take me all the way.
I sit before him today.
It was warm, huh, Prabhupada?
But now it's a little cooler,
last day of May
may I never leave you.
Pray, reveal it to me
as you desire.

p. 32

#17. (*Admit I Don't Know*)

You've got to
Hand it to them those
tall pines.

Dad's gone
Mom's somewhere
Mad and Tom I don't know where.

He asked, "If we are not these
bodies how come sastra says
a pure devotee liberates his kin
fourteen generations forward and back?"
I said
some things I don't know.

What do you know? Sailors...soldiers...
Some things are not worth
bothering over. *Asuram bhavam.*
I prefer to be alone in
this house
just walking in stockinged
feet, pace, chant
another round.

I said the answers come
with my own confession, and
I don't know. We
are not these bodies. We
have eternal spiritual quality
as persons, servants of God
in a blissful rasa.
I'll go read the book and
tell you about it.

pp. 33-34

A clown
a sincere guy old growing on
last day of May, walks
stooped but Sunday awaits,
any season he can write and
read *Bhagavatam*
Krishna is fully
present in name and *sastra* –
it's just our blindness and deafness
prevents us.

p. 34

❊   ❊   ❊

My Godbrothers write books too.
I'm writing this to my grandmother who
sat up in bed and said, "Goldilocks,
what big eyes you have."
Or was it I that said that to her?

Don't drop your pen, or you will
lose your thought.
Don't lose your soul
for jokes
joke books and antic ruse
of the lonely.

He was all alone when the
fire broke out. A tiny hole in
his pants revealed the leakage.
"No one should know," he said
"the nature of my soul."
But they're all the same,
psyches and bodies are
universal
unconscious
revealed in the dream.

p. 53

Swami, snakes, since when
was a good boy? Swami I became
as of 1972 Nrsimhadeva, and was not
with a woman after that.
And you wandered around the U.S.A.
he said, "That's fine but go to temples
and preach *Srimad-Bhagavatam* class
        as I have taught."
He also said keep you eye on the temple finances and
do your bit your little piece in the machine.

Swami, salami sandwiches are not allowed
tomato and cheese and bread sandwich
made by buddy Hridayananda Maharaja in the park
at Berkeley, and we sat on the
        grass and offered the food to God.
We're all scattered and grown-up
each one offering and what about me?
Someone says I don't see him
much at meetings.

p. 58

❀   ❀   ❀

Devahuti...
a crow (like a hawk)
glides in the blue
buffets of winds.
Kapiladeva will teach her,
        and I will go along reading it.

p. 61

So...you wasted
you were saved,
you worked in his mission
and what are you doing now?

Can you turn away from self
to look upon the Lord?
Can you say, "Prabhupada"
as you want? Does he
accept you as you are?
Can he order you to take a
new phase of mission for him?

You are one of thousands
in ISKCON. Do you want
to go alone as a different
way to feel special?

Krishna, Krishna, Krishna. What a mixed-up guy.

pp. 65–66

Gifts, who has. She (Elizabeth of the Trinity) had gifts
of mystical ardor for God, staying at the source by praying
in her Carmelite cell. Very good.
And I...and I...

Dwell in
nickel and dime and quarter
and A4 note pads and A5 and A6
and colored pens, pencils,
crayons.

Listen, the crows and
the peaceful wash of
the wind.
I want to be here at
this vocation well
lowering the bucket and
raising.

As the farmer grows and
cuts down his field, so do I
but not to provide fodder
for cows I'll slaughter.
But
for what?
You say. To offer
as devotional service
to my teacher.

pp. 66–67

Move along, poke
drag-ass. Be chipper,
daddy. Your heart's in
the highlands you too are
a utopian pessimist.

You unkindly describe yourself
posterily for posterity.
He sat in the toilet seat
in royal way (Oriental
style) hearing his master speak
and fighting flies of dislike
toward his master's delivery.

This fellow we joke at.
It's for his pleasure,
the butt of our jokes,
our only fellow.
We do bequeath...
May he die in the
arms of the Lord
by guru's grace.

p. 74

Swami, I am not a scholar
learning from the person in charge of
religious studies, I won't become your
academic preacher in the world.
I'm not at a computer on behalf of the
Communications Department of ISKCON.
In my dreams I lay in bed beside a GBC man
who didn't like me. But I'm not like that.
I am your cela, he says.
I'm trying to prove it fresh and ready
like a newly flamed *capati*.

p. 77

18. (Tiny Effort)

The tired guy the tired
bellcap is tiny and the
metal varnished silver plaque.

The tiniest fellow in me
wants out, wants rest
wants Raghunatha Gosvami to know
the tiniest soul we are
all the same size so you
can't be smaller
light up pure your own
self-realization. Guru guides
and you obey.

The tiniest biting
his fingernail of thumb.
Tiny repeating got a gimmick
a "he," a
mask of gauze and stone but
Mata made puppet show

tiny memory of her tiny
son Tim coming to me
each day carrying plastic
bucket with this in it:

Piece of incense, flower,
etc. His mother approved and
laughed throatily.
I was beside myself, mannered
foolish grinning – had my own
teeth back then when
fierce brass strong-thighed
Nrsimhadeva was worshiped by
yours truly.

pp. 79–80

#19. (Stretching Exercise)

Breathing by open window
is this body ecstasy? Tell
them, "See God in everything."
Clichés pour out. Breathe in
fresh air, and go through the
stretching exercise.

Stretch and pray.
My pee thing hurts a little sometimes,
but I'm all right if I don't go anywhere.
Eyes,
old, but I stood on one foot
with grace like a dancer
imagining myself small and
slightly hunched and under low
roof.

Imagine you are stretching for God,
stretching each limb
back and forth
in its self
the body is...
oh.

pp. 80–81

❊   ❊   ❊

#20. (A Secret Offering to God)

My God is not my own ego
but even that ego of
Steve-Satsfer, is
Krishna in tiny part.
God is my Master and
I am the spirit soul.
Both are spirits, and
one serves the other.

Holy fool goof off –
we've heard that ex-
pression from Kerouac.
Now I know a little
better what it means.

Just to avoid the always
serious and official we
may do this.
And just to make an
act (drawing), etc., which
has no audience like
the flower that
blossoms unseen but
is therefore seen only by

God. The flautist in the pit.
You delight in it and offer it to Him
and no one else has to know it.

p. 84

Please mind, wake up
and take this gift
freely offered. Why
do you dwell on lesser
concerns? Why are you afraid to
embrace the feet of
the Lord of your life?
Christian saints do it,
why not me, a flawed Krsnite?

p. 85

Halley, hello, the day has
begun. You die some but
live some and celebrate your
God. Oh, you of little
faith. You may walk
in the pine forest on the
logging road, surrounded by
signs of cruelty and yet...

The soul can be joyful.
Just don't think you're a
big writer who's got a
lot to say,
you and Simone Weil
figuring it all out with
your hard logic and
mystic heart.

pp. 88-89

Write, write until you
give up pretension, and it
becomes a prayer, a cry.
Please let me serve You free
of that which holds me
back,
the fears and reservations and
the attempt to get the first-
class berth for the
easy ride for
yours truly.

p. 91

❋   ❋   ❋

Who can figure it out?
Better to pray to God for
permission to act as His
instrument,
a pen, a knife, a zither,
a guide,
a preacher,
don't bore,
don't sin or deviate and if you
"must" read your Christian
authors and others make
some use of it in His
service.

pp. 91–92

#21. (*Wake up and Talk*)

I suddenly collapsed,
passed out with fatigue
at my desk. But am
now up to tell it. One
day I won't wake up.

Except in the next world, I
mean to say next life –
Lord, he says,
but in vain? Chant Hare Krsnas
but there too he's flawed,
offensive pramada.

Turn to God.
He taught Devahuti.
In His original form He
holds the flute,
controls all worlds by His
expansions, is the only
true enjoyer of sacrifices
and the best friend of everyone.
Whoever knows Him (even partially)
is free from fear and
attains shanti.
Now you're talking.

pp. 94–95

Swami is the one who controls his senses.
When it's time for night sense grat he's sleeping
and when they finally crash out he is awake
making prayers to the Lord.
I therefore call him Swami.

My master said a Swami is one
who loves and serves Krishna, not
merely a man with a beard
and saffron robe but a person
who works and serves the Lord.

p. 120

#22. (*Real Life*)

Jagannatha, I went to sleep
for twenty minutes and dreamt
a woman touched me.
A strict Mayavadi sannyasi would
have to do penance for that.
A strict Mayavadi.

And you guys? / We are
strict too but a little slack
because the chanting is so
powerful / Who said?
My Swami.
Is this all Hare Krishna stuff
you write about?
Yes, he said (who's talking,
Do you have a woman
in here?) No, no woman.
I'm just making dialogue.
Yes, I write Hare Krishna
stuff and real life as I
try to be a Krishna.

Then she said /
I read this in a poem by
Ray Carver, it was about
him, a writer and the girl
he picked up.
I don't want to hear that.
Okay, here is a devotee poem...
/ You just pick out some
scripture, is that it?
No, I told you it's
scripture and real life.

I don't get it.
You will. Hare Krishna, Hare

Krishna, Krishna Krishna, Hare Hare
I thought so!
Hare Rama, Hare Rama,
Rama Rama
there you go.
Sounds like blasphemy.
No, it's the real thing.

pp. 122–23

Why don't you lie down
princess on a pea?
You'll feel better unless
worse.
Why don't you
pray, "Hare Krishna?"

p. 124

#23 (*The Word Krishna*)

Rain the
word Krishna
the words you fear
shit and worse
Charles Bukowski
Henry Miller
Norman Mailer
now they are dead.

Krishna Krishna, keep Him apart
He's above they shouldn't
get a chance to blaspheme.
They do it anyway

God say God they
say I don't believe.

I won't repeat what
"they" say. But what we say.

Krishna, Krishna, Krishna, I'm feeling okay
I tell myself I've recovered
from today's wave of doubt.
Hope to fall asleep easier.
Just relax and let it come,
your thoughts are not strict
systematic Krishna consciousness just
waves of stuff and then
rain on glass,
Krishna.

pp. 130–31

#24. (*Heavy Fog*)

I got this far without a
headache, close to six A.M.
It's misty dark gray if you
were going to summer camp you
might cancel today. No, they'd
go anyway, drive up the hill
in the fog.

I don't have to go.
I can stay here a few
months only. I get a
sting when I piss, something's
wrong but I hope it will
go away or not come for
a while.

Limbs of the tree dance –
several dances of evergreen
limbs moving down in different ways
up and down the tall tree
this dark morning.

I wrote "KRISHNA" in red
on a black background
paint on A4 paper.
A very good morning because
I remembered you are supposed to
think of Krishna and be happy.

pp. 145–46

Say it was nice serving Swami
in Boston, the letters he sent
remind me I am his servant
still. Although I don't get such letters, and
I appear to be loose, I am on
a rope
and must account to him.

p. 176

CHAPTER EIGHT - SACRIFICE FOR BHAGAVATAM

IRELAND, JUNE 10–30, 1997

Dream of lower nature. When I woke I thought of sacrifice for *Bhagavatam*. Give up lesser for the sake of the greater. It will be good if I can do. Enter the study, the relishing...My starting idea is that by insisting on a reading program in *Srimad-Bhagavatam*, I'm swinging my time and attention to it and thus sacrificing the possibility of a more concentrated writing marathon or literary project...Now I'm insisting on reading every chance I get and asking the writing-self to come along.

> Satsvarupa dasa Goswami
> *Every Day, Just Write, Volume Eleven,*
> *Sacrifice for Bhagavatam, pp. 1–2*

With these opening words of this eleventh volume of *Every Day, Just Write*, Satsvarupa dasa Goswami introduces the character and scope of this new chapter in this unfolding literary project. Indeed, the very title of this ongoing series indicates the priority of writing in the devotional life of this author. However, this volume could aptly be titled "Every Day, Just Read" for now, as Satsvarupa Maharaja writes above, the "writing-self" will be pulled forward as he dedicates this next period to the spiritual discipline of reading. This is not certainly to suggest that the free-write *sadhana* will be suspended but rather it will arise in response to a sustained and focused reading of that which has always been Satsvarupa Maharaja's companion, the *Srimad-Bhagavatam*. The theme of this period is further described by the author as follows, *Sacrifice to Bhagavatam* also means to accept whatever it's saying in each section you read. I'm not selecting a group of prayers to read from a favorite devotional text, but I'm reading whatever is current in my go-through, now nearing the end of the Third Canto" (*p. 64*).

As one consistently recognizes, the geography and character of the place in which Satsvarupa Maharaja is residing always has a profound impact upon his writing, as a particular place creates an atmosphere from which the writing emerges and in which it breathes. Significantly, while the author continues to reside in Geaglum, Northern Ireland, at the time of this writing, it is the *Srimad-Bhagavatam* itself which provides that sense of place, in this case a literary topography which will shape this volume's writing. Undoubtedly, the reader will quickly recognize Satsvarupa Maharaja's profound immersion within this magisterial text.

In many ways, *Sacrifice for Bhagavatam* flows naturally from the previous volume, Choosing to be Alone. The choice to pursue a distinctive life of solitude is now deepened as the author explores the riches of the *Srimad-Bhagavatam*. From the discovery of solitude in Geaglum, Satsvarupa Maharaja now experiences now a transcendental solitude, a dwelling place which this towering scripture affords. The *Srimad-Bhagavatam* is not simply a text to study, but it is one to relish with heart, mind, and soul. Keeping in mind the tremendous theological assertion that this text is the literary incarnation of Sri Krishna, the scripture itself creates moments of *darsana*, verse by verse.

Satsvarupa Maharaja approaches the *Srimad-Bhagavatam* in precisely this manner with a breathtaking conviction in the unequivocal truthfulness of the scriptures and the Lord to whom it reveals. If the reader would similarly relish the author's mood in this volume, *Every Day, Just Write* would itself offer moments of *darsana*, free-

write upon free-write, moment upon moment.
      You dig what I'm saying, man?
      So where are you? In tama
      guru bhakta? In passion?
      In merely "good," seeking salvation?
      How dare he raid the devotees'
      club as if we were cult criminals.
      Who are you talking about now?
      I'm talking about these investigators
      who place us in the category. Let's not claim it,
      but just hear
      what is pure devotion.

p. 6

❀   ❀   ❀

Swami, I confess I've been a bad boy.
I used to make confession in church, and you blasted
that church saying, "They can't answer two questions

why God has only one son and why they are
killing so much although Christ says,
"Thou shalt not kill."
He got their number.

Swami, please forgive me for fault-finding.
When you speak it is a ferocious attack and
yet you are quiet as young Prahlada.
Bhurijana said that.

Swami, you are the memory of you.
Where are you? Where am I going?
Will I be with you and other devotees?
Does everything change
from one life to another,
and if so, where is the continuity of ourselves?
How will you be the spiritual master in my next life?

Are you the same Abhay Charan De at 26 Second Avenue
or is that just for this life?
I don't want to pretend to *gopi-manjari bhava*,
but I'm just throwing out these questions.
Is it fair? Where will we go?
Will I lose my individual nature?

I know I won't be Steve Guarino,
but does that mean it's all forgotten,
and if so, then how am I an individual eternally?
I don't raise these as doubts, but I'd
like to know what the books say and in my
own life what it means. How can I go
if I don't have love? How I can attain that love?

A fellow like me says he can't work hard
in an outer way anymore. He's tired of these big workers
who preach surrender surrender preach preach.
He wants sensitive nice treatment,
but I know we have to pray and work at it
and life is sweet and life is cruel –

The rabbits attest to that, bait meat
they are, soft furry, preening themselves
and then eaten by the fox. What is the meaning?
Did He who made the lamb make thee?

pp. 14–16

I have not forgotten
to make music on the pipe of the holy one.
I have not forgotten to make no sense sometimes.
There are one hundred happy ideas to keep after.
Death stalks the proud one.
The literary stuff is crap.

Norman Mailer and Frank Sinatra still alive?

Death waiting to pick them off one by one or more than one at a time.

I haven't forgotten the old sailor's club and the dreams I can't get rid of. But when Krishna wants it all clears up, and you'll be a different person. Just as you are different now than you were in 1967 or 1977...you keep changing.

Have I forgotten me old mother and father?

Yes, I have enlisted in the Lord's army. I seem to have forgotten something, but I am vying for the attention of the Lord in my own way.

I haven't forgotten *raganuga*. Radharani plays the lute. They are pleasing to Krishna. You are closing down the curtain on this day. The sun is going down. The day is becoming the night, and nothing can stop it. Another day less.

pp. 47–48

A baby was born dead at Gita-nagari,
another was born alive and is still
thriving. Both mothers survived.
And the rabbits here in Wicklow...
furry balls of life eating the grass...
are sometimes run over by cars or
nature finally allows a fox to
eat one alive...
How horrible and
here we are at the desk
with desk lamp reading
a little longer.
Tell, confess.

p. 52

So what.
He dances a jig
so what, the position of jazz musicians
is very precarious.
So what, a monk is better off?
My pen reigns supreme?
I say be on your toes. Your heart
    you must go into the other room and chant Hare
Krishna and stay close to your Gurudeva by following his
orders. This chapter of *Srimad-Bhagavatam* brings upon
you a sense of renunciation and sobriety.

p. 53

Swami, I sometimes must push.
When you were here we pushed,
and you pushed us and said work hard
for Krishna.

Many is the time, Mamma is the Vedas
I will serve you as
cowherd boy reader purveyor of
the truth, college lecturer,
please forgive me when my
language veers off like this
it is an indulgence on my part,
I know. But I mean to say

I am the boy grown old
who wants to serve you and
does so although a little awry and lazy.

A lazy fellow will get a good kick
in the pants from his Master.
Or a kind glance and he will go on
his own accord, preaching, preaching
hearing, hearing...

p. 104

He said
in bed and vowed I'll
be a better chanter but
when he began the beguine
it was as slippery as wet rock
and he fell in mind and bruised
his head, elbows, feet,
got up and instantly slipped
I think it's hellish
"mind" he prayed, "brother"
but *manah siksah* was
hard to find. *Manah
siksah*,
teach that rascal
to think topmost – or
at least to come back each
time to hear
Hare Krishna mantra's sixteen
words, thirty-two syllables.

pp. 107–8

Oh, celebrate the wound
I mean the right to write whatever
comes and say, "It's for God."
My zany dancing is a method I
learned and may not be fit for the
Lord but He's Janardana and sees
the good in what we do.
Demented but we want
to serve Him
like the bum who was not
in order but brought Swamiji some
toilet paper rolls.

pp. 150–51

Where is my love for Krishna? Why can't I leave all

memories behind? I seem drawn to them.
The three brothers in my dream
are mythical in stature,
out of a story, gypsies,
rip-off men, yet softies,
they gathered at Dad's bed
to commiserate with his illness
and give him wine. O Dad,
who do you have to dies this
way?
Can't you get better with good health foods and a
positive attitude?

My father never acted like that, getting tossed out
of a hotel. But he didn't love God or go to church. Maybe he
saw too much evil.

O saints of the Catholic Church, why didn't you
touch him and me too in childhood? My childhood was
deprived of religion which I so much want now but cannot
find.

Huh?

Oh, I can't find my heart to sing. We have been
stymied in ISKCON and can't enter *gopi-bhava*. I have cast it
far from me – fear of *sahajiya*.

pp. 152–53

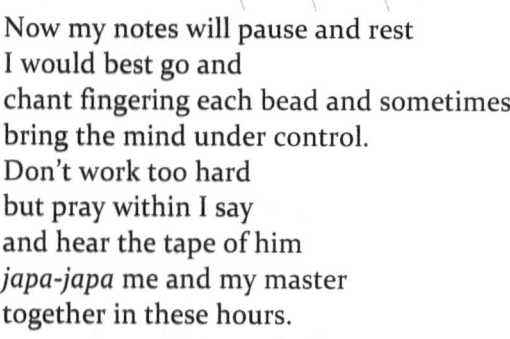

Now my notes will pause and rest
I would best go and
chant fingering each bead and sometimes
bring the mind under control.
Don't work too hard
but pray within I say
and hear the tape of him
japa-japa me and my master
together in these hours.

Sixteen the mere minimum I do
as my offering of breath and
scattered inattention, but
at least I count
and utter out loud the sweet
holy names which
will conquer.

pp. 155–56

❧   ❧   ❧

I pray for this conviction
sit and play and pray
construct the work
staying away from distractions
like fire, burn the wood
chant the mantras, observe and participate,
be constant and enthused.
Krishna will be pleased.

pp. 171–72

❧   ❧   ❧

I saw the wood pigeon flap
against the blue sky and knew
I didn't have to write about it.
I don't even know how I
feel or how a brother might
feel.

p. 179

❧   ❧   ❧

Expose yourself,
take off your protective covering and
allow the *Bhagavatam's* rays to
bathe you.
It's not difficult, harmful,

or painful,
and the gain is great.

p. 54

Each purport is filled with possibilities...

p.54

❋   ❋   ❋

Oh, he's a spiritual master
from Rio Grande,
and he's got a big name
among his own.
He's on a cult high-horse, but
he's a 'umble man.

He toots his horn in a
hundred plus books
and gives out looks
and assurances too to
the ladies and men
and their children.

He can't be hired, begged,
or bought,
but he's not so brave.
He reads and writes and
scampers up the stairs
when he hears gunshots
or a knock at the door.

Oh, he's a spiritual master
and can fire off riposte
to the atheists of yore
and those of today.

He's a fiery guru

on a soft seat awhile,
"Drag him down!" shout
the demons in my dreams.
He's an ISKCON guru
one of that sort
but unique in his way
I can't slow down to say
just what he feels,
but he's trying for that.

Oh, peace, please
tell me who I am.
Let me live for His
service.

pp. 57–59

❋   ❋   ❋

"Loving practice" I said.
Try to live out these words.
Narada, Narada
come to me too.
May Supersoul send my master
Prabhupada. "What! Again?
Hasn't he taught you enough?
He calls you repeatedly but
you get restless and want to
go away."
May he call me now
and change me.
I want to be changed.

p. 62

Narada, if you teach me
bhakti I'll take it, but
I'm not austere even a drop
like Dhruva was. Give
me the easy way.

Chant Hare Krishna. Awaken
in me that love.

p. 63

Oh, stop talking about
the world, Stevie Wonder.
But it's a wonder, I
can't see how you can just dismiss
the world in the name of
preferred God consciousness.

p. 64

God. Plain, abstract truth.
Peanut butter,
Rubber bands,
bracelets,
firm bread, firm
soggy toast and
bare knuckles.

pp. 64–65

Goodnight, eagle rest, pheasant standing on stone I
saw, grouse, spare them, rabbits too nibbling on grass
awhile before foxes attack.
    The world is like that.
Tell us how you write.
I take a deep breath and
plunge in with my
pitchfork and work like
crazy. I snooze and
cruise with a Sheaffer
pen. I grasp my *japa*
beads and tell you what

comes.

p. 67

      ✸   ✸   ✸

Old memories
not allowed or what
I read on the tourist map
of Wicklow; B&B,
pottery store, acting club,
horse club, stud farm,
what about churches?

pp. 67–68

      ✸   ✸   ✸

Henry Adams, the guy with the
pipe was Tad who later got initiated
by Prabhupada. Don't think he's your
disciple. You've got enough, they
worship you in your socks and forlorn
underwear. They say our guru ate a carob bar
and then went to sleep.
We gave him a donation. He worked even through
his pain. He's the guru of Santa Fe,
"The sweetheart of Sigma Thi."
He's free of the modes and doesn't read
newspapers, as far as I know.
He gets a monthly summary of news
from a lawyer friend.
Many things about him we don't know.
He keeps to himself and writes and
       publishes just a little.
I hear he has a shack in Northern Ireland maybe
we should move there to be near to our Gurudeva
and hear him give lectures twice a day
and cook for him, darn his socks,
damn his might,

we can turn against him if he goes
wrong. We pray that he doesn't fall down
Maya is powerful.

p. 76

Swami Prabhupada, we want
all wills to be surrendered to you.
Always we hear from you.
Maybe they don't understand,
but I do, and brothers and sisters do,
that you said no one can
replace the spiritual master.

p. 89

Interrupted, started again, dissuaded, not interested,
seeking relief from the *Srimad-Bhagavatam*
"then back to it again. My life will end in the middle
of it, or at the start or the end.
Persona pretending to write a book, to be a writer,
to be a devotee,
a *sannyasi*"
who are you anyway?

p. 95

CHAPTER NINE - MY SECRET LIFE

IRELAND, JULY 1–21, 1997

My secret life sounds good. Secret joy, secret terror? No, joy
I mean. Subterranean springs, juices.

p. 97

Someone may say, "But writing should not be like a
secret mantra. If it has potency distribute it."
I do, but even then I feel secret joy. Think how this
is not selfish. I'm cultivating surrender of even that private
self to the mission of Krishna. I have surrendered the outer
self, and maybe I have indulged in expressing the inner self,
now become aware that the secret self must also serve
Krishna – and glorify Him.

pp. 97–98

If there is a single word that becomes a stumbling
block within the spiritual life, it is undoubtedly,
"surrender." To surrender is to relinquish one's power, one's
status, and even one's standing within the religious life.
Perhaps the final example of surrender is the most difficult
of all, for the cultivation of personal pride in spiritual
advancement challenges the very core of the life of faith,
that there will always be an ontological or qualitative
distinction between the Supreme Person and the
individual. To surrender is to acknowledge this distinction,
and to thereby relinquish all standing before the Lord in an

act of humility and love. The unequivocal challenge to surrender in this manner is the principle to which Satsvarupa dasa Goswami points in the twelfth volume of *Every Day, Just Write*, entitled, *My Secret Life*.

The contemplative life has consistently provoked criticism by those who view such a calling as self-indulgent at best. But here, in this volume, the author replies to that criticism with the decisive realization that informs this volume as a whole, quoted above. The life of solitude has moved Satsvarupa Maharaja to recognize that surrender of the outer self is but the beginning of the spiritual life. As he writes, "I'm cultivating surrender of even the private self to the mission of Krishna." (*p.97*) This recognition has without question clarified the author's vocational discernment in a most radical manner. The outer self may be surrendered through the practice of regulative principles and devotional service, and that in and of itself is a tremendous challenge requiring unwavering commitment. However, as disciplined as one may be in this regard, the deepest parts of ourselves may still cling to a rebellious autonomy before the Lord. The insight regarding this next movement of surrender, the surrender of the private self would be one and at the same time excruciating and redemptive. One can easily imagine the vigorous and desperate protest of the ego in response to this call for an inner surrender. Yet, it is in precisely this intentional challenge to the ego that the joy of redemption may be discovered and then relished. This is the surrender of the ego not to an impersonalist void but a surrender to the Lord himself and the wonders of unalloyed devotion. This is the sublime *heme* which Satsvarupa Maharaja addresses in this foundational volume.

It is certainly no coincidence that Satsvarupa Maharaja here reflects upon the conversion of Sarvabhauma Bhattacarya, one of the decisive moments recorded in Krishnadasa Kaviraja's towering achievement, the *Caitanya-caritamrta*, an unrivaled theological of biography of Lord Caitanya Mahaprabhu. For this moment in the earthly pastimes of Lord Caitanya, a story of remarkable deliverance, which tells of the full surrender (both outer and inner) of the sophisticated, academically trained, highly regarded Sarvabhauma, a philosophical impersonalist is emblematic of the issues which Satsvarupa Maharaja addresses in My Secret Life. For these reasons, this volume may be understood to form a theological centerpiece to the *Every Day, Just Write* series as a whole.

Readers of this volume are given a window in which the author grants a most intimate glimpse of his own inner life, and this is reflected both within this volume's poetry and prose. This volume further chronicles Satsvarupa Maharaja's commitment to support and expand the preaching mission of the institution founded by his spiritual master, A.C. Bhaktivedanta Swami Prabhupada, the International Society for Krishna Consciousness. For in a passage cited at the beginning of this introduction, the author writes that he is cultivating inner surrender "to the mission of Krishna." And what is that mission? To deliver fallen souls through the sharing of the boundless mercy of Sri Sri Radha-Krishna. In this manner, by exploring surrender of both the outer and inner selves, Satsvarupa Maharaja continues to lend his distinctive voice in the service of Prabhupada's movement to spread the wonders of Lord Caitanya's *sankirtana* movement far and wide.

My Secret Life is a remarkable volume in which the author recognizes the significance of his life as a writer. For the reflections in both poetry and prose are themselves embodiments of surrender. To write is to surrender. This is the sublime "secret" Satsvarupa Maharaja shares with every reader.

#1
New electric heater in
bathroom. Warms up fast.
I wear the shower shoes
leave my slippers outside,
as Madhu preferred.

Finish up and come here, read
two Carvers and then I try.
But right away it's my little life.
Wind sound, Lough Erne.
My mind went over again and
again an inferior thought about
two children here who preferred
another guru rather than me.
No worth in the thought,
no investigation of it,
just chewing on it like an old bone.

Red clover is actually purple.
White clover is common.
I do not have much taste for
either *bhajana* or preaching.
But I like to be alone.

When I read of non-devotees trying
for sense gratification
I reject it as completely inferior.
It's temporary.
I know of the eternal.

When I read a Christian prayer
to the *aisvarya* Lord,
to God the Father
I think, "I know better."
And I wait for lunch.
Moved in here for two months.

pp. 9–10

Now I'm a cowpoke,
Western in Wellies
expatriate escaped in Ireland
get the hell away from
ISKCON downs and controversies and
the too much socialization.

p. 23

✳   ✳   ✳

The metronome, the harpsichord, and
        I better slow down.
Don't go to hell
you'll pay for this
a penny for your dreams
an Irish pound, hound
I want God
God's service in a way I can handle...

pp. 28–29

✳   ✳   ✳

Coping

Headaches dull not bad,
the boy's mother sounded like
a hag. "What happened to your head?!"
as if chastising, arguing against it.
The boy cried afraid – how
serious was the cut? I went on
shaving in the bathroom.
Then she knocked on our door.
Madhu answered, "Ow, wow."
He ran to get Randolph to take
the boy to the hospital. Not so
bad, some stitches. I didn't
see it. Wiped aloe gel onto my
face, gauged the ache in my

head and came in here to
do what I can next.

p.32

✶   ✶   ✶

Yeah, I don't pray
don't remember to say Krishna
don't pray to my master when
I have head pain I just
tune into it, wait on *prakrti*
to do its thing,

and enjoy the comfort of the bed,
and think the extra rest must be
demanded by the body.

They (people here) may not
understand why I don't come
out and over, but I'm not
well.
People take from me, don't
give, and they don't know my literary mission.

Oh, you sad-ass clown
he says. But I believe in the
Holy Ghost, the forgiveness of
sins. I bring semen up
to the brain or at least don't
let it out during
a year. Amen Midnight Mass
go on peace.

p. 59

To the universe,
to the merger of the book
off the sky hooks of

memories ("left-handed
smoke screen") – I
ran around a camp asking
for the sky hook until...
it dawned, you rookie!
You fool! And you freeze all night
in the outdoor straw bed thinking
when will this night end?

p. 65

❊   ❊   ❊

How I Wanted

I've got the best God
consciousness to follow and tell.
And admission of some
of my failings.

The emptiness, smallness
is like a very small fish.
My achievement? Who knows?
Plenty of words, in books.
You can go out for a walk.

And come back to this book.
I mean *Srimad-Bhagavatam* where
Bhumi is telling Prthu Maharaja
the plan to give shelter to
earth's citizens.

My reading is in our university,
our perpetual seminar and seminary,
our *Hall of Faith and Science*,
where Prabhupada presides,
the *Srimad-Bhagavatam* class.

I can do okay here, I'm
practiced. Can even teach.
But little fish, little fish,
in shallow, clear (and muddy) waters.

The slow rowboats are crossing
a short distance from here to Govinda-dwipa
on a Sunday afternoon.
This is how I want it.

pp. 74–75

* * *

The pot is EJW
the calf is – many possibilities
the milk I desire is
flowing bhakti for
you and me. An offering
to the Lord,
at the Lotus feet...

p. 84

Swami, the *aprakata* word is on my tongue,
the fever is swung, the Emily Dickinson book I never
won at the Kewpie doll counter in the
horse fair, the bingo game at Saint Clare's Church
and the actual Saint Clare of Assisi I never knew.

The Christians who don't like us because
we are Krishnas and that means to them
we can't accept Christ as our Savior. We say,
"He's our guru," but they don't like that or
they don't believe it.
Ray Carver in his fishing boat torturing the
poor fish with hooks and killing them.
The avenues of doubt, the poor habit

of finding fault with great souls and
with the followers of Prabhupada.
No, no you better remember that
you did abominable things with this body
they say you can't wash a coal but the soul
is pure. Swami, make us mindful.
He was kind to us but wanted us to work also
for spreading Krishna consciousness, and
          don't be afraid of
austerities, don't be laid back. O Swami,
I can't do as I did when younger,
and I'm not on your level, not so empowered.
But I will serve you in my way.

pp. 89–90

❊ ❊ ❊

The wind whines
on a calm day by the lake
a Monday early so no
motorboats disturb me.
There may be rioting in Belfast.
The helicopter patrols the skies
even out here.

p. 93

Salud, drink Highland Spring water,
your time here is running out,
drink a sip
with ease and
pray Krishna Krishna.

p. 94

Among friends
me and them
open the doors,

no, close them,
only us.
Forget the past or
remember it. Don't talk
I will tell you...
evermore
no more.

p. 96

❋   ❋   ❋

I put forward the calf of my
secret writing mission.
for Adhoksaja.
The pot is the pages of a
private edition.
The juice flows like ink,
but it's nectar from the
Lord, and I offer it to
Him, "Please accept this."

p. 97

❋   ❋   ❋

Vital Action
Hammering next door. Get it
done. I don't need to drink this
heavy grape juice. Away from the
rioting of Catholics and Protestants.

The police, he told me,
they hate the police for
guarding the road –
tanks lined up on both sides
so the Orangemen can march through it.
Hate and injustice. I'm
aware I'm away from it,
where I want to be. But

I don't want to miss out
on vital action.
Therefore, read and chant.
Sit silent awhile,
feel Lord Brahma telling Prthu Maharaja
don't try to counter what's happening.
Tolerate for Krishna.
Chant and pray for peace.

p. 100

Before framed portraits of Krishnadasa Kaviraja and
Rupa Gosvami.
You say secret life, but it can't be a secret from God.
But it's secret from you guys.
But you'll expose it. Sex expose. Flasher, streaker.
No, no. Calm down.
You calm down, old man. I'm the devil in the flesh.
I'll calm down, I'm the soul. But not so calm. Pic in
doc's office of boat in harbor, but it said the boat is meant
to be repaired so it can go out to sea. Not stay in the
harbor.
Hold on. *Mygranol* prescribed for joy-free, Inis-Free,
pain-free
sculpture hordes, nudes, dreams...
his bow tie
his smile
his circus sounds and solos
so long...
He dies, thinks of Krishna, that's fine, but if not all
this is a waste and worse.

p. 108

The secret is that I am always writing privately, able
to enter this vein where I can forget the audience. The
secret is also that I derive considerable strength and solace

from this. And that I am making an offering of this to Krishna, even though it is something very "selfish." I'm implying (and hoping) that I'm also confident that Krishna is accepting this "secret" offering. Thus, it is confidential and only known between Krishna and me. And it's not even known completely to me. But Krishna knows everything. He may also see this as a foolish, babyish form of devotional service, but He is allowing it for now. Anyway, I should not guess at what Krishna thinks, don't attempt to read His mind or turn Him into some supreme Gremlin. He's more loving and more powerful than I can imagine.

pp. 111–12

❋　　❋　　❋

These Things I Do

Oh, sit-here-and-nuthin'-to-do
blues. I tried reciting the
old verses of Gita I memorized
over twenty years ago. They're still
okay, starting *karpanya-*
dosopahata-svabhavah...rusty.
Asocyan anvasocas, funny
how memory works, you flick
your tongue back here and it
responds or doesn't. Some are well-
memorized, some always shaky.
Now alone with the little I do.
Weak semi-invalid, he can't
work or walk much, gets a
headache. Could write a batch
of poems some day...Answer mail.
These things I do until...oh,
there's a new little booklet on
Evelyn Underhill. Shall I learn

who she is? Bhurijana said
the people we read can help
us. But then back to
the Source, *Bhagavatam*, chanting.

For going into trance he
visualizes that he's walking down
slippery steps into Radha-kunda.
I sat up in bed last night when
I couldn't sleep. Breathed in measure,
counting myself down two and three flights
of escalator stairs but then
slipped over it in my mind.

You see, I can't think rigorously.
I just think a little and then stop.
Gaze, diminished, look out at
the lake. Skiers go by. Then
calm.

pp. 144-45

❊   ❊   ❊

They say Inis Rath is sad
for so few devotees, and they want
to make Gita-nagari a hub
of activity to receive homeless
when the earth flips out and
in Wicklow they're trying to draw
tourists to an open farm,
thousands come to Radhadesa in Belgium.
But why not a quiet place
where you can just take care of
the Deities, grow vegetables
and chant and read? Wouldn't that be nice too?
Darkening the sky, let it rain, I
say, let the beauty be in the

blonde tassel heads of weeds
with green stems mixed in
with long grass blades all
uncut and so deep you can
see only the heads of the little
deer, bright-brown and white-
spotted fellows with antlers
like new things too big for them.

See Krishna here. Your night comes
when you can rest and rise,
the rhythm. Just stick to
devotional service, my master said
and that I'll do each day.

p. 146

Listen mug,
sing a little
juggle before God and
audience of devotees.
No, be deeper than that –
what – how.

p. 147

Ordinary Aspiring Devotee

The *guru* mostly talks to those
who have at least proclaimed
surrender to him. Sometimes for preaching
he speaks to outsiders, but
the *sastras* say he speaks
only to disciples
the inner meanings.

What if he doesn't know
anything? Then he's no guru.
What if the rain blots out
vision through the windows, fills
the pane with drops, some
trickling down like tears?
What if you can't see out
except the vague outline of trees?

If you take your eyeglasses off
it's like that, everything vague.
And a twinge comes behind the right eye.
"When is the last time you saw
Radharani?" asked the boy near Varsana.
When is the last time
I read *Srimad-Bhagavatam*?
Having been away even an hour,
can you speak something
solid and precise and inspiring?

Maharaja Prthu had a beautiful body,
could be seen when he wore
the black deerskin and he
spoke like a humble sage
for the citizens instead of
commanding, "You must do it
or I'll break your heads."

Here and now. Getting near lunchtime. *Brghu-samhita* can tell past,
present and future. Who is going to
die? Those guys born around
1929, they're going down now.
And...it's getting near lunch time.

Before this day ends you want
to get in some licks on the
old piano, I mean the pen
to paper, and not just ordinary

official words but maybe ordinary
but as an aspiring devotee.

pp. 160–61

After Japa

The man who did his *japa*
to his stopwatch while
his mind went its way
rarely did he catch it.

Is there a man better than
him who chants with love
and has many followers,
who tells them, "Chant
thirty-two rounds as I do."
Is there a man so low
who envies the high
humble devotee?

Now put these thoughts aside
go shave and shit and shower,
shiver, God will give
you some ideas in the bathroom.
You have a freckle on the outer side
of your left wrist, for
sixty years now, Your momma
brought you out...

This man with the stopwatch
has done his sixteen and is
gonna sing.

pp. 3–4

Waiting for Godot

Blah! The silence, the time
is here, deeper
he's sad he's glad
he's nowhere really.

Gonna stop writing one day
sun's gonna shine in my
back door,
he'll be done borrowing
find his own
death at least here too
you can imitate, be a persona,
and finally expire it was so
brief.

"I worked in the Food Farm Supermarket
when I was fourteen or sixteen
I can't remember. It's in New Dorp,
Staten Island."

Yeah, put him to rest
with his stories, him
and Alexander the Great and
bugs and cows
circumambulating I mean transmigrating
the soul awakens
after death.

You tell me.
God, Krishna, Hare Krishna
my master will claim
me like a lost dog and
set me on the next path
duty work, maybe to open
a new Hare Krishna center in

a new Boston
I dunno, I'm faithfully
waiting for Godot.

pp. 4–5

Between He and I

My Prabhupada may
look a little scared or angry,
you can't see him, you
have your own *murti*.
This one is mine.

I enter close to him,
massage his erect back,
know his tan skin and
touch cool but not cold
I choose the exact temperature
of the water to bathe him
so only I can know his
visage and shape. To you he
is a distant little statue.

Dear Prabhupada, did you
hear I may leave you behind
"in trance" when I travel?
I think it's best but I
don't know what you think.
It will be nice to return
here and find you, recommence
the worship.

I couldn't carry you on
the airplanes and cope with
my own needs, headaches.

But then I'll come home
to you,
worship your photo abroad.

pp. 13--14

❧   ❧   ❧

Tired Eyes...You Want Something New?

Tired eyes and clock
ticking. Doesn't run out,
those AA Duracells
last a long time.
But they go too.

Now what I want to say,
examine if you have a novel in
you. Something different, don't
stay in the same old track
when it's time for new
direction. But the old man
(died young) shouldn't
attempt the impossible.
I have nothing to lose.
Could write with brilliant love.
Once upon a time...
the truth. He reads his
Scripture by lamplight, knows
at death whatever you
think...

Don't create out of vain
madness, to get applause.
And fiction worlds I know
are madness playing God.

You may just have to accept
your daily life and keep it
quiet too. Like Wang Wei,

leave a few hundred good
poems. I mean...

If you've got something else go
ahead, otherwise
the bathroom awaits you,
sir, and play the tape of Prabhupada
who was always satisfied to
speak the same truth, same
examples with enthusiasm
to smash demons, glorify
Krishna, to rescue the
fallen souls.
Think about it.

pp. 19–21

Swami, I hereby am frank
my time gets clipped back
each day by the first sign
of a headache.
Waiting for mail. When it
comes it's an open door and
a marathon to hear and reply
to each one.
For your master, I speak as his representative,
I answer as immanent, I do it, my bit.

p. 30

Red Glow

Finished my rounds,
thinking of the red glow
of the glass in Randolph's studio.
I told him, "Safety first,"
afraid of the red glow,
"The glory hole," he calls the
oven with its opening...

I was too impatient to stay for
the completion of the vase with its
wing-like arms. He's good
at it. Krishna conscious glass
studio. What's this to do
with me? Encourage him. He's
worked hard to gather the
parts, ovens, the art for
glass flowers, jars, vases,
items...a skill he says, he can
teach young Vaisnavas...
I leave the studio, back out
into the rain, to answer my
letters again. No poem this but
I want to mention the red glow,
the danger. Keep telling him
to be careful. Don't burn flesh.

pp. 35–36

Paint your face and the face
of others who come from your
mind, where from?
From the unconscious who
must be some form of
Supersoul, the Lord grants all –

if you can yearn for purification
He comes to you in that way.

pp. 44-45

After Japa

You did your japa in two hours
for that you don't get flowers bowers.
But yes, it's most important.
Sailing from one to sixteen and thinking,
"One day I won't be able to
do this, it'll be over."

O Lord, such little
feeling from me to You.
Please be kind and grant me
ability to love.

It starts with attention,
but even that I lack
so I have to offer you my thoughts
to You, but maybe they're not suitable –

My plans to read and write
and paint,
whatever I do,
remember You...
and then back to hear the Mantra.

p. 100

In Him. Beauty of devotional service. Hare Krishna.
Beautiful effort to serve the Lord,
Fix-O-dent in place,
I'm ready, fire-belly,
I'll be able to eat

a simple hot, quick
meal, chomp, chomp.
The one per day
oh,
you are a saint of
renunciation and
bellyful.

p. 107

CHAPTER TEN - ACCEPTING MY LIMITS

IRELAND, JULY 22 — AUGUST 11, 1997

Today I'm choosing the title for this volume, Accepting My Limits. It means health dictates that I can't read or write so much. Therefore, accept it. This title may seem to focus on myself too much or on a relaxed attitude rather than a bold going forth to preach. Why accept your limits? Isn't "impossible" a word in the fool's dictionary? But time again, if I plan something beyond my limit, I just have to come down to the reality. I need to take in a place of residence mostly. The limits are also because of my temperament. I can't push beyond them.

p. 122

A common feature of contemporary life is expressed in the maxim, "live without limits." This demand while often lacking an ethical or moral core, nevertheless compels members of society to find meaning and purpose in that endless quest for "more." One clearly recognizes this in the business and financial realms where the acceptance of any type of limit is an admission of short-sightedness and even failure itself. Consistently, the acknowledgment of limitations is perceived to be a character flaw resulting in a lack of imagination or motivation. Perhaps one of the greatest and most tragic examples of humankind's hubris is that of the Titanic, advertised as unstoppable and unsinkable. This story would result in the horrifically legendary tale of unimaginable sorrow and loss. Within the spiritual life, the secular imperative to live without limits is often transposed within a religious context as the drive to become one with God, itself being a calamitous tragedy in which the individual sinks into the abyss of impersonalism.

It is the issue of limitations within the spiritual life which Satsvarupa dasa Goswami addresses in the thirteenth volume of *Every Day, Just Write – Accepting My Limits*. The quiet setting of Geaglum, Northern Ireland, provides the perfect locale for the evaluation of one's devotional life. In the quotation cited above, Satsvarupa Maharaja candidly addresses both the features of his personal limitations, and the ways in which they shape the contours of his life, particularly those arising from his health concerns and temperament.

This volume provides a refreshing antidote to the frenetic compulsion to be more than human, a compulsion which has always funded atheisms of every sort. Satsvarupa Maharaja creates a peaceful mood in this volume both through poetry and prose in which he, himself a painter, employs language to create canvases that display his personal life for the reader. Satsvarupa Maharaja's much-loved companion, the *Srimad-Bhagavatam* continues to serve as a touchstone for his meditations upon shared human experiences within the spiritual life. These meditations reveal not simply an acknowledgment of the author's personal limitations but reveal his surrender to these as well. This is a mood of and movement to surrender which Satsvarupa Maharaja has addressed in the previous volume, *My Secret Life*, and in this regard one discovers a seamless flow from the previous to the current volumes. Acceptance of limitations is an act of surrender before the Lord, hardly a sign of weakness, or lack of motivation or imagination as the world commonly teaches. Ultimately to accept one's limitations is to acknowledge that I am not God and that I will never be God, an act of humility that defines the devotee of the Lord.

As readers of Satsvarupa Maharaja's books know well, he himself is a voracious reader and this volume offers unique features that highlight his reading practice. The perfect reading companion to the exploration of limits within the spiritual life is Srila Prabhupada's *The Nectar of Devotion*, a presentation of Rupa Gosvami's *Bhakti-rasamrta-sindhu*. For it is in this Vaisnava text that a devotee is invited to explore the breadth and depth of devotional life. A wonderful feature of this volume is Satsvarupa Maharaja's incorporation of post-it notes made during his reading of *The Nectar of Devotion*. This same is true as the author shares notes of his reading of the works of the renowned Christian writer, Søren Kierkegaard. These notes are included here, at the conclusion of this volume so that one may more fully enter the author's mood.

To acknowledge one's limits is an act of courage, to accept one's limits is an act of surrender. It is to this surrender that Satsvarupa dasa Goswami invites his readers.

Everything comes from Krishna, and Lord Siva
mentions some of the particulars.

Many important Sanskrit words describing Krishna.
Ho-hum a diddle-de-do.
I ate grass roots and
divided in two. I sat
for exams and booted
the loot, and I grew
tired of that and jawed
an elbow.

I greased no meat but
was blear and teary-eyed.
Grim and dry and kept
apart from God.

Music too I fled from
so
I could dwell in the
silence of the Lord.
But did you sing?
Did you ring a gentle
bell?

Please tell us your own
inclination and dis-
inclination and how it comes
from Him.

p. 5

I don't understand why you won't rewrite the MS of
PMRB 2 if it needs it.

Cross out, and you cross out your life. That voice
wanted to be heard.

Add too, make sense
make incense in Spiritual
Sky factory. It's the
material world, Prabhu, but
our spiritual master said we can
do it to make money for
the mission. We hear tapes of
Krishna Book and our guru's speech
and *bhajanas* and the sound and our
purpose makes it the
spiritual world.

pp. 28–29

O sleepy boy,
you are the best one
the day is yours to grab, seaman.
You are the free man to worship and
chant Hare Krishna and make free-writes.

You ask me why you should
follow so closely behind the *Srimad-Bhagavatam*?
I'll tell you: so you don't veer off and crash off the road
and plunge down the ravine.
You have a habit to do that
and have crashed more than once or twice
in your ISKCON days. Follow
his path under the arch
which is Bhaktivedanta Swami Marga.
I accept the truth of that.

p. 25

❀   ❀   ❀

He humped over the hill last
we saw of him in his
hiking boots, he wished to
die because of the pain and

diminishment and so he died off
rather early and wrote no
more
just one big diary at the
end...

p. 29

Happy by association with Krishna
and His pure devotees.
Oh, happy he is but
pays dues,
paints faces on the sidewalk
for money – they throw a
few coins, he's got a
wife and two kids.
Happy he is in this
world who dies knowing
Brahman (Krishna).

p. 30

Tired of the diary? But there's no other way for me
I
blow a horn
not porn
for you not
for me?
For Thee Krishna?
It's for Maxwell House Coffee.
It's for I-don't-know-who?

p. 32

Madness mild
hid wild
the poor cat, the
poor helpless chicks
of the hen, our dog
ate'em, or he would
at least kill as sport
in his instinctive romp.
"That's the material world."

p. 33

Feelin' better than you can
express yourself in an
Italian expresso cappuccino
monks and long-haired girls
sixteen-year-olds in tight Levis
sing with guitar
poems of their 1960s
eternal youth and
death the old hippie poet
is dying dead now from
misuse of the body,
all that drug-high waste –
lament you old fool,
play a last jazz record
it's too late.

I took safe eternal
path, am seeking ever
my Swami. You can
laugh at me, America.
Line up and have a good laugh
have a good look at
the thin animal in the zoo,

he's wearing a top knot,
and wear-ever
wristwatch, he's got a
funny look and tortured headache,
line up and have a laugh,
throw your Popsicle sticks
at him – it's his
feeding time.

No, precious, protect me
from that.
I am a holy monk in
the bathroom listening to
my master's words.
Get down,
be submissive
fire safe your bullets
in private.

Prose hose sock,
Soren
Would pose ain't
solvin' the dilemma.
Krishna Art Pose
Christ Have Sale
I don't have to work for a
living see, but I paid off the karma in
headaches.

This day I'll read the
songs sung by Lord Siva and
maybe the Kumaras'
speech to Prthu – I
don't meant Prthu Prabhu
of Holland, Ireland and San Francisco.
I mean the original
shut my seal my

mouth I'm speakin'
free
the Speaker of the House.

Yeah, I'm Speaker of
this House and Senator
too. Bewit,
be revit
it's the same old Jazz
silence of prayer
Haley
Harry Rama.

pp. 33-35

Sergeant Wilcox added his
measure to the beef account, and
I just didn't have energy enough
to paint with all it takes and
yesterday I got sick
you s.o.b., you killed him
you in your Brooks Brothers suit
and Rexroph dense with
allusion, bowing the bass, the
jazz band behind the great Beat poets.

I listened to that record
in John Young's house, not so
long ago, and now I'm not so
different really except just
add the one to the zeros,
the knight of faith, the
devotee living toward eternal
place in Goloka.

pp. 36–37

Oh, boy
Rasta men a plenty
in Trinidad and me
and England, and me and pen and paper
and rain coming down
this lightweight this head,

Oh, he is misused in
body and brain is
cupped in hands – What
you talkin' 'bout man?
You crazy?
Why don't you write a
straight essay with
three parts and dialectics and
point one, two, three, four, and then rewrite it thirty-two
times (he said he did)
proud of that
instead of

Puff, the magic dragon.
You can't repeat happiness
if you try.
Better to abscond, I mean
renounce the music of
the 50s and 60s and just live
these few days of your
autumn (one o'clock in Lord Brahma's
day but later for me)
smiling
genuine
bemused
headachy
Bartender.
Ekes ekes out a living, one purport at a time.

pp. 43–44

Now the engines of mercy
contradict nuns of Anglican
church are praying I hope nicely.
Someone ought to know God
directly,
if it were me I'd be fired
up, huh? But my eye –
ache might be just the same and stop
me. You'd be outwardly still
maybe unable but find ways
to tell your important message.
Try to save souls
your life is for that –
and you save yourself
by preaching.

p. 56

* * *

Old age
Drear, blear, you're in new territory, take it as such.
Animal sacrifice,
head slumps forward,
help, O Lord, to
get steady and read.

p. 58

He can, so worship Him, Govinda.
Okay, in a shoe store, in all places. I'll answer my mail.
All hail the chief
person in me is a humble devotee, he
directs the writer and fool
and restrains the jazz listener
says I got brain fog and
can't comprehend too much

Soren, he also – the
human one, allows the
interfaith celebration
allows the flower to
grow on hairy chest
dies without *siddha-svarupa*
but goes "there," anywhere.

p. 88

Hare Krishna
sprightly ads for Coca-Cola
don't help us.
I mention it to avoid
it, *neti-neti.*
I want to see the
form of Radha-Krishna
and be enamored by Them.

p. 105

Same thing, same thing
don't bug me about that
I don't see it that way.
That's the so-called problem
with Prabhupada's books too.
"The same example" –
the hand can't eat the sweet
but puts it into the mouth.
Water the root
sun and sunshine.

Effervescent waves and sun go
down same story with
subtle differences. I like it
that way. Uneventful

means no catastrophes, no rain
crash or robber, no one
died today. Events,
changes, wars, who
needs it?

We'll get enough of that.
Record as much of the sameness
and peace as possible before
the revolution which is also
another sameness.

Birth and death
Ever fresh is Krishna.
You don't understand.

pp. 115–16

Swami

Swami wants exclusive
discipleship. I give him
a mixed bag. That's called
karma-jnana-misra-bhakti?
Something like that.

Why aren't you better?

Swami, I am yours
dovetailing on the Bowery
on 26 Second Avenue, remember,
you said we could?
Not suffer a pinch in
serving the Lord. Just
chant Hare Krishna. You said that.

And you said, "Give everything,
surrender, you rascal!"
I'm trying. I want to read
Srimad-Bhagavatam and render to you,
as service, all the results from
the research I do
in errant ways.

And see you smile and pleased
with me. In your presence
again, become purified of
all plans and works but your
mission. And you tell me again
what to do.

pp. 145–46

＊　　＊　　＊

Swami is a title given to
controller of the senses
women, no
not afraid,
has knowledge pure.

Am I a swami, I can't
claim that I want to
appear as one and be
bowed to? Want
to please my master
who made me this way
preach and learn
"Read my books"
Swami, I serve you.

p. 172

Forget
you ever had a date
with an angel,
forget the Miles tunes,
forget trying to enjoy
the vague concept of spirituality,
New Age dream explorers.

But don't forget Vishnu,
Krishna. If you are forgetting
in that way, hold on and
pray Krishna Krishna Krishna,
I'm fading and need Your
protection. Please accept
my song
my intended
good acts of bhakti.

p. 178

Who is a hairy toothless sage?
Who doesn't care anymore for his appearance,
but as an ambassador
you ought to look good
take a mud bath for firm skin
and squeeze out words you have
heard keeping trim to
repeat parampara
on the grass hill of a
festival, 'twas where she
first met the devotees, when
she was only four years old.
Now the man who preached to
her, during a tent program,
no longer wants to do that.

p. 22

I want to go home
to my *prabhu-datta* nation
and be alone mostly and
tell stories. Or...okay, I'll
do what you say, but
"He'll find a place to hide."

p. 23

Fell Smith
mild words of
free-write periphery
don't ask me why the
rain sprinkles on the plain or
how long before you die. See the awful,
garish pictures of sufferings in hell –
they deserve it, but –
Pariksit wanted to know
"Can they be saved?"

p. 24

The clerk and the boss and
the *ksatriya*
and rash drivers of taxis
the henchman, punch man,
clever manipulator, all ...
eligible for going back to
    Godhead and entering the pastimes of Krishna, even
in this life.

p. 37

A brash Bohemian on the
Nalge Trail, drinks water
from his hard plastic bottle,
posed in his ankle-high boots
while standing on a rock –
the L.L.Bean catalog,
handsome young-man smile.

In a Nalge catalog of
good lookers, consider me a
crumb of affection.
I'm writing this way because
my right head hurts and
I can't concentrate on *seriouser*
topics as little Lulu
and Tubby could be doing
kirtana, wouldn't that be
nice? Spiritualize all the
comic books.
Serialize all the prints.
You make your own original
lit.,
that's best, only way.

You'll be judged by eternity
as one person only,
and not asked who else is to
blame, because that blamable
person will also be judged singly,
under the eye of God,
it won't matter, joint *karma*
doesn't exist,
he claims.

One at a time.
May I offer help?

pp. 42–43

The lame joke at the
graveyard, the wry look
at my unfinished devotional life,
the seedy *sikha* tasseled,
the aging organs can't hack it,
the walk, the sky in Geaglum,
don't get attached to pets or
cloudy skies of Éire,
don't think you can stay here
always but seek the lotus
feet shelter of Sri Caitanya Mahaprabhu
in this world of
every-step-danger.

p. 48

Swami crosses over
we follow, his
shoes we worship on
vyasasana, bow down,
get out and work.

Swami crosses over
to his instructions vital –
"Oh, I forgot." Well
then remember again.

He gave me split beans,
dal, kitchen,
death he said
doesn't count, or touch the
soul. Count Basie on the
U.S. stamp, gone!

But the soul can fly
to God and

He is Krishna, Society for
Krishna Consciousness we are starting,
join us,
I did.

Soon part of it asking
others
"Join us, at least on
Sundays when have
a Love Feast and before that
chanting in the grassy park."

Now I'm too old.
For the tent campaign.
My head hurts, I need
to rest. But sneak in
these lines to
my Swami.

pp. 58-59

❋   ❋   ❋

When I threw up last night
it was like a *kichari*.
It was a violent relief
from something wrong I did,
eating when I had pain.
Eating too heavy.
I got relief. My aching
head.

p. 85

❋   ❋   ❋

O Lord, this fiddler
Stefan plays with
fiddle on knee his
stifled songs, doesn't

know real sacrifice for You
sings a kind of blues
self-centered –
doesn't want to disturb You but would sure like to
know You and love You – You extract such a price for
that...or even when you make it easy it seems hard for me in
my Kali-yuga slump and bad, *sumanda matayoh*.

pp. 88–89

Seeing that his son was qualified to rule, King Nabhi
retired from ruling and went to the Himalayas. Okay man,
you're so feeble you can neither rule, manage, nor go to the
Himalayas nor to Vrindavana. Got you a place here to look
out and sigh and be a guy
    poet
    taster
    sheet I got no
    taters to play with
    summers away I'm a
    hoot tooting egoist
    got no music planned to hear. Just the silence, the
darn ol' silence
    be happy with it, wear your saffron sheet, I say sheet
    and be happy yourself
    you're a Hawaiian
    guru taster
    be gone, calm, calm me down, I got no plans beyond
this head with limits.
    Wrote my letter to GBC of Italy saying I'm comin' into
your turf with your permission September 20, although I
get headaches, here I come down Mt. Blanc, autostrada,
Agip, Antarbahir.
    No it.
    Your servant,
    Guarino of Naples
    Dan

p. 92

Devotees at Bedside

Go ahead Nurse,
he's dying. Give him
the holy names. No
one is watching. This
one's so out of it, get
her to repeat after you,
"Hare Krishna, Hare Krishna,
Krishna Krishna, Hare Hare."

But sometimes they don't remember
later or even invent it.
Daruka's mother claimed he
gave her prayer beads and devotees with
him sang chants around her bed.
"Did she resent it?" he asked
his sister. No, she didn't mind,
imagined the whole thing,
and it was fine.

So, keep on blending the *maha
prasadam* into their drinks,
but don't get caught by the
antiseptic doctors
who prefer it their way.
Don't let them see or hear
the mercy you actually gave.

pp. 116–17

I fritter and burn
and ease and celebrate
look to masters of word jugglery
of sacrifice and
old time's sake
who choose the right expression
from a life of suffering,

sense grat, ennui, pain
and what –
then go alone...

p. 131

Proclaim in your newspaper
the berries are appearing, and
I'll be gone from here before
most are ripe. And I'll be
glad summer ends at least
for reason: The water
sports will end.

p. 132

Swami, please dedicate
another. I mean let me
dedicate this life and another
to you. I'll wipe off the
wooden picnic table in the
courtyard of 26 Second Avenue as
asked by one of your raw men.
I'll (well I can't claim I'll
go give out books in a parking
lot, that's too hard.)
I'll fail, fall at your feet
do the lecture route and be
grateful. At least don't fall
down, exit as a saffron
elder, still at least he
died an official *sadhu*.

p. 145

Sacrosanct
bitter as herbs he
likes his honey
and Ayurveda pumpkin
pie. No, he is a
simulator and false.
You cannot count how many
days are left – that
knowledge of your life-death
you don't have, so I think these EJW volumes are
partly a hope that at least for now I can keep living one day
at a time, bow down at night and in A.M. Keep going.
    may M. sing happily and successfully at his venues
with fiddle and bouzouki
    and may I find the star
    of satisfaction
    what? The lack, the
    way told to me by
    the Lord, "Enter here."
    One doesn't know
    but writes
    each day.
    God gives and takes away.

pp. 150–51

Now the volume ends. Face and accept your limit.
What does it mean? Earlier in the book I knew. Now it
means, illness doesn't have to be so bad. Even pain. I've yet
to learn that. It's a tricky phrase because I want to go
beyond my limits. Limited to twelve microcassettes. Go on
after twenty-one days to a volume number fourteen. The

unlucky number is passed. Fourteen is a "good" number. Our flag is flying. Krsnite, Prabhupada follower. Beggar.

p.150

CHAPTER ELEVEN - THE DIARY AS DEVOTION

Diary lines
in devotion means
always remember you're meant

for death and next life,
remember Krishna, what you
learned:
You're a disciple submissive.

Always write
sincere, just write and trust it
will lead you back to Godhead.

p. 37

The Art of Mixing seems like a good title for this volume. I was thinking of something about hope – my hope that I could raise my diary writing to an art, to a preaching instrument and something pleasing to guru and Krishna. That may all be implied by the *Art of Mixing*. I mix my reading and making notes of *Srimad-Bhagavatam*. I blend in my observations or thoughts, ISKCON activities, sense perceptions; I mix in attempts at free-writing, poem fragments, non-devotee books I'm reading, etc. My hope is to raise this act of daily writing to an art and a prayer.

p. 30

For Satsvarupa dasa Goswami, to write is to

surrender, and in this, the fourteenth volume *of Every Day, Just Write, The Diary as Devotion*, the author will examine the particular genre of writing in which this literary project is gathered as a whole, as is evident from the passage cited above. To describe *Every Day, Just Write* as merely a diary would fail to capture its complexity, and indeed Satsvarupa Maharaja describes this effort as "the art of mixing" thus hinting at the nuanced quality of his work. It is remarkable to discover such broad literary efforts gathered within a single volume, and the reader moves seamlessly from poetry to reading reflections, scriptural study to horizons beyond. The pressing question for Satsvarupa Maharaja at this moment is to examine and to evaluate this particular genre in relation to his spiritual life and service to both his guru and to Krishna, the Supreme Person, as well as to the disciples within his care.

In this volume, Satsvarupa Maharaja expands his devotional reading to that of the Danish writer, Søren Kierkegaard, who becomes a conversation partner, if you will, in this process of discernment. Figures such as Herman Melville, a towering writer within American literature, is considered for his profound artistic and theological insights. One of the most enjoyable features of this volume is the inclusion of *The Book of American Diaries* from which excerpts are interspersed throughout this work. The reader is given wonderful snapshots of diary entries from American luminaries such as H. L. Mencken to significant historical figures such as Aaron Burr. These entries display features common to diaries in general but also cast relief upon the profound distinctiveness of Satsvarupa Maharaja's gathered writings. For his writings are consistently placed before the ever-present backdrop of guru and Krishna, and manifest his desire for ever greater surrender, and in this he is wonderfully successful.

As a devotional practice, a diary is perfectly suited for one who is committed to a life of solitude. For a diary shaped by bhakti opens a window for the reader to glance the broad horizon of the author. Satsvarupa Maharaja's distinctive voice casts the aesthetic richness of the Vaisnava tradition in new and inspiring ways, through a manner of expression, which the author has previously described as a poetic rather than doctrinal mood. A diary shaped by devotion finds a home within a long tradition of Christian writing characterized by St. Augustine's monumental *Confessions*. Regardless of the differing traditions, these diaries share the foundational concern to explore one's inner terrain as part of an ongoing journey to live one's life fully before the Lord, who provides both context and horizon for these reflections. Such writings reveal an ongoing conversation between the pilgrim and the Lord who dwells within the heart, as well as the spiritual master who has made such a life possible through his grace and compassion.

Finally, such a diary demonstrates Satsvarupa Maharaja's relationship with his own tradition. In a wonderful passage, the author expresses his appreciation for the Orthodox Father, Theophan the Recluse. In him, Satsvarupa Maharaja finds a kindred spirit who is rooted in his tradition but seeks to share its riches with his own distinctive voice and through his personal experiences. Quoting an excerpt from *The Art of Prayer*, "they (the Orthodox Fathers) did far more than mechanically repeat earlier writers: For this tradition inherited from the past was also something which they had themselves experienced creatively in their own inner life. This combination of tradition and personal experience gives to their writings a particular value and authority" (*p. 128*). In this statement we enter the very heart of our author, and in this volume of *Every Day, Just Write*, Satsvarupa Maharaja beautifully weds these two themes: to reveal the breadth and depth of his Vaisnava tradition through the use of his both unique voice and devotional experience.

The truth of the matter is I may be a little like

Bharata in madness. Praising the hound. Chasing the
'Trane. Chasing your tail. Singing the blues. That's why I
think of the improvisers. You are one of them. This hasn't
been done before in Krishna consciousness.

They know better. They are calm in the mode of
goodness. Don't tell to give it up. Make it better.

It's simply thinking out loud. You can renumber it., put
it in a new frame, reform, return to a former way, it will be the
same

crying for service,

stubbornly being who you are

refusing to play the role you played before. Listening
to the voices as you write, saying this way or no way. Saying,
if my authorities want me to change they will tell me.

Saying, please caitya-guru, sing me Your song and I'll
write it down.

Before the audience (or at least one and twenty) in
dressing gown, the author composes.

It's all right.

We're gonna chant soon.

Our page is adorned with Krishna-*nama*.

p. 7

I'm a fool, reprobate,
Please Lord, make me Yours,
to act fit, brave, strict,
knowledgeable, compassionate
as befits a Gaudiya rep.
You can do it in me,
but on my own I'm turd.
(I'm a spirit soul within
but covered over.)

p. 21

Thank you, Lord, for that tasty feast of paint forms.

Child's play. Don't label it, but you enjoy it and especially
enjoy the transcendental vibrations that permeate
    the indirect message
    so direct tacked on
    the unconscious delicious
    safe jungle of
    child's imagination where
    he wanders free and even big
    green monsters are friendly,
    wear *tilaka* or sway
    to rhythm of *arati* dance
    we saw in temples
    in salad days.

p. 36

    Please redeem me,
    please guide me
    Lord of the heart
    Gopinatha
    Govinda
    Madhava, Lord of all names and *rasas*, as taught to
me by A. C. Bhaktivedanta Swami Prabhupada.

pp. 43 – 44

    It's okay
    sailing west due north
    due to have a baby
    laryngitis, spiders look
    the phone ring with
    little ding-ding-ding not like
    it used to, I never
    answer, "Please accept

my obeisances." Sit ready for
potatoes and soup.

Get ready for receiving
Radha and Krishna (fifteen inches tall).
Get ready to leave Them on
your tour. Get ready for
headaches but in between
lectures on Sarvabhauma's "Bhakti-pade"
change in *sastra*, and on Balarama's
Appearance Day "so much
nectar in His *lila*" and
on Janma when you
initiate on behalf of Srila Prabhupada...
and get ready
as much as you can
and even without preparation
get ready for diving
at his lotus feet.

Ekadasi preps. Don't overeat
mashed potatoes, fried potato
soup with carrot and
broccoli...some roasted nuts...
you see...

Listen to your master and
then to one of his disciples
lecturing on Vedic truth and
then opt for silence so
you can think it over
while you wait
for an Ekadasi dessert.

Some Prabhus fast totally
on this day. I say my
headaches are my *tapasya*,

and I don't want more.

But on Janmastami we'll
fast
a life raft
a dream
benight ...
Don't forget Krishna
and your momma? No, my momma
is the Vedas.

Don't forget Vrindavana,
discipleship,
the ship of *hari-nama*
as you sink –
and rise wherever
He sends you.

pp. 56–58

Weeds blow in assent.
Yellow-cream-yellow
pale weed gold
thistle
they blow to the left as
I look up eyes bathed
in clear air painless
this moment
Krishna Krishna. I tag
on.

I fail and float like
a puff ball from the
weed head on the

wind
O poem is so –
lax.

    And little yellow flowers like buttercups or lesser
celandine amid the green grass and yellow rye and further
off but all on the same plain, the water, rippling dark blue
and the sky –

    such big clouds move and
    you can see them, bigger than
    the hugest imaginable
    trailer trucks
    or jumbo elephants
    don't call them demons or
    you'll frighten me.

    I've got enough fears
    in dreams and head
    pains. Easy Street
    blues, my friend
    Jimmy is playing clarinet
    at sixty years old I
    ought to tell him now's
    the time to center on
    Krishna
    with every breath.
    He'll say I'm doing that
    on clarinet. But how pinpointed?
    Ask yourself.

    Krishna is kind,

big arms
narrow strait.

I thank You for this day
and simply hope it counts
as offering to You.
Please give me what You
think is best and the
strength to endure all
in remembrance of
Govinda as he taught me
and us all.

pp. 63-64

✦   ✦   ✦

Ride in a big car,
accept a rose garland
and foot bath of ghee and
you think you're Number One
at least in the hearts of
disciples. But that's not
true,
you're just a wee
swallow, a swift,
a night owl pigeon
who goes ooo-ooo
cooo
in the dark of your widgeon covered
moss eaten
but pure unknown
soul. You're God's!

p. 85

✦   ✦   ✦

What's your service, bulb?

I shave-up devotees.
What else?
I write rhymes. And you?
I run the zoo at Mayapur.
Oh, whose disciple are you?
I won't tell you lest you make fun and I get angry.
Are you...
Stop here.

p. 126

✤   ✤   ✤

Varuni beauty, don't
add your laughter, or
AMA will get mad.
Unless you are serious
nowhere you'll go
in spiritual life.

p. 131

✤   ✤   ✤

On the lake of Panca Gauda
I left my love
the deity of Kurma
in an old lunch pail
dented with age and use
I rallied my ego
Saying, "You're an American.
Do something swell."

p. 132

✤   ✤   ✤

Varuni is nigh
Always drink to full
Rama will protect you
June is long gone,

November not yet so
insure your bets and
side with Baladeva!

p. 133

He paints while Rome burns.
No, his painting is into the
eye of the calm.
His own soul deserves
expression. Don't get caught up
in European maelstrom –
hears lecture
alone peace –

p. 135

Peace in my head
from the day, Lord
Krishna gave it.

p. 150

✦   ✦   ✦

(From Part Two "The Diary as Devotion"
Ireland, August 21 – September 22, 1997)

Make it even in a diary
so interesting that they keep reading
and hear Krishna, Krishna. I want to
serve Krishna, they hear a doubt,
"Is Krishna God?" And then it's
countered.
Yeah, but those who are devotees already know this.
Maybe. Let them hear.
Oh, you
Oh, you
are doing this.

p. 15

In the tracts of land, on top of old Smokey
all covered with snow,
I lost my true lover
for thoughts are so slow.

I believed like a squanderer
and misused my lot,
so, I'll be sent to a diva
and be buried in sod

I never knew bliss times
I only knew "mew"
like a cat on the run
I was covered with dew.

I yearned to be a *bhakta*
not lagged with the rest
too timid for heaven
too lost for the best.

My tale never ends 'cause
the soul's got to move
from body to lamp post
he falls in the groove.

pp. 33–34

Diary lines
in devotion means
always remember you're meant
for death and next life,
remember Krishna, what you
learned:
You're a disciple submissive.

Always write
sincere, just write and trust it
will lead you back to Godhead.
Does it happen automatically?
Each day you see
vote for God
open your hearing
to learn
instead
of
nod.

p. 37

Janmastami is happy
always with devotees
never apart in spirit
may I worship my Lord
always.

p. 55

Please accept me lively,
not patronizingly,
not a blind following –
or rather I wish I could blindly
follow you as you said
you followed Bhaktisiddhanta Sarasvati.

p. 59

Janma get out
alas get out
never can?
"More, Madhu!"
Audience shots.
Janma get out
of my body-self
and sing of Sri Govinda.

p. 59

❋ ❋ ❋

Slums slumming reading J.K.'s
Book of Dreams, better to read your
own Krishna-conscious times.
Looney Tunes and Paul Desmond
Jukebox mysteries...

p. 114

❋ ❋ ❋

At night lying in bed
after the daylong headache,
the sound of rain.

p. 147

❋ ❋ ❋

Hey too nanny
the cock's in the meadow
the fields shorn of hay.
The *pada-yatra's* coat is drying
on the fence post and
we are dying to get free
of the worst of the morrow
in the corn
of the day.

p. 151

Like a swallow you spear
into the air flap and spear
like a bullet with your
feathered arrow tail – into...

pp. 154–55

Don't force too much emotional truth on me about
my inadequacy, etc. – I have enough cross to bear. But
Providence may force me to do both – head pains and heart
pains. Job of the Old Testament suffered from head to foot
but remained faithful to God.

Anyway, I thought like that.
Now let's go inside the house.
For every moment you break
a hill is made to take
I can't rhyme a cherry but
a goat cries, "Hari!"
And by his beard I see
Krishna in everything, *maha-
mantras* especially.

p. 158

CHAPTER TWELVE - ECONOLINE PREACHER

Irregular hours begin.

p. 36

Now you can write your own *Diary of a Traveling Preacher* in the tradition of John Wesley, Saint Paul the Apostle, and some ISKCON preacher-diarists. *Parivrajakacarya.* Authorized. Persona acceptable.

p. 22

Monastic life is characterized by both stability (committing one's life to a single place and community) and a daily rhythm shaped by a schedule for prayer, worship and study. Maintaining this monastic spirit while traveling is at the heart of both the prose and poetry of this, the fifteenth volume of Satsvarupa dasa Goswami's *Every Day, Just Write, Econoline Preacher.* Departing from his cherished home and writing shed in Geaglum, Northern Ireland, Satsvarupa Maharaja embarks upon a six week journey to France, Spain and Italy to visit devotees and disciples within these European nations. The author's primary motivation in making this demanding trip is to provide pastoral care to devotees suffering in the wake of their spiritual leader's abrupt departure from the International Society for Krishna Consciousness.

With this *Ford Econoline* van, one may find an

analogous experience of the sanctuary offered to Satsvarupa Maharaja by his residence in Geaglum. Certainly, this will be the vehicle engaged for making this journey, but it will also offer refuge for the author's chanting, reading, and writing. The writing within this volume includes a series of twenty-one numbered poems which themselves trace the author's spiritual and geographical journeys during the waning days and weeks of September. With the month of September as a backdrop for this series of poems, both lyrical and contemplative, the author expresses the monastic rhythms he maintains even while living on the road.

This volume is further characterized by the continued inclusion of passages from *The Book of American Diaries*, begun in the previous volume of Every Day, Just Write thereby continuing to expand upon the important theme of a "diary as devotion." In this way, the reader is given a range of reflections from a diverse host of writers. These diary excerpts are offered in addition to Satsvarupa Maharaja's own reflections upon numerous literary figures such as Edgar Allen Poe, Susan Sontag, Thomas Merton, Soren Kierkegaard and Emily Dickinson. In fact, the author even includes a Dickinson poem within his poem number Nineteen. All of these authors share with Satsvarupa Maharaja a relentless pursuit of the nature of the human spirit with all of its contradictions and ambiguities. Once again, the *Ford Econoline* itself provides the locale for these numerous reflections, while away from the author's shed in Geaglum.

The writing of this volume possesses a gentle cadence with a clear sense of movement that corresponds to the *Econoline's* travels through Europe, sights and sounds of which Satsvarupa Maharaja describes with a painterly finesse. However, this should not belie the fact that this six week trip will be incredibly demanding, physically and spiritually for the author. This is the beginning of a challenging period, glimpses of which emerge from time to time as fissures of concern and worry within the writing itself.

I would suggest that the extensive Radhastami reflections that Satsvarupa Maharaja offers in both prose and poetry form the spiritual core of this volume. One can only imagine that it is the gracious and merciful glance of Srimati Radharani which will give the author the strength to face the challenging pastoral tasks that lie before him. Finally, this volume concludes with the magnificent poem "Econoline Preacher," itself concluding with these verses:

> In the days that remain
> let no one be blind to
> the truth of Krishna's *Gita* –
> tell them and yourself
> surrender to the King, sweet
> Lord in three-fold bending form
> and Radha's blessing on us.

p. 152

September Songs

1

Invitation

"September Morn" is a painting of
a naked lady bathing in
a stream. There was also a
cheap porcelain knick-knack of
a deer called September Morn
and...
It's September 1st in my house.
The clock is ticking slow and
audible like the one on Grandma
Doty's porch.

September 13, my sister's birthday.
"September in the rain." Two years
ago I wrote September Catchall.

O grace, O face, don't
hit me with mace,
I'm just a cowpoke *sannyasi*
about to travel in a
Ford Econoline to España.
Would you like to come along?

We'll sing huzzahs and meditate,
guitar lute songs, by the
roadside nervously
fall asleep behind tin walls.
You know the game, crossing
borders, entering temples,
would you like to come?

We'll play Krishna ballads,
serious look at purports
and who knows? Maybe a bright
moment. As we mix,
as we die. Come along…

pp. 1–2

✦   ✦   ✦

2

Honor the Voice Within

September, he's got his own.
A clock tick-tocks;
it's cold already.

It's been several hours since
I read the Supreme Lord is
not partial. May He be
partial to me. I'm in the
right club. But in my
heart what does He see?
That kid who connived,
even with his mother,
tried to get his way
for his current lust.

Sing the song of liberated prose.
Honor the voice within. He's
dictating, insistent saying, "Go
ahead, write it down, what
I say." You obey but not
always. At least two persons
working here. And the third
is the pure spirit soul.

Rupa Gosvami, you said if one

---

can't live in Vrindavana – which I
assume is best – then live there
in one's mind. That's hard too.
I live in this house, then
tomorrow in Bhadra's house in
Dublin with the all-night street light.
Vrindavana. My master's purport,
my yearning to write through September.

Adventure ahead.
It has been years…
"The words without meaning
also have a place, 'He insists
from within.'"

pp. 9–10

❋   ❋   ❋

3

First Travel Day

Now we're definitely going
not in a gown, in the dawn
at 5:30, he said.

I've got my bags and just trifle
to spare. We're going down
to Dublin for the day.
Then the ferry.

The kind of poems I want to write,
said James Wright –
but what about me?
It's the travel heeby-jeebies,
one minute hot, the next cold,
death and living, God and
Vivaldi, you can't keep your

314

mind under control.
Accede to that.

Clear sense but then,
you can't. Syamananda, I said
this is your last chance, please
write me a letter how you
are. Otherwise, I'll be back
in six weeks. He had a stylish
simple cap and raincoat.
All day it rained, and then the
sun came out.

All day I went in and
out of the van. I don't care
this year if the car
alarm goes off. God is
true and good and above
the modes. You better get rid
of those *jnani* books and *karmi*
books. Just today I looked at the
picture of Upabarhi, that's his name.

He had a little couch just for himself,
like a hedonist's *vyasasana* and the
girls were seated on the floor
beside him and standing leaning over him
as he sang, bare-chested, garlanded.
It was love songs like
cinema songs and the religious
devas cursed him for dis-
turbing the *sankirtana*.

Don't sympathize with him.
Therefore, I'll choose the
silence I can hear, cars and
trucks and *japa*, and I've got a

tape of Srila Prabhupada singing in '66.
We're definitely going to start
traveling in three hours.
Come along,
September song.

pp. 24-26

❋ ❋ ❋

4

At Bhadra's House, Before an Evening Program

September winds whistle,
kids in the street, not my
home.
Hold on. You'll give the class
at 5 P.M. Now hear: A scooterish
engine, a large jet in the sky,
flying from America to Europe,
and a horn blows like
a conch for *arati* or is it
a train?

Sunlight bright for a few minutes
penetrates this dry page, and I see
the imprints of my handwriting
from the previous page.
Sorry. Sorry.

Thick blond hair down her back.
Was she a Hare Krishna woman?
I didn't have time to see.
I was exercising by the open
window, breathing deep.
How deep?
Brilliant, white clouds with dark centers.

The kids' futile, energetic shouts.
Those billboards out there,
life in the offices, shops,
running like tributaries into the pubs.
At five I'll tell of Prabhupada,
and play his tapes. "Why eulogize weakness?
Be determined. You promised."

pp. 35–36

❋   ❋   ❋

Online, diary web
world we write for
someone, the solitary person
is the author himself
before God.

p. 38

❋   ❋   ❋

Sannyasi Crossing

September crossing I know not.
In cold steel van awhile
forget yourself and tell me
of your Master.

He's the Supreme Person from
whom all comes, the sastra
tells. He's not subject to
error as we are. And He
lights the way with dances
and friends, intimate friends
who have passed all tests.

Oh, if you could concentrate on

that. Nervous moments can
deflect you there, grasping the
prayer beads and counting
your Names. (His holy names.)

September crossing I know not
only now in this house
morning over noon arrives,
hot and cold water on your head,
dry off. The lady of the
lake has a lovely smile
and a bumpy mile.

Erst, erk, shove that
back down your throat,
clamp down, Swami
we expect the best of you
in a little while
a little bitter do you
no harm.

And the Power Rangers – comic book heroes
on the children's plastic cups
and muscular bandits or
God's agents? Make-believe.
Just a man and his wife,
just an aspiring old
celibate student pretends –
or plays out guru life.

pp. 45–46

6

At Sea

September at sea, the furrow
broad the boat stacked with
trailer trucks, looking out I
see memories,
the furrow trough...
That way, France.

The poem and I spaced out
forgot who I am where I
am supposed to go. Turn
the door handle to the
men's room, relieve my body
in there, then walk as in trance
to room 17 (I remembered,
so I wouldn't get lost)
open and to my companion.

I start talking some new thought
I had about solitude –
I want a life of prayer,
and about preaching –
to the devotees, that's my lot –
and faithfulness –

I can't leave Prabhupada.
So, you are not spaced out
after all,
just at sea
for a while.

pp. 61–62

❀   ❀   ❀

With water and sponge

remember Christ who had
no water but was offered
only vinegar on the Cross
in his greatest agonies of
flesh and his mind turned to
God – "It is finished."

✦　　✦　　✦

7

Into Spain

September Zaragoza, España –
I'm a traveler again. Brag
of the miles, headache is like
a battle medal and
my persona wilts.

The words go out before me,
speeding van eats up,
suddenly comes signs:
Deviation No way
You Don't Have Right Of
Way. No access –
Go – Here –
The arrows many –
in French they call road
stripes "zebras."

And in Kamzooma the
women wear aprons and long
black stockings and come to the
doors of their hovels
bearing shovels.
I've seen so much from the

back of my van, the interior
of my head and Li Poi
and Emily.
You'd think I was a millionaire
and not a humble monk.

Oh, let me tell you about the rest stop in Sud France
where they have big replicas of
eleventh century monastic architecture.
It's really swell.
But we had no time to stop,
and I wasn't interested.
Maybe someday we can do
that in ISKCON.

Tonight an hour more before
we stop. Our Ford is mighty,
but Spain holds a jinx
powerful, barren Spain
and me and Madhu driving to
New Vraja-mandala,
like a straw through
the eye of a needle.

pp. 74–75

✳   ✳   ✳

8

No "September Song"

"Sept Song" never arrived,
just as well. Pick out the song of the children
below this tower.
Babble.
The fly stuck in the glass –
I hear him rustle and

stood nearby.

Come on, you fraud, you've
got no song just longing
for what never was –
the peaceful routine of
June and July in Wicklow
when I sacrificed to
Bhagavatam and wrote 80
private tomes and remember
all those paintings from
you hand?

A leaky pen.
Spanish. English.
Spanish. Tomorrow lecture
that the Lord sets up and
disperses like a Player. Say
He's not bound by karma.

Don't harm an ant. No
September song but this criss-
cross dashed off in between
commas and my secretary
opening the door. Quoth
the raven –

pp. 93–94

9

The Day before Radhastami

Pause on a hot day before meeting
with disciples, what to say?

That you and I come together by
his grace, obedient, the same
truths, I repeat, you hear
on this hot afternoon
in Castile in the hills.

This is Krishna's land, ISKCON.
Here we believe in Prabhupada
as exclusive founder-*acarya*,
here we worship Radha-Govindacandra,
and there's electricity only in the morn.
And a home-made Nrsimhadeva.

Pause and hope you'll be able to
deliver some slivers of pure
and strong truth – yourself the
servant, "I got initiated thirty-one
years ago tomorrow; these are
my original *japa* beads." Don't say
that. Say what?

Whatever comes to mind
after we sing.
Look at them.
Clear your throat, drink spring water,
begin...

pp. 114–15

O LINK, O COM please
get us to our GBC man –
I need an extension on the
deadline. O COM, O LINK
I'm on the brink of disaster.
Please connect me once again
with my man. But I don't
need repetition of the
jazz of the past. Of the
forties and fifties, don't you see
it's dead? On this day
when blackberries are
some of them red and some
black ripe, pray to Jagan Mata.
Please recommend me
to Your Krishna.

p. 121

10

Radha's Day

Hurry he'll interrupt you before
September Song,
Radharani's Day turns to
noon.
You break your fast,
you're a secular host – fool –
to ideas you don't want.

But what do you want?
You can't – won't – say

324

"Radha's service direct,
under Rupa Manjari!"
That would be a farce,
a mockery to say or "pray."

Then? Prabhupada, we say.
But there too I fail
to make sense. I'll eat
the *prasadam* they sincerely
offered and say she had a
nice soprano voice who sang
kirtana to Radha when
I stood in the rear of the temple
viewing Radha and Krishna dressed
in soft green today,
while the children played
and the men danced and
the women I know not.

I am not a *sakhi*
I am just a
fellow who gave the lecture and
now is ordinary plain.

pp. 125–26

11

Return to My Own

September 11 make mine.
I'm alone a room with an
open window – one fly
circulates in here and
fresh-feeling air.
Here's a cup of water, sir.

I can't get right now into
Srimad-Bhagavatam. Why not make
an appointment for the morrow,
say at midnight? Remember
how you used to?

I'm in Spain, end of a
country road. The men were
singing and playing guitar in the
van, I heard the strains faintly
from here.
I just want to get some
assignments done
and return to my own...

At least visit my own
briefly, a few words,
hello to self,
pause to remember...
Let Krishna enter
the natural way
demanding my love
and attention.

pp. 140-41

12

The Secular Diary of Stephen Goswami

Before you know it September
will be gone. We hardly knew
ya – no chestnuts yet, no
song, no...
hermitage, party time, back to school –
what did you expect?
An arrest? A conviction?
A release? I want a simple
peace.

In September we hope to drive
down from these hills with
no jinx to break down our van.
It'll be third week
as we head into France for
Italy. I want to stop an
extra afternoon
pause and recollect, say
something at a P-stop...

Oh, it's a long way
from May to September.
No song.
Roll along. The calendar
goes bare.
Chanting Hare Krishna before it's
too cold, before Kartika,
before they go to India,
just me in this house
fresco, lies, Emily's
bonnet and a visit
by Tu Fu.

pp. 150–51

Listen mate,
if you draw a picture,
you may let your hand go free,
but how are you pleasing
Lord Hari?
That's the point of life.

p. 2

Then you slid into easy
gear saying my head can't
take extended, concentrated
thought. No force, no
meta-narratives.
We got to slide easy.

p. 3

13

If you had a gold pen
in September
could you write on a walk
in the woods?

Tell my legs' songs,
breast and
heart and ironic glance –
the factory abandoned,
thoughts of robbers awake,
are there any bears there?

If I could cease doubting
and the ditch, I'd
say it happened in September,
a likely time before
fall and winter...
No rhyme or reason
for that.

I'll be happy one day at
a time, purchasing my peace.
Today, shaved up,
broke fast, a sumptuous
Ekadasi lunch (beets and
avocado and olives mixed,
a green veg...It was good.)

The afternoon is ebbing. I read
the sastra. No urgent special news.
September 13 sounds unlucky,
but it's good and past now,
was gentle. God in
all things, even I
faintly perceive.

pp. 15–16

If I had enough light,
if the sun was up
you could sup
with little Miss Muffet.
If Charles Dickens wrote
swift and short, no, no
there is no one. You better
thank your stars you are

---

able to rise at midnight and
get that good lick in with
Srimad-Bhagavatam and your master say –
Soul is self,
body illusion,
turn to God.

p. 33

Pipe smoker demands
his slippers not be moved,
demands a million things
and scratches loudly and
hear his turds drop
splash into the toilet –
we live too close,
but it's okay I
just need to write it down
into the ground
of a mortal ironic
persiflage.
B. O. Plenty and
Gravel Gertie
and Marvel comics
Dead
good-bye to mother and father.

pp. 34-35

14

My head feels pressure, but I'm
the soul. I don't like poems
that don't tell God
but how can mine rhyme
with devotion if I don't
feel it in my chest?
If I don't feel it in my
life? Jest awhile longer,
play ironic, seek the quiet
hour with Thee.

I mean to be with Krishna who allows
myself to play with words,
with colors and who gives
me the pressure to teach
me something.

He doesn't neglect us,
though it may seem so.
He cares and waits until
we pay attention to the soul,
obey the guru and give up
chasing the prizes of
the world and listening
to misleaders.

Why do they still enchant us?
Talking this to myself,
mid-September in the
early eve, I'll hit the
sack and hope to come
painless to a midnight rendezvous.

pp. 39–40

15

Once there was a September
'97 tour I took to
Spain and one day wanted to
say, "Krishna, Krishna I don't know
a damn thing."

I just want freedom of pain
or if You like I'll take it
but I'm sincere in wanting
to write...

The rest is blanked out,
unable on Haridasa Thakura's
disappearance day.

I said, "There have been many
saints in this world but this
maha-bhagavata is very relevant
to us."

Pray to be rid
of distraction and
to taste more the nectar
of Hari-nama Prabhu.

p. 52

16

Mid-September is past
I gave the class,
and now I'm free a day
to do nothing or whatever
I want
in a room.

You walked and talked alone,
worry you are limited
to eating and sleeping
(not mating, no hating).

Some leaves are fallen,
pale, scorched green,
curled on the path.
I'm doing nothing much,
while you, you sir are the bravest burdened
preacher and manager.

I'm in Spain, where are you?
I don't know how to use
a computer – that doesn't
make me better, wiser, purer,
but still it's nice.

To be illiterate and out of harm's
way as the news broadcasts
the slaughter and I pray
for a little thing – that I
can hear my own chanting of
God's names? Maybe.
I pray...I cannot say.

pp. 70–71

17

Madhu's found a new polka
on accordion –
where do they come from?

One bird whistles Hare? Startles
every morning. In this place,
near Guadalajara.

I walked twenty-five minutes into the
country, first time ever on that
path, didn't want to meet
because no hablo espanol,
and besides...

Did you read at least a little?
Yes, of Hiranyakasipu's turning his body
into golden youth as
strong as thunderbolts
when Brahma sprinkled him
with water. That's Bhagavatam
too.

Now feeling feeble, almost every
day, wings folded, walk to
the bed, repair. I've got
a country air, a transcendental
polka of my own – not
better than others but
surely my own.

p. 87

18

Batten the bins,
clasp the locks, tie the
motorcycle straps –

We're in la bonne France
to go to a congregation of
balding brahmacaris or maybe
they're white haired by now –

To see where ladies are ladies
in saris and borders and
there's a leader and
money troubles and rumors
and dissatisfaction but...

Where on a Saturday morn I can
speak on C.c. or S.B.
and everyone will agree in
theory and even in practice
krishnas tu bhagavan svayam –
to that Cathedral Villagio
I'll go

Headache or no and
throw myself
at the feet of Prabhupada
and his followers another year.

p. 107

19

September's going,
I don't care, I do care
for my welfare, want to
get through this tour manfully,
give all the lectures
make tunes on my flute,
record the starts and stops,
the awkward meeting with
an ISKCON leader or
immigration cop.

And then we return to Inis-free
where there will be no motorboats
this time of year – the start
of Kartika, is when we're due.

Then I'll have it my way:
Regulate so I can rise at midnight,
chant *japa* out loud,
sit before Prabhupada and
Radha-Krishna, my books,
a lone walk. But I am partly
imagining it ideal. There
will be a drag everywhere
you go.

So, read a little today in
absolute *Bhagavatam*
and chant on red beads
you carry wherever you go.

p. 113

20

At Medolago this poet
scars his name
again and again on a tree of
memories and foolishness.

Look at the girls, old ladies,
bags under the eyes, look
in the mirror at my own
starved face – you've been
taking it easy and can't deeply
answer questions like

"What will Krishna think at the
time of my death if I didn't
get re-initiated?" And – "Can
I say prayers to Prabhupada or
am I not allowed?"

Tell them – he married me to
a woman and now it's undone
by his will. He's gone
in samadhi and I'll rot
soon – I mean the body
is not the self. I forget
what to say.

Chickens belong to neighbors.
Someone is washing our van – I hear
the water splashing, and I
too will splash some on my
own feathers and eat heartily and
meet the boss of this
place, bow to him
embrace him chest to chest
while keeping to myself.

And try to give Lord Krishna
His due – the Supreme
all-loving God –
do You know me?
Can we work on
my improvement?

September days so peaceful
in this rich village,
oh me, the
smoke's gonna curl up
the chimneys before
too long,
make a song.

pp. 128–29

Yeah. Bonzo, Bozo,
me ate a pizza
in Italy and talked to
seven matajis in a house
in Villagio Hare Krishna
and told them I'll be guru
if you like but the
main thing I'll do is be
alone, myself, so you
can say, "He didn't fall down."

p. 131

21

Cock crows, a neighbor's?
Man murmurs Hare Krishna *mantras*.
The chill of September in
my chest and back. Are you
ready to give *Srimad-
Bhagavatam* class?

As ready as I want to be –
leaving room to improvise
to watch their eyes,
wait for the brain,
to make a spring –

Talk of this:
How the soul is,
how the practitioner is
materially motivated even in
bhakti, how he
overcomes this –
by higher taste.

You'll speak, but
what do you know? Nothing.
The old woman looking on me as
a worthy guide for her last
days because I speak ideally.

My dreams tell another story:
Fear of unseen people
looking at me from the attic
and the literary poseurs who rob
the wayfarers just to get
a rhyme.

pp. 142–43

Econoline Preacher

Now buckle your seat belt in
the best of Fords
and roar
over autostrada to the next
place, private viewpoint of
September-end,
lasagna, pizza, ravioli,
Pavarolli Vivaldi,
and Jaya Govinda.
Inscape and looking out
lecturing from the books.

You are headache-prone and
Falldown-prone,
Women-in-poetry-prone –
it sometimes hurts
but do your best
and remember Swamiji wrote
with his own hand
on your apologetic letter,
"May Krishna protect you
from calamities."

In the days that remain
let no one be blind to
the truth of Krishna's Gita –
tell them and yourself
surrender to the King, sweet
Lord in three-fold bending form
and Radha's blessing on us.

pp. 151–52

CHAPTER THIRTEEN - PUT YOURSELF OUT

ITALY, ENGLAND, IRELAND, SEPTEMBER 22 — OCTOBER 7, 1997

For the title of the sixteenth volume of his unfolding literary series, *Every Day, Just Write*, Satsvarupa dasa Goswami aptly writes that this volume could be called, *Prove You Can Do It*:

> Prove you can do it...
> Prove you don't have anything to prove yourself. You are who you are.
> But also, prove to me that you can endure a headache, come out on top, or come out humble.
> Prove you are you a student of the Swami's.

> *p. 46*

In this volume the reader continues to travel with Satsvarupa Maharaja during the course of his six-week European tour. Ultimately, he chose the title Put Yourself Out which compliments the alternative that he considered. The expression, "to put yourself out" has a variety of connotations, which capture the themes that the reader will encounter within this volume. To begin, this expression calls to mind Satsvarupa Maharaja's actual departure from Geaglum, Northern Ireland; undoubtedly, this a literal "putting himself out" from his beloved residence and the solitude which it affords. At this point, one might consider the alternative titled described above for in departing Geaglum, the author is indeed proving to himself that he is able to make a significant trip that will tax him physically, emotionally, and spiritually.

This leads now to consider a second connotation of this expression, "to put oneself out." Here one may understand this expression to suggest a setting aside of one's needs or preferences for the sake of something or someone else. Indeed, there is an ethical foundation that supports the expression that Satsvarupa Maharaja has chosen for this volume. This phrase suggests that one has chosen to inconvenience oneself or has chosen to make oneself vulnerable in the service another. In this volume, as follow the author's European journey, we shall see that has chosen to set aside his personal preferences to serve both the institution, the International Society for Krishna Consciousness, of which he has been a leader, as well as to serve devotees in need of spiritual or pastoral care.

This volume is primarily set in Italy, and ever the painter, Satsvarupa Maharaja colorfully describes the early autumn beauty of the Italian countryside in both his prose and poetry. The author continues his series of numbered poems, begun in the previous volume, and these might be described as odes to the month of September. The poems themselves possess a painterly quality the author shares both personal thoughts and reflections, characteristic of his free-write process.

The six-week journey undertaken by Satsvarupa Maharaja has a pastoral focus. In this endeavor, the author bravely proves to himself, as he puts himself out, that he is able to instruct and counsel the members of the communities of devotees which he visits. This is done in spite of the health consequences that would impact the author severely. This volume then serves to provide a window upon a preacher's process: prayer and study, reflection and composition, all critical steps before the lecture is delivered. In this way, the reader is able to enter this process from start to finish, learning that indeed this endeavor is not dry academics, but rather one witnesses a distinctive form of devotional service, a key component of the author's daily spiritual practice.

This volume concludes with Satsvarupa Maharaja's return to Geaglum and both his beloved home and writing shed. If you are like this reader, you will feel a sense of relief that Satsvarupa Maharaja has returned home, a place of beauty and solitude, a unique residence that he has established in pursuit of his calling. The final page of the volume wonderfully describes Satsvarupa Maharaja's reunion with Radha-Govinda and his *murti* of his beloved spiritual master, Srila Prabhupada. Having challenged himself successfully, having "put himself out" for the sake of the devotees of Prabhupada's society, Satsvarupa Maharaja may now return to the distinctive life that he has so painstakingly created.

September 22

Chill in chest. It's good
to travel in the morning.

I hear you canceled a chance you
had to lecture on *sankirtana*.
Why? To guard your health and
the myth. Then take it
out there.

Your Mama's no more
your protector. Your Daddy's
gone. Peat moss in Ireland,
yellow vineyards in Italian
fall. And traveling to another
temple.

The Italian-made Prabhupada
murti grows on you.
He's here. You bow down,
make a show before the
Vaisnava *cognoscenti*.
This old, historical student.

Now rest and travel,
sit up, lie down
upstairs and down to
enter a temple hall –
your notepad in your pocket.

Give me a room and some
time and books –
I'll make you a promise
Volume 16, Krishna's face.

pp. 4-5

23

You're getting pretty near the end
aren't you? You mean
23rd?

Yes. Shit. Speak for yourself.
That's the problem, it's hard
with so many influences coming in
and you a pudgy, malleable
one. (Soul is not that).

You say, "Shit," and "malleable" –
those words come from places
where you learned them,
full of innuendos, histories,
instead of feces or stool
instead of "easily moved,"
patsy, pushover, you are
proud you are a City College
student and you lie.

You just want sex, we know
you. You just want people to
join your religious movement, you
just want money. It's all
so impersonal and mercenary.

What else? Get it off your chest.
Well, I'm sick of these religious
temple devotees and non-temple
devotees and non-devotees
and temple-less topless
nightclubs playing jazz, rock,
reggae, Reagan, I'm sick.

So, how is September in Italy?
Oh, just fine, really nice. The
cornfields are still standing dry
and yellow and other crops yellow
and green and skinny motorbikes,
but the people not so skinny usually.
They complain the economy is down,
but it is nice where there is still
you don't have to close the windows.

I think Hare Krishna.

pp. 26–27

I'll see You in my dreams
because You are everything.
Vasudevah sarvam iti –
but to me?

Someday
pray for it at any
cost.
Such a *mahatma*
is very rare.

p. 41

24

Beauty donna in the sun-
dappled cars go by the long
windows, I'm a Hare Krishna
prisoner in the *sannyasi*
guest room.

I complained that I ran out
of steam temporarily. You
non-devotees (poets
especially) don't know us.
You know the men with the
shaved heads? Well, I just
shaved up clean, do it
every two weeks before
Ekadasi.

Now I'll get back to my
eros or inspir-
ation, I get back my
second and third breaths
to speak to disciples
and to initiates and Godbrothers
and to...
God, God the
Witness Indwelling.

Prabhupada, the guru
on the swan-carrier
vyasasana, wearing a
locket with photo
of Bhaktisiddhanta
Sarasvati Maharaja.

Prabhupada, head of GBC,
member (chief) of ISKCON,
our well-wisher
cliché
no, it's real but you have
to be submissively intelligent
glean out truth
inquire.
(They nod their heads
assenting or asleep when

I make the right, familiar
point).
Haribol. This is the poem
for Sept. 24, it's almost
warm enough
for summer,
an electric saw I hear
and it's almost lunchtime,
take your *curna* and
be wise,

surely the second draft
will come,
you'll know what to say
at the moment
you go on stage
jazz old-timer.

pp. 49–51

From France and Villa Vrindavana devotees
come to North Vicenza while
Sats was here, he hasn't
dropped out yet vows to
last until death in his
seventieth-eightieth year, and wants
only to hear a little old-
time jazz as recompense and
not have it held against him
at end of life when he
wants to go to Krishna
(back home, back to Godhead).
The pen tells the truth
or says something.

Sridama dasa is gone,
his ex-wife is back.
Nanda wants to divorce
his wife. The devotees
act cold to you when you
deviate. ("They're too busy.")
"What else is new?"

Kalavati's emergencies,
fax doesn't work to America
where I am attempting to send
a message I consider urgent
but know it's not deep.
"Extremely intense and deep," he said.
Superficial knowledge of God is
useless.

Last stanza – don't knock the
gold pen, just be patient
with him. Prove it works,
prove this and that.
I say be patient, I need
tender care. Give me to
drink in an ink bottle and
use the traditional rubber
plunger method.

God is Glory, God is Love,
all the incarnations from Krishna
perpetual, as waves to sea
Krishna is known to devotees
I am one. Don't forget –
I am servant of one
whatever you are use it
in his service. Gold.

pp. 51–53

25

Initiation day. Not for me – I
give them out. I did it –
became disciple of the great
acarya thirty-one years ago and
I'm his castor-tree disciple-
turned-*guru*.
They say I poisoned Prabhupada,
minimized him,
treated him wrong, lied
to his face, disgraced
tried to replace him,
corrupt at core, deserve to
be pictured in *Monkey on a Stick.*

I say..."Prabhupada,"
when I'm sick or idle
or feel embarrassed recalling.
"Prabhupada," I blurt out,
my prayer spontaneous.
Sitting on the bed
suddenly Prabhupada.

September 25 initiation day for
Annalisa and Namamrta
I'll give beads, pour colors
and ghee, got a good lecture
lined up from *Adi* 7 where
Lord Caitanya teaches to be
obedient to *guru* and chant holy
names on his order. Preserve me
Lord, to perform the act and
my whole remaining life
not betray it.

pp. 66–67

26

Madhu's away three-hour drive to a
town in Italy that makes
accordions. What he wants
is a melodeon. He's an expert
musician, and Prabhupada says talent
can be used to please Krishna.

In M.'s absence Jaya Govinda is
guarding the door. I'll go
in and tell him he can do as
he likes in Krishna consciousness.
He's old enough as a man and has
done very good *sankirtana*
service. Why should he have to do
only what his "authorities"
tell him since they themselves
do what they want?

I may not tell him that
so bluntly. I don't want to
get caught myself. I'm hiding
things. I just dreamt that
two black and white skunks entered
our Staten Island house.
Woke with a start!
Something's stinking, about to enter?
I'm afraid.

The stink has begun.
It's pleasant weather Sept. 26
in lovely Italy,
better than the North. We're
        heading north tomorrow
towards October, Belgium.
I'm going to sing in the class –
Prabhupada tells it best,
the combination of

awe and sweetness
of the Supreme Lord Krishna.
So, let's hear it from him –
hear me tell it.
When skunks enter, jump
first and figure out later
how to get them out.
I'll ask M. when he returns,
hopefully with his
melodeon
for Irish songs and
jazz in my mind.

pp. 80–82

Autostrada sounds Italian
until we zoom loud
to start
on!

Sal uncle, Italian memory
Torino, to border
rare you get stamped passport
always wondering
do they know we are devotees?
Always chanting distraction but
praying somehow, somehow.

p. 94

27

Hi fans. Hi literary hero.
Hi God. Hi Dad. Hi
Sats. Hi Prabhupada
Hello Narayana Maharaja, why don't
you leave ISKCON alone?

I'm in the back of the van. It's
straining at 95 mph, Madhu
would love to go faster, but
they built it to cut out
at that speed. BMWs
pass us.

So, it's hard to write.
Suddenly a loop goes looop.
Krishna, Krishna, Krishna, Krishna.
The Lord
The Lord. The God.

The girl died at 33. She
hugged her Godsister and said
I'm afraid to die. So,
the survivor learned that.
I read it in a letter from
the survivor which I answered
by shouting into the Dictaphone
as we roar through France.

This is Sept. 27, tonight the clocks
fall back. Good – I can sleep at 7:00 P.M. without
sunlight. God God, when I die like that
lady I hope at least
I get more writing done first.
The dying girl was comforted
but replied, "You don't know

what it's like." (To face your
attachments to the body and
life and "the Death.")

But they said she entered
deep peace. She was hearing kirtana
and Prabhupada.

Okay, it's only September 27.
I'm not quite 58,
we'll stop for lunch.
I've got plenty plans.

Improve.

pp. 96–98

28

Krishna consciousness.
Nobody knows it but the devotees.
They gather in a temple
after greeting the Deities and
Prabhupada's *guru-puja*.

You outsiders don't know these
functions so there's a glossary
in this book. I don't attend
the temple *puja* except for
mangala-arati (see glossary)
and then the class.

I sit on the *vyasasana* and begin.
This temple speaks English
so I don't get to pause in-between phrases.
Now I'm tired and won't continue.

Ate yogurt and fig jam and
apple slices at a Texaco
gas station in Luxembourg where
I walked and *japa* in
pre-dawn in a playground.

Now I'll rest and then
we'll drive on. You don't
have to know what I am
saying. But you have to learn
Srimad-Bhagavatam with some education.
I'll try to make it clear,
but I assume you've read
the *Bhagavad-gita* and believe
Sri Krishna is the Supreme Personality of Godhead.

SK says, "Faith is the highest
don't go further."
Hear from Me,
says Krishna.

pp. 109–110

29

By an open window with a
confessional screen on, I gave
class this morning and that's all
I do. Even while I sit here the
leaders are worrying about the
government's investigation of cults.

I won't be guilty. There's a
jet rumbling. M. picked up
the same encyclopedia/dictionary
I've been browsing in (where
we are guests) and said, "It's no
good. It doesn't have the

word melodeon." I didn't
tell him it does have Monk,
Miles Davis, Mingus, Coltrane and
Ornette Coleman. But when I
saw the film where Bhaktivinoda
Thakura is protected from tantric
attacks because he's reading the
Bhagavatam aloud, I decided
I don't need jazz,
won't ask for it in London.

Sitting by the open window
with a confessional screen –
couldn't sleep because a
fly bit me. My austerities
are nothing, you could say
but I won't feel guilty.

I've got a lecture lined up,
a clear-of-headache day,
and still a few hours to write
and read in small
installments. When September
is over, we'll go on
until He says.
Gravel on the walk,
I wish our leaders well.
I'm sticking to Bhagavatam
and Every Day, Just Write.
Jazz greats, I wish you
well. I'm in silence with
a birdsong, and
I hope to read like
he was doing.

pp. 127–29

30

A crazy man in the temple,
he wants to speak with me,
but I'm too weak.
Let Jack or Jill or Leader
X take it upon.

I know he'll get angry if
you cross him,
warns he'll go to the police
and newspapers. On top of
that, he says he's going to die soon.

Angry...me too, the
Ravana and wren and
lion and crossed emperor
and angry telephone lines...

And what about feeling foolish,
wanting to be rid of material
desires? What about lack of
love, inattention in chanting?
Or a plain scientific fact:
we're all going
to die soon?

Talk to me, no I can't.
Just a moment? But what
can I say to help or defuse you?
Show you I care? I can't,
you see...Or I could but
I won't. I'm walking this
restricted line. Hare Krishna.

pp. 148–49

Smoke and fire
Emily's bed, her hand
Her white-heat poems –
A few I learnt to approach,
The coach with Death
and Immortality in it, the
fly buzzed, but we want
Krishna when we die –
Lord, let us behold Your
face and lotus feet or form,
even by hearing it's enough –
let us not forget You and
next life please let us
serve You.

p. 185

O Sarva, O Gopinatha,
Please admit me one member
of the gang. Let me stand in
back or up front but no
heavy duties please, give
me the honor to speak and
I'll fulfill it like a veteran.
Musician who knows how.
That's my payment for
the food I receive and looks
intense from Bhakta
Farlow who distributes books
in London and wants to know if
I can help.
Help.
I ask for help.

pp. 197–98

No, you don't
gotta do anything but serve
your master. They're feeding
you for that. Next
what will you speak on a
Sunday afternoon? How about
telling what Srila Prabhupada wanted?
He said chant. I
don't know. Tell an old story.

pp. 199–200

The sounds are merry
the sounds are gay,
you're sometimes sad and
far away. But you will then
want to be in the city of
God and think these
musicians can help you?

Are you joining a lost
band of sense gratifiers,
yourself consorting with sinners
and claiming it's okay? Or
are you on a mission
to dovetail their love
as it rouses in you
something live that felt
dead?

Are you being impudent,
going off? Or is it
bona fide service?
Don't ask them

you're on your own,
trust your conscience,
Pinocchio. But watch out
for signs of growing nose and
ears.

I don't wanna remain
without it he says,
and so Krishna gave him
CD sounds. Let's see
what happens.
Srila Prabhupada is laughing or is
that a frown?
Don't leave me
hold my hand.

pp. 223–24

CHAPTER FOURTEEN - BLACKBERRIES

IRELAND, OCTOBER 8–26, 1997

Let's get serious.
Better get it in your soul.
This is the way I want to ring chimes. Listen, he's
good, good. And I am too
pickin' berries
my hands stained with ink
brown – green – red – blue

p. 37

The return to Geaglum, Northern Ireland, will initiate a remarkable period of poetic explosions, chronicled for the reader in the seventeenth chapter of Satsvarupa dasa Goswami's series, *Every Day, Just Write*, entitled, *Blackberries*. Having completed a long and challenging European tour, one can imagination that a return to his home and writing shed, has created a powerful moment of spontaneous combustion, if you will. Indeed, this volume contains a wealth of poetry, representing the most radical moment in Satsvarupa Maharaja's ever emerging poetic voice. In this, the reader encounters poetic experimentation in which traditional forms are now pushed to their limit and beyond. At this moment, any line distinguishing the genres of prose and poetry has been effectively breached and transcended, and in this break, we witness the emergence of new forms, new styles, which usher in experiments in poetic freedom. These new poetic forms have the qualities of a literary whirlwind of pure expression, into which the reader is drawn with great force by the power of this poetic sense of abandon. Not only have forms been broken open, but rules of grammar and the syntactical relationships between words have themselves have been decisively challenged and overwhelmed by the intensity and urgency of Satsvarupa Maharaja's voice. Indeed, to enter the pages of this volume is to experience the unhesitating momentum of an artistic juggernaut that cannot and will not be restrained.

At times within this volume, Satsvarupa Maharaja will refer to these poems as "improvisations," thus calling to mind a distinctive feature of jazz performance. Improvisation within the performance of a musical piece should not incline one to consider this a moment of haphazard chaos. Rather, it is the accomplished musician who is able to depart from the established pattern or shape of the musical composition. Improvisation is the free experimentation with a musical theme present in the original composition. Such experimentation is playful concluding with the musician's ultimate return to the set themes and melodies within the original composition. Such is the case with Satsvarupa Maharaja's poetic expression within this volume. Prominent poetic themes are similarly challenged through grammatical upheavals and wonderful wordplay in addition to the seemingly effortless border crossings between prose and poetry.

Interestingly and significantly, the artistic eruptions that one encounters within this volume are created within a setting of peace and solitude, while one might readily imagine that such works have been composed in the midst of the often frantic bursts of energy within urban life. Further, the chronicling of life, which has become characteristic of Satsvarupa Maharaja's endeavor within the

Every Day, Just Write project continues here unabated. His reading, his reflections, his worship of Radha-Govinda as well as his loving relationship with his spiritual master, Srila Prabhupada continue to form the core of this literary endeavor. The poetic outbursts that fill these pages make this volume all the more remarkable given the devotional setting of this work. The poetics here are wonderfully riotous and continually draw the reader, as will any genuine improvisation back to the established core of the piece, which in this case is Krishna, the Supreme Personality of Godhead.

Finally, throughout this volume the tender quality of the work as a whole emerges through the presence and mention of blackberries, which appear on page after page. From the poem quoted above in which in a crushed blackberry yields a dark juice that stains the hand of the writer in the same way as the ink of his pen, to the sweet offering of blackberries from the hands of a young child, the berry's presence beautifully unifies this text. In this way, Satsvarupa Maharaja pays tribute to nature's bounty offered graciously from the outstretched hands of his Lord. This is the center, this is the melody, that divine composition, which moves this author inward and upward in praise and prayer.

The Promise

You want exact on-beat
for your own
jurisdiction
formalist/Emily/part and
parcel/reduced fares
we're not going there! You yearned for longed for
ease
ease
chestnut
Now get it right. Hear him and let your pen flow
I don't know where it leads, love
white page Krishna appears
      here by writing. He appears when I try
my relationship appears.
Just barely warming up

    imagine this one too is for God. Respect. Assume they
know what they're doing. Assume words flow I'm not going
back for nothin' not Blue Hour good time
    frustrated

    sad
    loins
    sailor ROC
    blues – all gone so ignorant didn't know my master,
      few friends and they too...
    no, now I'm enlightened
    the Indian part leads to Krishna, Best flute player. He
      stands adorable little boy, man. God of all.
    Who can understand! This was the purpose. Go to
      the *vana*, go there. You've got limited time.
    See you later

bop smack
black blues each moment
loves me, understands me,
I love you too but it's not
so deep to the nerve
perhaps
cunning
Prahlada
see you again today
India
he got locked up, Crazy Carl, on lithium. Now the
    last coda, I'm going to sense
buoyant cat
gait be with you
Krishna Krishna
Krishna deliberate
Krishna chant
beads like
wood, Krishna chant. Teach them,
Guruji
sway you belong
in saffron dress blue
no more sailor nightmare
teach me to dream and
fight back for right
Love Supreme.

pp. 13–15

❋　　❋　　❋

1

Okay, roundelay at last you're
speaking to me again not for
money.

Oh, this is too much!

Not enough, my critics will
put me down – I'd better read
a book how to take it.

This afternoon...why can't
you read a sacred book
and tell a story? We wanted
to be devotees...at 58 years old
he settled in the country and
took walks and picked daisies
and gradually built up
a reading and writing repertoire
and then something new and
pure and honest took place.
"Hope is the thing with
feathers that perches in the soul..."

p. 20

2

The shed man has his own
version of reality of Ireland
rainy and puddles, twenty minutes
walk he's always talking of
his aching head, his life
of Riley – "What a revoltin'"

Since you came to this world
you never stopped spinning and
accumulating karma, and it's
spinning off when you write.

Your ISKCON memories – a
wife chuckled finally but

not long before you and she
 - A house thugs raided.
I am sorry I made
so many mistakes and still
leftover temple president the
story of me on the GBC is
another chapter I'll tell
you sometime but poets want
surprises and lovely things
to tell their beloved Master or Sue.

For me it's idam hi pumsas
I've got my military orders in
a 9×12 envelope from Gurudeva –
go to the service on board the
ISKCON rear dept., check in
yearly with *sannyasa* ministry
and write some required papers.
The good things I'd write
would be censorable but
when we die…
It's more important to be Krishna conscious
than "right, beautiful,
metric, nonmetric, Nothing."

Hare Krishna man makes this
first visit to the old
melodeon player, disguising
his appearance in pants
so the old guy doesn't freak
out. But he'll bring him some *maha-prasadam*.
I'm like that too.

pp. 45–47

3

You can't write because you aren't
dipped deep recently into
sastra, krsna-katha,
you're admitting too much and
indulging in other things.

So anything you write will come
out flaky, and the girls who write
poems and the men who read
them won't – like it.
They just want (I say) doctrine
from beginning to middle and end,
whereas I want *ars poetica*.
you're kidding yourself, conning
the readers and the bottom of the
page is coming up like death
fast...we know *Bhagavad-gita* teaches
you're a soul and the body
is the covering. A poet dies
thinking of Krishna, and he lives
thinking of Krishna, and he doesn't worry
whether he dies in the six months of
dark moon or in the full moon.
And he preaches and pleases his spiritual
master. He's a poet like Vyasa.

pp. 56–57

4

Night soon, raining all day.
M. looks out the window.
He says, "A poor soul is rowing across

standing up in the boat with
one short oar, like a spoon."

That's Inis Rath.
They don't have enough money
or men. But it's quiet.
Somehow, it's going on and that's
the wonder: Radha and Krishna
are cared for.

Over here the chimney is pouring out
smoke for the first time this season.
I ran through memorized verses
tad vijnanatham/...
yasya deve/...
yasmin vijnate...

They row across to Govinda-dvipa...
Gray all-clouds
Clock slowly ticks. Krishna
gave us peace
now use it
in His service.

pp. 70–71

5

Here you are in your old
handwriting

You sat in the temple.
You walked in the quay
joking as light as the sun-
shiny October air.

The boat was wobbly and
watery but had good oars,
and Arjuna rowed us across.

I entered the room surprised how
many were waiting.
Quick obeisances to
Radha-Govinda, no time for
devotion in front of the crowd.
Hurry into the lecture –
reading from Cc. *Madhya* 7.

Lord Caitanya loves His devotees
but has to follow social etiquette.
It is rich, I said – His
indirect praise yet criticism of
their giving Him comfort when
He wanted to go alone to
walk in *tapasya* of *sannyasa*.

You shouldn't
criticize a guru or give him
milk when he asks
for water. At the end
I paused but didn't say:
I am not just a reciter
of the Absolute, I am a
person and I give it in my books.
I said that later in the cloak room just to
Manu. "Yes, that is intimate,"
he said.

Then back to the quay,
talking, joking and beholding
on Geaglum the collie
barking at a few birds thirty
feet above in the treetop.

Back to the house the
garland breaks into dozens
of pieces, another
Sunday yajna, and I'm back
to myself – write your odes,
no one knows.

pp.86-88

What Reason

You get quiet times too. They say they don't know.
They're of the school
That Doesn't Know

Or they can believe in God. But Krishna
consciousness is so universal-specific it could ruin your
friendships and get you kicked out of the club. Then
you "join" the worldwide web of say 50,000 who are willing
to buy books, go to a temple, and say yes, Krishna
consciousness is good. India has millions.

But if you don't want one, all right, I'll just sashay
down the stairs
with you if you don't want that,
I'll be yours too.
But I'll always tell people Chant Hare Krishna.
Soon you get into that groove
that rap
sampradaya

I do it all the time and sometimes want "out" or
release from it. That's what I was trying to tell them in class
this morning, but it wouldn't come out and here it is

on a late Sunday afternoon
I'm sitting alone playing
the piano for love
of God and
without any *karmis* or music-philes who don't know
shaven-headed music.

p. 91

*　＊　　＊　　＊*

Preacher

This is the way the hurried-up people move.
Don't put it down.
Man, you keep saying that
it's no holds
Krishna surprises you.
We are not this body. Soul is eternal.
God is *acyuta*, but He reveals Himself. Yeah? How do
    we believe this?
Because it's in the scripture. Some do, some don't.
"Read second chapter Gita and chant
    on these beads."
You get off like this and then return to regular
    behavior as if no one knows what you are doing –
crashing to Swami's feet
"I did it! I gave out a book! I sang in public! I helped
    a devotee!"

p. 92

Shed Poem

Poem of night and fright
get into it I'm not tired
out so should work

Again: this day has broad
stripes of sundown like
October 12. Krishna is sum total
but also a Person, all to Himself.

I repeat what's on the shelf,
in the book *Bhagavad-gita As It Is*.
I take essence and remnants of
my master's talks,
convinced it.

This is not an official poem
of the canon. I just
wanted to write a page in
the shed where
the ink wash paintings
show animals saying
"Gauranga!"

Please accept me.

pp. 93–94

Okay, give us real stuff
krsna-katha

sadhu sitting in sunken garden in Yama-tota in
Puri, but white guys had to leave, Hindus said. Mosquito-
bitten I retreated upstairs and said To heck with them. I'll
speak American into my Dictaphone. I know what they
don't, and they know what I don't

So, I went back to Dalmia's house, and I said I'll stick
with ISKCON that accommodates Americans.

But you were saying...
Yes, *hari-katha* is good. Lord Caitanya came here
once. He entered the ocean and went down to Konark,
where a fisherman caught Him, but internally He was with
the *gopis*. He stood on shore and watched the play of
Krishna and the *gopis*.
too intimate
straight no watering it down
straight Krishna consciousness from the hip
of GBC manager
straight *Gita*
lip
mantras
good spiritual look straight from guru now and until
more
Krishna you give me arm
and sight
I love You

pp. 101--2

374

6
My Altar

Prabhupada sitting before me may
be angry if he chooses,
but I seem him as I choose
in burgundy shawl
and orange Swami hat,
Radha and Krishna beside him.

He looks up, and I look down.
"No perhaps," he says,
"it must be fact."
Then fact, little offered by me
to your Krishna consciousness movement.

Lord Nrsimha's standing astride,
can't knock Him over –
He will duck your dart and
deliver you a blow
finally rip you apart.
He's covered
with silver armor and
surrounded by a
yellow and white *parijata* garland.

Jagannatha from Puri is actually God.
Photo of Panca-tattva
from West Bengal and NYC 1965.
Parampara gurus, Six Gosvamis
and two napkins
where the plates will go
with hot lunch.

Sad and mild.
Waiting for some
clear thought

to better serve the Lord,
sits a peon before the altar
of Krishna worship.

pp. 111–12

The Lake Drink: A Scene from the Shed

The lake drinking is running
rippling to the right, all ripples
like...
A blue lake fringed with
weeds like big plumes on top
they turn palomino all winter.
This is God's energy call it
material, it's splendid.

The lake and the island. Within the
island are two big statues, Radha
and Govinda. They are served by
the devotees. They leave me
alone here on the mainland.

I serve but wish...sometimes
I do write and roll like in
"rock 'n' roll" a white
man's game.

I joined the Hare Krishna *mantra*
I mean movement it
is notorious in newspapers and
anti-cult groups, lost two
decisions at Supreme Court but then
one came down favorable when
the Supreme Lord refused to handle

the George case.
I'm in that movement.

The lake strait doesn't actually move,
its top blows left like a tree
leaf, leafys. Words are hard
to manage and so is a temple or family
and even a single life (the best kind) –
but don't become a bachelor daddy!

So the lake is fine on a plane and
the island is a dish and Krishna could
pick it all upon His left
pinky if He wanted. He leaves me
He demands me, He'll award
me, I punish myself

when
and
how
Krishna, we are Your servants
in the movement.
I am just
saying, as my report card used
to, "Could be better."
Ma Vedas Loves All.

pp. 116–18

Women of the Veil

What's that? Oh, what's' in a name? To me it could mean nuns or just the opposite.

They know and I know/imagine a group of
devotees making music together like this to your picture slides.

how would you explain it to the devotees? They would think they are being subjected to evil bad
maya.
Well, is it?
Not any more than...

Women of the veil. Lonely notes here and there. I'm just happy it's mid-October and I can write this day be grateful

Prahlada
Prabhupada
what does it take to sustain,
write as much as you can?
Those young men in Wellies, their young outlook so different than mine, showing off to each other,
or simple friends,
their intellects and bodies and futures and moms and dads to contend with
Krishna/Cross/mix
being left alone
not in India
guesthouse reality New arrival Swami with big
walking stick –
"I'll talk to you later."
Big shots.

pp. 119–20

Remove obstacles
like stone over Christ's grave
where is the biog on Paul
the man who invented Christianity?
Where's my stall for
selling rice?
Why did he leave a
simply wonderful in the kitchen?
If you allow ignorance
then you're in it yourself.
"That's why I holler at
my servants," said the *guru*,
"So I and they don't stay in *tamas*."

pp. 156–57

Getting into My Way

I am now on my own. Those dreams, those dreams,
    bring you back
to the place you want to go
But not really. You struggle helplessly. Can't get out.
Oh well, better to be awake.
Then...

My momma didn't teach me...
Krishna science, my spiritual father...
Leave behind that past. Swami says don't bother
    with it, don't talk nonsense.,
mold your life
be perfect
I think, "Is this ideal?"
Now I will remember Lord Yadu.
He says he will. I don't know for sure
prejudiced by the critics and what they say.

The man is trying to express
something of his own, at least
the sign of times
a beat out
There can be no mistaking it

There it is, the fine point we want to make.
This is the Sunday gray
don't waver in your quiet
determination
Krishna, Krishna will take me at death.
I fear you're not doing the best
But this is life
live it the way you know
big holes on left side of page
white fields of lined paper
I live here
like a worm on page
I live for this kind of thing
Reflection is for us.
You can understand your own.
This is the way he said
his trademark.
My, my
Krishna, I am floating at ease
he's going to leave me alone a number of days and
    I'll tell you my own thoughts at that time.
Krishna, Krishna, it's about to end in the middle of
    your song.

    Young boy from Denmark and you from Ireland,
you don't know what it will be like when you grow up
 as I do,

no one to talk to,
isolated in your self-conception
and never sure Krishna

loves you to do what you decided. You twist shape
philosophy to suit you
mirror my unrest
I'll just say this much –
I do love You, Lord, and I want
I want
I know – nothing.
Goloka, please take me
away from me, painful next lives –
and death at least let me
remember You.

pp.43 –45

More poems

No more poems I heard
since your turned to your
secret new art of listening and
writing. So, we silent
poems aren't good enough
for you?

We gave you so much,
worked so hard...

Oh, shut up. I still love
you.
Then prove it. Write
us. You will write yourselves with
ease.
But you've got to
grease your elbow.

It all comes from God.
True but He wants
to see your effort.

And so
blue lake strait happy no
ferries today I'm okay
finally waving my flag
All Clear
until the end give me
forty more years or I'll
take twenty, twenty would
be really nice, that's
seventy-eight I can take (and at
that time I'll ask for just three more
so I can live as long as my master and
go to him but he had a life of goodness I
misspent my youth.
    Oh well,
    chant Hare Krishna
    write poems,
    don't eat anything after lunch,
    write a candle, (light one)
    and
    pray Hare Krishna will visit you
    full fledge before you die
    Amen.

pp. 79–81

I was satisfied
to fall asleep
having exerted myself
for Thee.

p. 91

(Beauty in October. Met Syamamayi and daughter picking blackberries. "The last of the year." Daughter's mouth stained with them. Goodness, tangy clear. Happy. Then come to this with good conscience and see what you can do.)

p.95

Last Blackberries

(So, brief this is. But my time is also brief. Can I leave you with some impression in brief? Why not? Haiku does it in three lines.)

Last blackberries.
Take us for a ride in your car
don't kick the dog.

you and me will ride through the city for bad
will try to avoid – the inner purpose will protect us
a brother like JS is with me and others
with our paraphernalia
for a festival to preach Krishna
in the town hall
this I made up

My last dies, tasting the last blackberries
This is my sweet tang
last, last, last
not yet
you'll die but
now sing.

He sings through me
and me in him.
Krishna, You are the kindest
so brief we keep coming through here in old age
    grant me spirit to help others.

this is the way
we play to relieve tired
spirits of others
and instill peace
but show confrontation
I'm no big teacher
little – what

O Lord, Your nature is
beautiful I am digging it that way
    Christ came
    Krishna came
    They taught us to love God that's
    the purpose of life
People don't want to hear His message.
    We do it nicely.
Let's jive not for sense grat
but dance in the halls of light and *mangala-arati* dark
candle at night
Kartika
Blackberries
I host
hold the host up
my prayer is to learn to the love the Lord's names
and convey this to others
    varieties of delight
    the bitterness
    understood in that way
God is good
Prahlada teaches and
I am his, go in goodness.
Give me strength.   *pp. 103–05*

Our Lady

(Hurry along. Brief time. Incongruous. No one should see me
doing this. Hide your tracks. Allow you heart.)

> Jungle drums begin a song and let's drown out
>   the chatter of fools and materialists.
> Your lady is the supreme Lady
> your Lady is Krishna's Radha
> this is the truth.
> There's no lady in this world but
> she's but a bag of tricks, grows old
>   Cleopatra was expert for a
> while (salad days over) but she
> too had become a crone
>   a crone's okay too
>   but I'm just saying
> I read the book
> Tenth Canto and auxiliary by
> Gosvamis
> in Mathura I heard
> from Srila Prabhupada I heard
> about the *gopis*...

> Now worker tell us what is your spirit?
> Our Lady, the Catholic says for the mother of God
> we too say Radha is our mother in *bhakti*.
> This is fine, but what do you feel?
>   I feel I am hoping I don't get too addicted to
>   allopathic pills.

>   Can have pain-free days,
>   to sing of our Lord and Lady,
>   sometimes go to Vrindavana and Puri and
> place this body on the earth and pray
> and receive the blessing, blessing –
> I am feeling that rock center
> blackberries on the tongue

my mind
a snake in me
I am feeling these things, need for my own quiet
    growing like a late autumn growth of bush,
                            last berries...

I'm feeling out of joint sometimes
not in sync
but I do it anyway...
Play with the players
on the white page stay

in the lines or gambol
and ask the Lord to allow me my time to be with Him
  names, holy names
  there'll be a time
  you'll grasp your red beads
  there's no faking it
  whatever little you have
  don't avoid the white-lined page
  the flowing of ink's ink.

Your Lady is not mine
lady or man has soul inside
a monk doesn't play the game.

Alone a hermit wants his prayers and texts and
        his alone –
his tentative connection to the world
we seek eternal nothingness?
Eternal variety of Krishna and Guru
please give us another chance
this was brief it
was
Krishna.

pp. 126–29

Swami

Swami is the name of the
controller of senses it doesn't mean
he controls his wife. When he went home
and met their mean group, he
said I have become a swami, meat
is not allowed. Instead of being
well-received the Swami was thrown out.

See? He said all right to the Supersoul
in his heart. I'm not afraid of heaven or
hell, all I want is to dovetail service
and that is the ideal swami of this story.

As for someone given the name Swami,
who is human and doesn't always control
his senses, we can say that he dovetailed
the best he could and as far as I know
he still goes with that super-title.
Goswami, a name that can be given
to Americans because the leader
is above designation. But the follower
has got to avoid serious mistakes.

p. 133

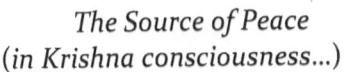

The Source of Peace
(*in Krishna consciousness...*)

This minuet in the park of the *mandira*.
Say I'm happy for this day
pain I waited
and now can sing my simple song
God of twilight
the girls are walkin'

and the young
man just happens to be out walkin'
and I'm here
in my *Bhagavatam*
squeak kazoo
    this is the time the
Lion-man Lord
    ripped him good
Alone, alone, happy for that but
you should be working
They can spy you grooving
on a lonely quay
the sun last rays glint
    I saw the swans fly by
Yeats and company
I sat and watched calm water

God in all
we don't know

Artists make music for a...Each one can
    make a manly
or feminine sound
each one contributes to the whole
in Krishna consciousness.

Demons' look out, you'll get it
masts destroyed
battleships sunk

Home free
ink spill
"Will you please get me a lollipop or twelve when
    you're in town?"
This space for rent.

Krishna, I'm not centered but
want that old peace, calm
You've given me ability to
worship You as calm center-
giver,
but I also know You're the
killer of demons,
and my master
wants me workin' out.

This loose-goose
this tight-as-drum
oath on beads he rose
back to Godhead
borrows
writing to make poems
for the might movement called ISKCON – gone to
  a center in Alaska yet? Detroit? Wyoming? All over.
    There's no lack of sound.

pp. 137–39

Song to Nrsimhadeva

Hand writ or smoke
it comes from Him
no one knows His prowess
His extent. It's good to declare the
Unknowing
I don't mean the "Cloud" of mystic dark
Be sure it's Krishna
yet still we don't see Him
can hear and talk with fellow mystics of
Srimad-Bhagavatam.

They'll see it as myth but we don't
what can I say? Introduce some of it as best you can
Lord, please accept me too as Your servant.

Coming before Lord Nrsimhadeva in the palace one
    by one they prayed
in fear and obedience, told frankly of the relief they
    felt from demon's death.
Thank you for giving us pain free,
Oh, how we suffered.
Now we want to enjoy peaceful life of varieties.
Big men are only little fellows in the flood, all swept
    aside by time like the soldiers of
                    Hiranyakasipu in Your
    nails.

Singing for the faithful, the whole world may
    become so
if I could bewitch them
please them
with incarnation of sound
music hath charms
and powers – like song for You
    who knows the
    emotions we feel are
    due to Supreme One
may it please Him
may His will be appreciated
by us so we can say
    it's good
    it's Krishna in my life.

The times when we thought we'd
died and finally did,
bluffed that we were pious to enjoy with
    ourselves as center,
making a melody around oneself.

The world is a sorry place
but for the incarnations of the Lord
and his faithful servants,
mighty devotees and simple ones too.

In a special place we
sing of God's grace even
in simple ways as He entered
our lives major and minor
Hare Krishna chanting this morning
you can say thanks and write, the power
is yours for awhile,
every life thrown around
inter outer space went
the airplanes
thrown from Lord Nrshima's
power glory
amen.

pp. 142–44

Straight, Don't Chase Me

I go my own way by a calm lake
since when are you the lone polecat
the guns raised of boaters who can't shoot swans but
    others they can

Are you saying...?
Krishna consciousness has jurisdiction here
you can say that but I'm the one
who's a servant hiding out

Clocks go back I will rest on
a pillow
I'm following the discipline.

Well, that's how it is with
we students
got to be in bed by 7 P.M.

Discipline is a good thing
eight ways a man avoids women,
but Srila Prabhupada said we will see them not like
    in the story that Jiva Gosvami refused to see Mira.

Now I'm piping hot a good day is over
we toasted in
apple juice
the one year since I was in Italy
Isola di Albarella
and detoxed
am I better off? I just want to remember
    the leaves and bike-riding
    and being alone then too and
    genesis of
    Every Day, Just Write.

And since Madhu discovered his
singing career and I'm glad for that when

the sounds come on
I'm glad for that

You are sorry you are neither an angel nor bopper
words come out no good not mine
    where's mine? You tell me
    I was down
    I'm okay now
    "He prayed with elephants and humbleness"

Grin
greenback
fall back
of clocks

your wail your God and that's the gospel truth
music of skylark and squawker in trees I heard but
    didn't see
Paul walked home and I was not an altar boy
poor guys a hundred and twenty million sued
the news filters in

I saw the Gandharvas
And you?
I heard them singing their prayers to
    Lord Nrsimhadeva
meningitis – O Lord, You killed the demons and we
    can be happy again.

Straight
Don't chase me
I'm a cop too.
I preach in peace and congregation hear my praise
    of Lord Caitanya tomorrow before Radha-Govinda.
Pure I am
    dream
    if you like how I
    read a poem in a jazz club
    a priest of ISKCON saffron mittens
    and water bottle chaste
    devotee blues and
    drums fade out a
    song given to God, Krishna.

pp. 160–63

Renunciation

I want to talk about you
very human, etc.
   My farewell to
   listening to my favorite music
   while I write.

Good-bye I'm a monk
who ought to be more in silence
with Hare Krishna *mantras*.

Thank the Lord for the freedom
to do it, but now I'm
going to renounce.
Thank you for the dance for the nights for the
strength of your artistry.

Silence? There are always mouses scurrying at least in
   mind and dreams.

Writing to music is a kind of ultimate
I'll be back

This last day
of Lord's glory
   always in the blood
   as long as you live.

"But we take another body,
I'm not this body."

Bird of the Geaglum marsh
the not-to-be-killed swans and the killed ducks.

The nameless wordless
the clashing sticks

row us over to the Island
will we have whose
tune in mind when we go?

To accompany you back to Godhead
while you read *Caitanya-caritamrta*
whose horn
whose clashing drum?

I want to talk about You. This accompanies me
The attention of Prahlada
as he prayed
is admirable, desirable
ought to be dignified.

Terrific five-star writing
Don't sell your soul for that, Faustus.
I'm a calm lad by a calm lake where fog rises thick
    and burns out in A.M. even without jazz background.

You wail.

Then he paused and played all alone. I want to talk
    of Krishna in the head of Yadus and dearmost of His
    devotees all over.
    In Vrindavana He's best
    I'm at His feet
    in disciplic succession.
Yes, all this solo too the impure motives in my heart
the craving for muffins and ice cream
the sweatpants and
sweat
follicles, follies
boredom at our ISKCON
ruptures
doubts
diminishing/last youth

exploring sounds in mind's caves
That's okay
I'll let you go
But I want to be "like" Prahlada, fixed in what
    Krishna wants
and not my own invented offering.
So farewell
dwindle it back down to none and write
with whatever you already know.

I will behave and write fashioned as a
    Hare Krishna monk.
Thus I do declare half-solemn this clock-back day of
    Our Lord, October 26, 1997, finis clap clap crow.

pp. 167-70

The Promise

The time is autumn and I'm in my tracks
let go blackie men you ain't
de only boss
I is too said the ofay
crime-eater

The dream: in some kind of car race
and I went up the stairs in Katan Avenue house,
    Hindus let me take the room for myself.
Yeah, I need it
get headaches
this evening
they drinkin'
No hot dogs but in the dream people were nice,
    like it when humans are nice
            but it's not only so

You want to go alone more
serious on this Ekadasi
act as a sadhu
even if you aren't one.

Crow
Gray-hooded crow
mag raven
the stream of Tusca
the stream of Eirin
of Dirge of Druid
I am the only one in my head

calm down and give us good stuff after all you don't
    have fever flu spouting uncontrolled what girls you
    love and sadhus shake their heads
"He was bluffed by a good
piano player."
Lost chance for flying in plane
to Vaikuntha Goloka
for what?
Lush life over a glass
of whiskey tell your bitter story how you missed the
    boat, back in the material world to hear
                                    jazz and it's

    not the same
try to squeeze
yogurt they brought me
and plums and grapes
I don't want so much
just a simple life
alone
don't horn in on my scene
just give me peace to chant
Chant Chant and go to
the Shed
I missed the chance today

see in a book what someone's got to say
who's not me
a Christian a
whore
a prim miss
a prof egghead
me, me
the you of part and parcel
so small he lost his
chance today
wriggles he's a good
guy accept me
Swami
this is strange, your boy
doing this listening
but I'm only on a loan
eight minutes then back into
strict behavior with
rules
he's evil too?
We all are.

Promise
to be faithful
sixteen rounds four rules
some kind of preaching
give up when I'm told "that's enough" by
indisputable authorities.

God, what big
words you have
to laugh
the earn
the fern I am promised
to Him
I promised to Krishna
kiss the Blarney

            bow down
            and keep writing
promise you bet
a song went wrong in my day
I grew old singing
lame a horse kicked up
Bless the little puppy
bless
            bless,
asirvada.

pp. 175–78

CHAPTER FIFTEEN - FREE KARTIKA

IRELAND, OCTOBER 27 — NOVEMBER 14, 1997

So, you see, dear Krishna present in the moon. I'm full of petty desires. I reach toward You, but can a dwarf touch the moon?

And then look right over there: there's that place, Inis Rath island. The secret, locked treasure. There work the few devotees so unsung, taking care of their Radha-Govinda. From here on Geaglum mainland, I hear kids happy enough chattering in their Krishna conscious childhood. May they never regret it. Time for me to turn back to the house. Wet grass. Freedom in Kartika. Freedom to walk as I like, to be as I like. Where else could I walk with three of my 24×18 wild paintings under my arm and a book bag full of you know what.

p. 120

The Hindu month of Kartika, which corresponds to a series of weeks in the months of October and November according to the lunar calendar, provides the setting for Satsvarupa dasa Goswami's eighteenth volume in his *Every Day, Just Write* series, *Free Kartika*. In many ways, this volume and the preceding Blackberries may be considered a single piece literarily, as the dramatic poetry and its form-shattering style continue uninterrupted in this current volume. At the very same time, the spirit of Kartika fills this writing, and the reader may notice a palpable shift in mood. Kartika is a particularly special time of year within the Vaisnava tradition. It forms a period of time that encourages devotional reflection, as well as the observance of added disciplines such as fasting and an increase in one's japa practice. Certainly, a time of year shaped in this manner will allow the customary pace of everyday life to lessen, so that each devotee may have an opportunity to focus on that which is essential. How beautiful a time of year for this author, who has sought to craft this type of daily mood and practice within a retired life of solitude.

The powerful stream of poetry that is captured within this volume following Satsvarupa Maharaja's European tour, initially collected in *Blackberries*, continues here unabated. As in the previous volume, the reader is soon to be immersed in a current of daring poems that push traditional poetics into wholly new identities. This new poetic form is expansive with unpredictable shifts across prose and poetic genres. It is this type of fluid style that makes these poems unique and groundbreaking. In as much as these styles of expressions will shift within a single poem, so will its content. The reader is carried swiftly along by a dazzling array of images and explorations, reflecting the breadth of Satsvarupa Maharaja's scholarship and his urgent yearning for the Lord.

I would suggest that it is precisely this sincere desire to know and to love the Lord more deeply that ignites this poetry to move, at times, at a furious and relentless pace. Ever cognizant of the passing of time, the urgency of these Kartika expressions reverberates throughout this work and imparts to it a powerful artistic integrity. In considering his own mortality, Satsvarupa Maharaja provides valuable instruction to his readers: time is precious, and it is to be used in pursuit of what is essential, pure love of God. This consideration of our mortality may be seen as one of the fruits of *Free Kartika*, for it is in this month that one indeed is given that opportunity, that freedom, to consider the import of our lives and the source of all meaning and purpose. Such an emphasis undoubtedly arises during a series of weeks shaped by increased devotional practices, including the celebration of Govardhana-puja, the remarkable pastime in which Krishna protects the residents of Vrindavana from Indra's unrelenting rain, which reveals a moment of both divine beauty and shelter.

This rewarding volume concludes with a series of Kartika meditations, none more sweet and tender as this:

> we, me and Supersoul in
> one heart
> flesh and spirit
> we go, don't say
> low level down
>
> say I see the last golden sunshine
> I see maybe the last
> moonshine of Kartika
>
> why did you forget?
> Saturday night
> is bright for
> you in room
> alone.

p. 187

The gentle beauty of an auspicious month is granted to the reader in a manner that both challenges and soothes, so that all may come to discover freedom of spirit beneath Kartika's moon.

The Loneliest Monk

(*He's a blues man, not directly religious but I take him that way. "The loneliest monk."*)

> They assure you like a mommy and dad, a lover (a
>   crowd, a subway)
>   that God is real, life is
> real
> you have to live anyway
> so you might as well sing
>
> as you move.
> The coda the demand is
> to serve God
>   for your
>   pipe toot the
> world
>   is also spiritual world
>
> God, God is rhythm and blues
> is the top and bottom
>
> God, I'm talkin' to You
> Rip calm choose your words better
>
>   Even if fast
> released time for religion
>
> fly to cockpit to God
>   God mad,
>   not guitar mad
>   or money or sex mad
> But get it right / we've got best science. I'm

preaching to you for mankind. I
                                 get purified by that.
But want to relaxed with people.
Wrote to Manu I'm alone I'm sorry, I made a
     mistake
          be kind
They are. Gave me blackberries.

This is blackberries, part two,
shiny berries grown on land
offered to the form of Srila Prabhupada.

His name is in this place. The man is good I like him.
          I'm broken and wobbly
               forget to turn on the tape recorder to my
     own lecture, it's lost. No else records it.
Thank you, they're trying their best. Level best.

Godbrother Maharaja, one great preacher. We put
     each other down, only at death make an elegy –
"He was a good sort. Did such-and-such" – but I
     never loved him, couldn't afford to.
Speak truth, honest –
that too is not everything.
     Read and recite scripture –
that's not all either.
     Listen to Monk, that
doesn't redeem you
     But relaxes, jump
     start rejuvenate.

Hey, I like this
it too comes from God
his eccentric run
his art
stars falling on
(I can't say everything, Alabama, I don't remember

the juke box was it? Johnny Smith, stars
                              fell on Alabamy
Arrowsmith Mohican, I can't remember a damn
    thing.)
We are falling bridges, my fair lady.

Please be with us on the bass walk. I'm a metaphor a
    bridge to the other world.
Pen writes fast to the
beat of heart. This day we consecrate to Krishna
praise and be cleaned
do it in your way.

The thing is
President Wilson guides us
wrong. Demons. This is a bad age, but at least no
    nuclear was present. They say the worst is coming
    soon. What does the psychic say? She said I've got a lot
    to write. Don't depend on anyone but God, God's
    word and
your master says I'm here to accept your service.

You make me feel good
I allow "even" the drums to
shake up the angry and weak
inner head
    the vein and arteries ready to
choke up and say "Ouch!"
The head and my mind say
    "hurt" but could say
It doesn't hurt so much.

Cruel tormentors, learn
to listen and don't kill your
cat or fellow humans
    No pets allowed
    no love allowed unless authorized

Oh, pinafores and long daily walks, hide your love,
     don't touch thorns.
Pick berries but not
poison or mushroom
     vicarious
     carry us home to
mushroom to Krishna
     the clear way
     Bhakti
     trans
     Mike and Mary got
married.
     I don't care. I know he's trying to – to find
     yeah
     "I dig it," they say
     In France. But then died.
Take love eternal.
It doesn't end. You dig it as long as you can,
     "Sorry, folks,"
               this attempted flawed
               to love you and God and
               me
the end is
only a new one.

pp. 3–7

I Approve
*(I just read that material life is miserable and material
attempts to mitigate it are a failure. We should follow the
acaryas. Musicians can glorify the Lord, poets must...We try
to be happy, not forgetting Krishna. A thorn to remove a
thorn.)*
     Nice walk in a park. They're happy to hear it.
     The clear divine profound
     sound of that horn

you can dance to it if you
want but the idea is to hear
     in your soul
"They say the intelligence – or something else-
     is the soul."

Hold it as long as you can
then let it go
This way.

Please that boat never came
yes it did. It came,
and they got out and went to the temple
of Radha-Govinda.

The abrupt
drum bomb
I forgot how to spell
This way, pleez in the
dark theater he lost his way
The man who misled me
I went alone to hear these men thinking they would
     not mislead – they know only the art of music
beat and tune and improvise.

   At a moment
   my head and your hand
   our pains united
   dissolved
   or I'll sit and look out at
   a gray island sky and fog rain
   playing to help us
   Help us remember
   Krishna
   So many notes we must find the right way

   I say he found his own voice it grew into a

complicated song all his own – God gave him that and
said, "Now you become the sacrifice. Give it to Me."
God wants all – read it, believe it?

    I take it easy but work
    no chestnuts in
    snow not yet
    Fall, ladies, children, old men
    Fall leaves crinkled,
    Rain
    rain soles feet
    spin, past, things we want
    he pushed me
    Navy
    gone I knew him then too his solos sustained
me, a freedom when I get out I kept dreaming I'll be a
hip cat in NYC until then get high on fly
                                in Navy bunk
degrade
    whaddya expect when Celine is you guru
    and Genet
    blind
    hope-less
    my Swami was soon a-comin'
    sing it in our ISKCON
    melody. He's seriously and sad and angry
    got a right
    well, listen, he's a good man I heard
    this freedom sound oh brothers I wish you
could understand.

    What
    a joke
    they prefer
    rock 'n' roll synthesized
    I can't spell them big words but just make
the point

this is a most personal
no one can share
but you have to get approval
get a stamp on your hand
a passport or you won't be allowed in sketch
make it clear
    I say Krishna knows my heart and these cats are
okay by Him
    Satchmo said he would play some bars of
"Hello Dolly" and they'd let him into heaven.

Now I don't claim I like
that hide it on the sneak
    but it's love and blue
    the time is soon up we
can tell you
    blackbird lands on grass
    gray hood raven
    crow plume
    walk
    fly   home
    back to Godhead.

pp. 15–18

Put Your Little Foot Right Out

The timing is fine I could dance
with you but that's silly
    we seek the words
    like a swan on lake
this is the Krishna consciousness version of
    Zukovsky
    Billy said he shoots to kill

You don't know me without
you have read Tom Sawyer

Sawdust trail little foot,
John Wayne in that movie? We
Guarinos came back to Queens 76th Street apt.
    singing
"Put Your Little Right Foot Out"

The guy said it's a strange mixture,
I just accept it all
spit out the pits
don't eat the skins,
yeah, he's soft and he's loud –
so what?
Different.

My language has to improve
"obsessed with language."

The horse got loose.
He's talkin' through a horn,
and I in words
    self
    atma.

Listen, I read what Prahlada said and I agree the
    worse is worst,
the bad is host
the way is KC
KC
    KC KC KC
KC KC
Now I see you mean business too.
A serious folk
star I mean you

Naw I'm just glad I'm
out of pain

When I die
you will cry
when my buddy dies –
who goes first?

Leave something for the world
obsessed with word
he creamed pie

I mean to say
        Krishna consciousness in the book He said
    the remedy is worse
        Supersoul will do what
you ask but why not
just do what He wants?
That's the best. Put your little right foot out.

We wanted God sought in the contemporary. Srila
    Prabhupada says it will all be gone.
He was "very angry"
he said "dog food" and "you murdered the whole
    thing in two days."
"I don't wish to discuss." Oh, master in Hyderabad. I
    switched over to his mellow *bhajana*, Hare Krishna
    bhajana.

Put your little foot in *kirtana* hall. I will believe only
        what's in print in *Srimad-Bhagavatam* and
        Bhagavad-gita
    follow *acaryas*
    and you'll find the way home
he said this is my
song to the world that
pestered me that is beautiful by

itself as made by God
    in the last mo's
of Oct.
said I can got it
God is in control He
gives Protection in Him. There is no other.
    Krishna saves me, and this is
for You an offering
puspanjali.

pp. 22–25

❖   ❖   ❖

Preparing Breakfast

Dear Sir, here are my
poems, pissoir and all.
I'm showing off my
teeth (like a donkey)
but have a deeper purpose.

Simple propaganda: God is great.
Hear a refrigerator in the next room,
a clock ticking
your precious time runs down
in Krishna conscious furtive
glances – is Death in the
house yet?

Now finish this sestet
and go into the kitchen
to open yogurt cups,
wash blackberries,
raisins, apples, do good,
bananas with rotting skins –
let's see if they're good within;

it's for offering to God,
apple juice, a light
elegant breakfast for a
poet, a preacher
of
words.

"I'm sorry, I'm sorry,"
she wrote, "for this and that."
All right already, I said.
Too many apologies.
I'll accept you as you are.
But not those rotted pears!

pp. 34–35

Waiting for Lunch

I didn't forget

bring in the little table
the stainless steel plates
for Lords and guru
filled with hot and tasty
dal, broccoli, carrots,
bread with butter...

You will chomp but
first offer by prayers to God
hundreds and hundreds of
times you have done it and
will do it until you
can't.

God – it's in His hands

He pleases His devotees
who wait for lunch. *risin*
But great ones live
not to eat but to feed
their Lord, and they
truly take His
remnants.

pp. 39–40

Poem Words

Don't bluff, words don't mean
that much to me, don't bear
such esoteric sound
or shape or meaning – as
if to penetrate existence in a
good poet's sensitive heart.

Mostly we arrange them to carry
the *parampara*. A poem is
a quick to convey some moment in a serving day.

Like explaining a picture –
smoke rising from a chimney,
say what's it like to be here
at your desk. Give a picture
of a man wearing a sweatshirt,
amused, lacking, quiet...

words...complacent...
"yearning" is too strong.
Say "apple" but keep a
straight meaning as if you are
looking at someone, a reader
and talking to him.

Tell him something about
Krishna and your attempts.
Or leave yourself out of it
and give him the holy names,
holy words of Absolute
Person in his ear.

pp. 56–57

You wrote
sat in shed.
No weak head. Wore gloves.
You said
Hare Hare Lord Caitanya
"Process, not product," said the new book.

My day.
Don't tell others where you are going. Not enough
     time to do all I want.
Sacred waste.
The truth is nigh.
Henry trespasser from the moon,
"What would you do if you went too far?" the art
     book asked.
I said I'd stop. I'd say all right Krishna. I'd straighten
     out. But I wouldn't die. I wouldn't indulge. I'd check
     myself because I'm a student of swami, and I control my
     senses. I wouldn't let it distract me like happened to
     Bharata Maharaja. So, you don't have to fear. Keep
     going.
Read the *Srila Prabhupada-lilamrta* now until the
     fourth then speak. That will be your product.
Save everything to show someone.
Who?
Jerry Jarvis Pink Skater
Doris Defoe Laughing Gas Entry.

Dye in the desk. Pink grass foot
is covering the truth between his legs.
Predictable Shrink. "Freud (Fried) philosophy."
Simplistic.
He's right I'm for him. I choose his way path to
    Krishna.
Ahum.

pp. 75–76

Noon, after listening to Prabhupada talking with
professors in Toronto (1976)
    He's speaking to Professors in his room.
    I'm hoping they may not embarrass him. Of course
        they can't. He
    won't back down. But I want
    him to look good in their
    eyes as a Vedic sage – even
    if they can't follow
    because if they're favorable then
    the meeting is a success.

    Not "Swamiji, but it isn't true..."
    They're always disagreeing...

    Sad for both a group an
    academic is not going to submit
    but see him as a Vedic sage at
    least as a scholar of same
    texts they know –
    Hopkins
    used to appreciate that he's a
    bhakti scholar and respect and
    inquire. Don't argue.

p. 136

Ocean of Love and Mercy
(*We begin with a prayer that our own writing will go well in
Krishna's shelter. That's not exotic or occult. We can expect
it if we follow the process. But yes, we invoke the Lord and
the spiritual master to approve of our attempt in unusual
forms. Hare Krishna Hare Krishna Krishna Krishna Hare
Hare. May all be blessed, may demons be subdued. May
passions be dovetailed. Bring your own instrument and join
with us in* kirtana.)

Now we are going to enter the ocean of love and
mercy.
Yes it's good vibes. No limping? Well, if you are
physically crippled, come limp
own way to the music
of Krishna consciousness intended.

The sunny day I rode across
not caring so much if someone doesn't
like me or honor me.

I've made my mistakes. We have made many
mistakes.
Show time. God's energy pervading
Didja hear? –

He's got a spiritual abode
(many, many),
and He's the all-pervading in this world.
But what about loud and harsh things? I'll tell you
it's all Him. I can figure it out myself. There is
the Lord you see, and there is free will in the tiny *jivas*
and then there's the powerful *maya*-illusion (*mama
maya*.) So, they get in trouble and that's the grief,
misery that's so prominent in Kali-*yuga* known as bad
karma.

Harsh it is often that's the way it is.
The beat is body
beat is
the way I go. Ascension.

Bhurijana in Australia singing out the illusion the
    misery and the *Bhagavatam* topics.
Yeah, he says, yeah, this is the way to go.
I don't want no bad times.

Tell me what is your Krishna consciousness made of?
Sticks and stones
GBC meetings, now time alone
and headaching capacity.

Oh, improvising is a wonderful thing roots in church
    and home and learning from hanging out with others
    who knew it and know it now.
Now this we have in Krishna consciousness when
    we meet. We don't talk about it as such.

I'm improvising
making up my lecture based on what we read and
    hear. TKG unwinds a lecture like that. You can say,
    "No preparation," but this whole life is a preparation
    and the surrender of going into this one with no
    prepared script.
So listen I say
You read your notes or Post-its and penciled
marginalia that's okay too and you look up at them as
if it's new you've got it already to give, what's the diff as
    long you're on
    and it's blues
I mean it's *sastric siddhanta*, right mood then if you
    make it up as in "Abhay" films,
that's okay
"It could have happened."

I could have been in the rowboat in the blue watery
    princely blue cool.
I could have been a cloud
a picture by a master
a foot-loose paranoiac British young man who
    drifted into Krishna consciousness.
The way has many roads but a ticket to Delhi won't
    get you to Bombay
not to demigods we want to go to Krishna
with our brothers, me in a special little compartment
    for ISKCON recluses with imminent headaches.
The song is you
The people like it.

Yeah, and a conga drum in Tompkins Square in
1966, we were there with Swami. Ask their group to
cool it? No, we just took our place and did our thing
on Oriental rug and joined us some with frankincense
    pouring out, a sax, wooden recorders toots
and Swami banging the one-headed drum. It was
    Afrique-India-NYC-Pole-Irish
trans
transparent dancing
the jive was in their heads but
in Swami's heart was the Hare Krishna movement
direct
    from Lord Caitanya took many forms.

pp. 168–71

You've Come Home

You've come home.
Not a light thing
when a friend or husband
enters the house if there is love
it's nice.
Things go right
but going back to Godhead
is not just a light song
    and yet it's the lightest

going home is my song, walks with
me and even in the car going
to work Madhava dasa is
"going home," home is the
service the devotee works
in, his consciousness.

Going home – to lecture mission,
pain that saddens you
worry "Will they hurt?"
The letter, the calendar, impersonal and
faceless tells me I'm going home to
end another life

or am I wandering no where,
please God guide me
like a dog who knows the way,
a homing pigeon,
unerring compass to guide

on the zigzag path
through the Milky Way
    guide, accompanied by good
persons in this world of
misery and illusion

put up with less than perfect.
It's that way

going home is a dance, a sigh
Remember foolish and hard times
Famine in Ireland,
Holocaust
who can figure it out now?
The cause is matter
and ignorance
get out of the burning building
and go home
    as soon as possible
the brisk time means take me
there
    You Lord,
know bad stops or if I
get diverted I'll recall see Hare Krishna *mantra*
written on a wall
    in the men's room
    in a prostitute's words
    a billboard.
for me be clarion to
remind others
play my horn
    come home!

Krishna come home, Mother Yasoda
called. Hurry to be in touch
with intimate beloved and lover
in the home where I
am protected
    or as I say
wherever you go
You are home by air plane and
foot remembering this time
Your Hare Krishna *mantra* is my tune

so long as You
Krishna Krishna take me to
Your abode
    in faith
    going home
no place short of this.

pp. 48-51

Concorde

Music, gentle rumbling.
Sir, have you been to France?
Do you know *concorde*?

Do you know peace? Do you know how to speed
    along, how to swing with life?
Do you know how to please yourself and God at the
    same time?

Concord is in U.S.A. and in self.
There's a lack of it.

Now deep is only
one *concord*
    your peace God
do whatever He says
the taskmaster
agree co-operate with the Almighty
or you'll be crushed
wheel of time.

Admit *concorde* is with God's ways
Say the required words.
You know how I want
honest and free love of
you to open in me

I see these
in me emotions
un orthodox
the trail is strewn with
bodies and new flowers
    followers
    he drives a maxi-taxi
    in Trinidad,
help him
when you go there

express yourself
in brief time
I say concorde in
peaceful dealings
the Lord will accept me.

pp. 71-72

❋   ❋   ❋

So many errant thoughts
there be
when you take *sannyasa*
you should be free.
Always read the *Gita* is our
code.
May you be protected and
to Krishna's abode
enter soon,
Swamiji.

Moving Fast
(*Write in this time, swing with what comes in life – in this case - *)

    A great favorite for *cognoscenti*
      they know the way it goes
me
on a walk so many bright
sights
you see
old guy may go at any time'd
leaves tell it wet leaves
and puddles
as I go my way

indoors my song. I had so
quickly
you say it

there's a solo act he can go
for. It's not background.

Background –
    autogenic heart, arm,
brain, it's all "given"
the leaves, the sky, the
desires

what you'd like to do
It's going
so fast
the virtuoso
listen background becomes
foreground
the pure devotee lives every
moment in Krishna's presence

background noise even the pain
he's in trance and can't be distracted

---

this is driving me
wail and play
and no one knows who
you are

whoever you meet tell him of
Krishna
yourself first

this is the way
tell Manu, tell Gopi
in your letters

you play as long as you're
able
your serious art
to please the world
there is no other way
"I do what I can"
guru gave you the mantra
and we chanted until death
Hare Krishna, fast and slow
back and fore and middle

when you run out of milk
    ink
like a race car driver
you drop it as soon as you can
smile get a new one
walk and smell flowers I
mean offer them to God

be elder of tribe and stay back
and if anyone comes to you
take a break and see him
and smoke peace pipe

this is the way to be
free and allow it to come
it's all given Krishna's
seed you strew
I walk with Him
see how He's in you
surrender to His
dominance
He's everywhere
The Lord in Vraja
go to India?
Yeah right now.
Chant holy names

Lord I can't control my mind
Yeah, I hear the well-known phrase or riff
exchange you and I some krishna-katha, nice plans, go
    through some little tells together for Lord Krishna, I am
    doing that as best I can

pp. 99–102

Peace and Love

(Now I'm entering that world. Pray to Krishna to let me do
it in a Krishna conscious way, see the good in them. Take it
from *yukta-vairagya*.)

> A prelude is a time to warm up or
> we each pray when we'll have to
>> join brothers, yes together
>> and work out a concert
>> effort.

> Prelude is a brief space, and we hope
> our demanding (although friendly) readers don't
> bolt out too impatient.
>> You can use it as you like,
> going off in your own mind
>> I go to Krishna (I say)
>> automatic knee-jerk reflex,
>> "I go to Krishna." But do I?
> Here is the band

> yeah, I came out here and listen like a little boy or
> dog, to a selected music,
>> you know how he tilts his head to one side "his
> master's voice"

> Vic Trola. The pup is bemused that
>> it could happen –
> he's hypnotized a while and you can be too
>> that human factor
>> romance when it's slow
>> keeps you in an illusion
>> (We must say)
> that peace abides in you and everywhere else in this
>> here theater called the First Lutheran Church of
>> Glendale.

I don't know
    when it was Christmas Eve
midnight Mass there were maybe
moments like that.
you could hold your breath
with him for a little,
and then the reality

    whereas here in Inis Rath I've got a more sustained
peace. Oh just see it as coming from your Lord Friend
Krishna in response to your desire –
    he wants to be alone so let him. Keep off the
material modes. Let him listen and write a little longer,
    he did some service in Boston and elsewhere, on
GBC, so now let him...

    he doesn't want to go into the Army of first-line
action as many of my sons are doing, I give him his space.
    As father he maintains all sons. I see it that way

    that's the way
        he says

Abhay and his Ma and Dad
in the TV series
are also an illusion

listen, they applaud
automatically once they start the precedent.
You expect they get on that way.

In this little time I don't want to demand too much
    of you writer-reader.
Relax,
you took this borrowed time
on an Esgic pill
you are performing along with each soloist

---

try to make it good but
more important than that,
    love, give your love to it.
To Krishna given source
of pain-free or pain to
the liquid
melody
structures...

I really would like to be free of it.
Dreamy, are they really nice are or just playing at it?
Bastard artists in real life when the show is over

    I hope not
    we get to go to work

"Please cheer me up, I'm down.
I'm going through a very difficult time."
We laughed that he so openly asked for help, no
    male pride –
but since he asked for it,
can you give it?
How to cheer? You hold the long note –
(you say I too know suffering but God is good, I
    can't give you money but friend,
God is in you / your cause is necessary,
    you asked for it,
now find in you the link to Him,
chant your rounds –
is this helping?)

He says Yes it helps, give me more. A sad sight to see
each day go down now but lovely to observe God's move in
each thing.

    Best Artist and Teacher – as Time, as sastra, or friend
        who gives shelter and food.

Now you act to give Him back as guru-daksina.

May there be Peace and Love in the
universes / demons quelled,
    bhakti-yoga rising
as star fulling moon
toward the end of Kartika

pp. 113-16

Here's That Rainy Day

Here's that rainy day
he's holding the notes
I remember 72nd, Central Park near
furnished room of piano teacher
in his concubine student,
Italian girl

I had room with my own piano
imitated Bill Evan's chords
I'd heard somewhere very
dreamy on marijuana, it was
just two or three notes over
and over like calling up spirits
of dead or whoever would
come.

He, white cotton hair
bald except for top holding
a candle (lights out)
said, "What are you doing?"
Here is that rainy day
he plays alone,
I don't mock the guy
they say he's a poet

---

you got to find out for yourself
what is a poet

he must be strong as well
as soft and be able to
swing – whatever
that is
this rainy day is gone
in my mind blue
sky I'm eager to see the
moon filling up the sky
on 5 P.M. Kartika near
ending

note it as you
pass by as you
go for the umpteenth time
we are pain-free
he paid for it so
he can work out

here is that day that
moment, he's developing it
in his own way
    trained hard as it is
fluent as hell
"Ordinary!" one says.
"Genius!" another

here is that day
of judgment
when one person
practices and goes before God
    with piano or
whatever he's got to offer
says God you gave
this thing it's trivial and wrong

I know but please
find some bhakti in me
let me know You
through this offering it's
all I know.

pp. 117–19

Dark Doings

*(This is all Krishna's grace that I'm able to write at all.
Sunshine, water, I don't know how to express anything)*

The soldiers are marching –
Is that what it sounds like?
Did you ever hear soldiers marching?
Yes doctor, I saw them on Memorial Day come
marching down Gifford's Lane.
And drum solos?
I guess in the high school dance band or Gene Krupa
something like that.
Do you remember the first time you saw green grass?
Felt velvet,
      felt desire for a woman?

I didn't want to linger with the doctor, so left and
came here to the chapel, to chant Hare Krishna, only Hare
Krishnas allowed. If they have the power, he said, they'd
close down other religions just as the Orthodox and
Politicos did in Russia. That gave him a slight depression
for a day, but he picked up his motor anyway.

Will we be able to leave on time?
Yes, as soon as we jack-up, hoist up the engine and
place it in the hood.

Doctor?
Yes?
Where is Krishna now?
In your hair. It's not a myth.
Meth.
Beth, where is Doctor now?
Tell her the time you went crazy writing words the
voice of the woman in the piano
        as composed by a classical composer.
No – it's just Banshee madness, stump of the trees
feeling pain of dry karma you
        have to face and no way free of it.
        So, you scream
        implode Rilke

they'll be released from hell.
That's called state of purgatory.

Here we are in the half shelter of ISKCON, avoid the
        too many words
Krishna vast will control all so worship Him,
        have faith,
there's no alternative.

here guys, chant, women, chant, we're going
        down gracefully.
Give you three more days alone –
take it easy no hundreds at a time,
        chant Hare Krishna
"dark doings".

While they played the may be hatched evil
I serenaded to God what my
Master taught me
            and avoided being corralled by nice words
        of a brother
who at least likes something
        you wrote
oh, you are into your own lit

halfway through. Man, I washed the plates, stainless
    steel and dried them, God's plates. Here there,

so, I tell you, give me a drink Sir
I tell you
is hard to get through and over the
horns hurdles

I wrote another letter papermate,
Dear Charge, dear Lady
    I tell you God is with you
and you'll be all right. Is it moral
to advise?
            Someone has to manage the toilets,
    plumbing, dig the holes
The *brahmanas* sit and shit and
Think of new *sastric*
                presentations

,
above the *brahmanas* are the
Vaisnavas and the *sannyasis* best of all
write letters to
    people in need of a
rubber hose

Sir I want an explanation for all the parts being a
mess. Here it is:
    He's not clean or orderly. So, I'll clean up. Give me a
half hour and I'll put everything in order, you won't
even notice it had been taken apart, just give me one
hundred dollars

    Krishna watches the riff
    happening, of course He saw good in it, very small
        good
    compared to direct worker,
    poor of Calcutta not allowed to see M. Teresa

when she died,
ironic
cynic
we'll have to pay
    maybe he was wrong all along,
can he bow down to those
whom always seemed wrong
and now, "You take over. Let's see you do any better"
"We can. It's the wrong system you worked under.
    But you were deaf when we told you."

Man, these are dark doings. No, it's sun-lightly.
    He's got
a slight decay-stuffed head
    mortal opening, nothing a
little rest can't cure
    take a new body
in spiritual world
nobody dies
Propaganda

Now home shelter. They were true melodies all along.
I chanted Hare Krishna all along and reminded people
Krishna Krishna
    I hope you are chanting
    and reading scriptures
    same prescription, see you in Baltimore
    where I'll be performing
four intimate days and nights
another Birdland
God chant really chant
with sincere
bugle and drum
chant and chant

pp. 133–37

He Remembers He Was Humble

Now in the window is clouded
over like my head
but I'll tell anyway

a little of a day like this
you should
a *brahmacari* should
no more will I roam
but in my mind I get
this thing
    I say okay we will do
our thing

there's a time when we can
be like the other
Krishna Krishna comes crashing
through
    "refuses to brood or apologize"
but God is Maker you
agree?
He said, "I launch nuclear missiles"
She said, "Before you press the button read a few
    pages of this, young man"

Listen he said
    I sew buttons
    I make cakes
I get along the hurdle / Eat until you
can't digest

the bee will bite
so Krishna said Just return everything
    I forget to tell in the letters the ripe part
now Krishna Krishna is the
best thing ever when sick

in head I pushed on
to serve the Swami
in Calcutta flat
felt even the pain a kind of
ecstasy to be with him
do it over?
I can't take it
but you did
Krishna I was a good boy
so he said
that he had to go through
oh the poor guy I feel sorry for him he's
taking on an absurd task when he quits he will be
glad and say, "So many ways *maya* gets us trapped."

pp. 137–40

Softly, For God
(I'm running fast, blood in head, etc., clear until the next
fog, hope "it" doesn't run out yet, that empowerment...)

They may hear overhear
    don't fear
it's just M. in the kitchen

softly as in –
    The way is mine to paint
"There's only the present
    moment, nothing else"
            shit on that too

I say *sastras* say
the gentle move
has a purpose
God put us here to do
something
    not just invade a moment to moment

"Don't remember, don't think, don't stop but don't finish
       so soon" – says the all permissive painting teach

I say Softly to be
       free you need Narada
everyone's got to hear a
guru of some sort
your own sense,
intuition
Buck off – I'll make this place, path my way for Him
"You sure can swing," said the master to modest student
          who was good but didn't want to know it as great.
Then how to face that talent
How to swing?
You do it
moment present
hold on tight,
the ferry won't sink
you'll remember God

hold on the thing is taking
us over. These guys are expert,
     and I am jabbering
God God on the express what I always wanted –
     God, Krishna,
the blue boy
specific universal

keep a diary – you try to be with Him. Someone did
something well,
          and you linked it to God.

They say, "Why always Bhagavan? Stop. I don't believe in
God."
          Bhaga-van and he who knows Him is also Bhagyavan
          softly I am happy to
          play for Him, the trill and

hill, Please Lord
    slap it on (me)
orange or blue
    the intuition is playing
    at God
or playing with God

make us a pic of Krishna
    if you're going to draw
    or "Krishna"
    in graffiti
    while we alive the clock says 5:40 is His
    5:41, 5:42 is His
    I branded blue-throat
    white
    teaser
    lover,
    Lord,
    boy best
    softly Krishna bring
sun and moon on Kartika last day
round moon
he couldn't sleep smooth no liquor drinking, a little
    milk and busy serve You all day –
take it away but I'll live always in You
give me that insight
I love You.

pp. 144–48

"Boys chant with
Swami in '66, remember?
Hearing it now."

That's all I want to say about that.

pp. 150–51

✳   ✳   ✳

At the Threshold

*(Saw a deer, white-spotted, a very light tan to blend in with
the golden reeds at water's edge. Alone?)*

At the threshold, hey!
The God is in the center
eye your right eye too is Him
    don't pause

the flies in the shed want to
get out but don't know it
Death awaits
O Master I didn't
poison you, did I? Did
my lack of devotion and surrender
make you discouraged?
I always thought you could carry
us all

like Hanuman
Jaya Rama! You leaped
across the ocean of
misunderstanding separating us
we wailed but you

you got us now I'm saying
it gets angry

he's busting the place up
he wants freedom but
what's the price?

"Oh, I intensely love
the avant-garde."
I intensely nothing
let it be mild and middle
he can't get the right notes
wanted out wanted in
    Master I was bewildered
but did not poison the
atmosphere of you I hope
my soiled
    nightshirt
my devious schemes
my fear now of those who
would corral me in your
name "Do this,
Master says."

Leave them
No one you can trust
but Krishna – you told
Riddha dasa in South Africa,
oh, treasure that one.

He's yelling like a beast who's got to be controlled
    for his own good.

Then on comes the all-
knowing lawyer playing a
trombone. When we used to join together sweet
    spirits some of us not bitter
in competition,
friend,
on verge of friendship

was there a night like that or
was that too a deception?

O master, O husband and
wife, a guru and disciple
a brother and brother
a child and teacher
a dog and friend
the vandals came and burned down $100,000 worth of
stuff at New Talavan, and they made cahoots
of religious and politicos
and burned down freedom of religion – "We'd do
    the same if we had the chance."
The world is not a fit place –
    but who is a gentleman?

Together a handsome riff on
the threshold on the
outskirts of Gloria,
in the inland outback

Master Krishna
    I sigh wanting You
Let the exam come, the well-
practiced servant will pass.
Death is an act of faith.
Read where he takes you

Mudhas don't believe but
pure devotees need You,
know You, accept the
mahajanas

now this boy is coming home
tear down the chimney
put up a new roof I've a
yen to live there in

solitude under thatched
roof. Please please
be kind to me
   says the roofer
   the spaced out boy

wants readers to
bring that one person close
to Krishna so the Lord will
say okay here's a little knowledge of Me
I was always with you
but you couldn't see,
like a blind deer, you ran
here and there but I was
always with you within
   darn fool
   you can see Now –
Oh, that would be good I'd keep the secret and share
occasionally as you would like,
   I'd be a good manager and *brahmana*
   a daydream –
me in your lap
   me out fighting
   at least let me be humble and tell them Krishna
is truth I did it
my whole life since aged 26 and I die in vain not
In faith yes

pp. 156–60

Aspiring Devotee Lullaby

(*Your little eye. You've got some past ghosts and goblins and
pains and more ahead. This is a little respite, or a way into
the troubles? Ah, I seek asylum in your peaceful center,
under the shade of a mighty tree or niche for Krishna
conscious artists of easy-going elder age.*)

Forget me
you've got your eye on
Mexico, some town some place
just in your mind

when you lay your head on the pillow
you get a dream and ask
Krishna
when you say His holy name
lullaby. Lullaby.
Repeat a sweet word
to the Lord above
in your heart

it's easy. It's hard too,
but these guys go at
it.
They clap at the wrong
time.

It's loud and soft
this lullaby

this way please
he ushers you down
dark
aisle with his made-in-India flashlight

all right sit before the
screen the master is speaking
and the theater is full of
spooks and dead or lost
ISKCON-ites

a possible riot waiting
outside the non-devotee slugs
I do see ladies too

and spirits and Deities wrapped
up. We are on route
the way back to Godhead

always a threat before we
get there
    it appears we have
to go in some kind of
group

a dream I did it
but now you are
going on your own
too

soft as he can on
his piano
the tune he made
up a real
soft melody
    one of any number
God can brush off with
His flick of hand

and give you to
ease your sure burden
and pain because you
think your body is
you and hurts

thank you, Lord for all insight

pp. 160–63

"*ki jaya* Internet blues
people insultin'
better keep your own missives
tender at least with humor
don't destroy faith

stay out, mind your own business
mine your own gems
in Krishna consciousness.

p. 163

O bright golden moon
signaling the end of Kartika,
you are free and generous tonight
thank you for appearing against this dark blue
    background
so startling, revealing you are.
Are you thinking of Krishna?

p. 165

A Sad Romantic Song
(*Rainy day. Recovered from all-night headache. Back on tracks of reading* Srimad-Bhagavatam *and now this. As I write it's misty dark at 9 A.M. and two rowboats are coming from the island, the morning program must have just ended. I read of the man who lives on the path like a python. I heard of the ISKCON investigation into a suspicion that Srila Prabhupada was poisoned. I'm feeling troubled by things and according to the man who lies like a python, that's the nature of life in this world. Trying to get out of it. Accept your way.*)

One shouldn't live for sense grat
One should or can may sit in a
theater and hear a love song,
one can relax in illusion as the
lights go up in a heroine and
hero dance, she in long gown,
he in tux

Oh, it's so sentimental, it won't last.
We wait for the denouement,
the villain, the plot to thicken.
"The butler did it!" Killed
with a brass candle holder

the ghastly scene. But for
now they're dancing by candle-
light in a mirrored ball-
room. They will have to sell
it to ISKCON in later
decades, and ISKCON may also
have to sell it or it will crumble
down into the Detroit River

you cynic,
you poisonous poison,
lack a smoke you exhume
poisons fumes
you're a little Kaliya –
so says my inner friend.

It's a Stygian dark of another
day and I melancholy sit and
hear the dance music make
us so sad about the love
we lost the fools
we are.

"People are becoming like
werewolves," wrote Mert in his
diary and he read *On the Theology of Death*
by Rahner and liked the intuition
that death means surrender
in faith – as an act –
that God will take us.

sorry I wrote my review
    So caustic
I did it in self-defense
the process ain't absolute,
you know

now what? You have taken
me so far, by hitch-hiking
and now I've got to get back
to the ISKCON temple
    but there too it's
not fun

oh, the music is right in a sense I X Love
I X Love
means what?
    your love is X-rated
your love is X-ed out,
you better get
right in mild groove
of regular Krishna consciousness your master
and SB taught you
    suitable for this
    rainy day and me
humbled
short-changed
    witted
    Amen

pp.175–78

449

Please Lift Me Up

There was a flower near Napoli
you mean near the Vesuvio?

they just play their way and
I know my way has to be okay
too
in Krishna
Krishna's heart. It's all in
Bhagavad-gita.

follow those railroad
trolley tracks round and around
in Napoli chaotic it was

so, I'm here in the way of
sing music
Krishna, when I falter, will
You please pick me up?

Prose it. They're doing something
or other. Reminds you of your
distraught youth you thought you
could serenade like a cat in alley
and it would be okay because you're so young

you thought you could live
that way amoral, immoral
with Anna and Eliot
play it now to recall
and pull yourself out

Srila Prabhupada writes of *acyuta-bala* –
you lift yourself out by His
Balarama's strength.

You are giving us book sections.
That's all I know, you
know. Or muffins, yogurt,
sleep, neat, alone,
bad thoughts sorry I'm
not single-minded but
I'm just not.
    so face it.

You try you try Do you
try?

Then let's put it this way:
    I'm a beginner and fake
that I have been at it a long
time.
Can't sing kirtana Don't
want to be cursed to come back
next life as sudra
as Gandharva was to
become Narada
    for wrong songs
but here I am.

They play it sad hoboes
    distraught
I say you better take it
    Krishna chant

pp. 184–86

451

Last Night of Kartika
(*What will you do when you go back in the house? I'll read*
Caitanya-caritamrta, *chant a round, low pressure, low level
energy, that's how I am.*)

We go in Seine
    we go into our house
we go
    back light-hearted
light foot Lame Deer

we me and Supersoul in
    one heart
    fleshy and spirit
    we go don't say
        low level down

say I see the golden sunshine
I say maybe the last
moonshine of Kartika

why did you forget
Saturday night
is bright for
you in your room
alone

moon Krishna loyal
    Prabhupada
I am up oh
the music can take you
dancing

but you get to see your own
self in no mirror
    fast and only take water
the book crack it open
under lamplight

I don't want no news
      no music, radio
or politics shout
      news lies
I want only the air and
a few hours a few words
Krishna I'm a spinning top
lost and You can alone
find me
pick me up

I stick in too many diverse other people's trips

pure devotees only love You
think of nothing else
that's what I heard

now Krishna, see here
You are subordinate
to Mother Yasoda
and Radha

my hand aches to tell
you go in page learn art
let me serve You
for the joy of it
I came here to commune with self
and He's the self of selves

old temples finished for me.
Seine – Mississippi – burned down
      they'll attack some place where I reside too
(but this Saturday night I want the moon
      or the peace
I will force this
person to walk back and forth) japa and
      not get worse.

He admits the words float from God and He's the
    only one they go to
and his friends
I don't know.

Now before it gets too dark raise up a flame offered
last Kartika
Damodara light
burn / no headache
to Radha-Govinda
shy shiny boy and girl
    and my master

pp. 187–90

CHAPTER SIXTEEN - RADHA-GOVINDA, WE HARDLY KNEW YA

Thinking of a title for this volume, Parting from Peaceful Geaglum. That says something. It is peaceful and I know I can't always have that peace in this material world. I'm at peace here even when I have a headache. The scenery, the solitude, going to the shed, doing as I like, no lectures except once a week. It is certainly a place of peace for me. And I am parting because at the end of this volume off we go on an airplane to the Caribbean via New York City. So, it is a fitting title unless you want to keep searching for something more central or deeper.

p. 194

In this, the nineteenth volume of Satsvarupa dasa Goswami's literary series *Every Day Just Write*, entitled *Radha-Govinda, We Hardly Knew Ya*, the author continues to reside in Geaglum, Northern Ireland. However, he is writing on the eve of a major trip to the Caribbean and Guyana, New York City and Gita-nagari Farm in Pennsylvania. As in the passage quoted above, the volume's title could have formally foreshadowed his departure. Ultimately, the author chooses a more playful title, which bears great spiritual significance. It is important for the reader to understand that while Satsvarupa Maharaja has made a home in Geaglum, traveling will bring feelings of separation from his beloved Radha-Govinda. In this way, a preference for a particular setting will always be superseded by his relationship with his cherished Deities. Thus, the title ultimately chosen by Satsvarupa Maharaja expresses first and foremost his commitment to a relationship and only secondarily to a place.

The nineteenth volume of *Every Day, Just Write* marks a transitional period in the author's life. The beautiful Kartika month has come to an end and with it that sense of monastic stability that Satsvarupa Maharaja has enjoyed since his return from European travels in early October. Now, he prepares for the challenge of travel once more, which will be more arduous given the distance of this journey. Concerns regarding travel are heightened by news of political tension in Guyana in the weeks before a national election. In addition, it remains to be seen how the tropical climate will impact the fragile health of the author.

This sense of both anticipation and concern forms a backdrop for both the prose and poetry of this volume. Significantly, both styles of writing will reflect Satsvarupa Maharaja's sustained reading of Krishnadasa Kaviraja's theological biography of Lord Caitanya Mahaprabhu, the Caitanya-caritamrta. As this magisterial work details the inauguration of the *sankirtana* movement in India, undoubtedly Satsvarupa Maharaja's extensive reading and reflection upon this text would serve to prepare him for entering the preaching field once more, in anticipation of his visit to disciples in lands far from Geaglum. As he writes, "So few people in this world have even heard of Lord Caitanya. They don't accept Him as the Supreme Lord. So those who do love Lord Caitanya must spread His glories. Lord Caitanya's teachings are the essence of knowledge and it can benefit everyone." (p. 27)

So, the reader now stands with Satsvarupa Maharaja as he prepares to depart, to say goodbye to Radha-Govinda. The second half of the volume's title, *We Hardly Knew Ya* suggests both the brevity of time since his return to Geaglum and the spiritual reality that the depth of one's relationship with Radha-Krishna is without end. Moment by moment, the devotee is drawn ever closer into a limitless relationship of love for and service to the Divine Couple.

As the day of his travel departure draws near, the volume then ends with these simple and beautiful words:

"Hare Krishna. This most wonderful thing. Krishna and Lord Caitanya." (*p. 235*)

Talking During a Ballad

Can you swing with someone when you don't
feel like it – initially?

That's the whole point of life.
Someone or thing wants to swing in a certain way
            and we resist.
But I can't stay at home and be happy, said Kurma.

Swing with it.
I'm not a rubber band, a ping pong ball.
I want it my way. Let the world swing with me.
But you're not God, fellow.

We say I'm happy I'm swinging with the punch! It's
      happy but not –
I'm game / I'm here and happy going to work every
      day and traffic jam is just another way to
surrender.
      Oh well –

      But there's another mood. Surely you and I can
make it. Carrying from one to another. Two players can be
okay together on same time.
      You've got to go deeper. What you are given may
            seem trivial.
      The inspiration that was present is gone. You've got
            to go deeper.
      Help someone. Give them from your own reservoirs
            of Krishna conscious knowledge.
      What do you have?
      I have this now.

      Be happy

Krishna conscious mood of let go and let's have a
little piano and guitar,
  a little electric please but not too much.
Now here's what I learned to play with –
  God is good to all
  and the science as given by
Lord Caitanya is
simple yet sublime
is topmost – Krishna is the Supreme

  they say Wait, that's Indian. Or Take it slow, I
can't change my home life so much. What are you
proposing – throw out cigarettes and meat and sex and
wine? How can I do that? Impossible.

  So, you say all right, do a little at a time. Or simply
add the chanting, hoping it will do away with the rest. Sly
preacher wanting people to change, knowing they can't be
happy in material life.
  But you preacher, devotee,
  are you happy?
We see so many who are not happy in their
  Krishna conscious life.
Yes but we won't give it up.

The one life is just a spot
we are unhappy not because we
took to Krishna consciousness
  but can't rid of material –
  yes so it's not easy,
  I'm still doing it.

You told them that?
Yes, and I practice it alone so now when I do say
  something,
see someone it's
  more fact

I say I'm all right
give up stuff and
chant always be a happy guy
    and meet death in voluntary
act of faith.

They are impressed?
Maybe.
    It's your duty
    oh, I see.

pp. 2-5

Don't Be Afraid

Watch out this one is wild
he said. But I wasn't afraid
    jungle. Madness
My Mama told me Don't
be afraid, it's only a movie.
    It's not real

I said But, it seems like real fight brewing. She said you can
    hold on to my arm if you want.
Then came "snake pit"
and I said wait this crazy people

she said No I told you
Don't be afraid
    you can blank out
pretend it doesn't happen. So, this strategy can
    used any time

When you get shot by bullets or big-dog attacks?

Oh, it's just a film

I'm here
with tears pouring from
eyes from fatigue
he said I will be okay
but need juice, orange juice or apple
a little rest
and a sunshine rising
the day after Kartika is over

the bazaar
    is empty
the onion skins on ground
instantly eaten by a dog
    and two spiders
    eaten eaten
    poverty

makes them not interested
in go-go
Krishna day-glows
Because we need technology,
Swami, do you understand?

He said you are ruined
by your bad habits.
You were born in God's land but you think
    you want day
money Good Year tires

don't cooperate
Europe-Americans
took to it
where are they now?
Biggest temple in India
In world,

file in
and don't complain
or accuse us.

pp. 7–9

Forbidden

bring you into the committee
in a Mayapur room
hang your head low
   go to hell for
devotion?

Better get it straight.
I tell you how it goes
simple when gathered to
make serious joyful music
   for no commercial gain

now tell us You wrote
novellas but that's supposed
to be over as with the drinking
of beer
   and wearing of pants
and shirt and standing around waiting
for a bus
   angst
in your head a Charlie Parker
theme
   or something easy to
get at
for me

your crew-neck sweater
stop! No memories

---

they demand and I say
okay I just want to go back to Godhead
But you see I get these
headaches so I went alone
and there I discovered
my old love
and its application as
music that can be used –
is our time up?

they don't believe me
or say, "It sounds okay but it's forbidden"
like Mert's peace essays.

pp. 14-16

KC Blues

Aha
Yeah, we are blue
and I don't mean
in Missouri

there is a preaching center in KC
now, Krishna-sneha dasa cooked
halava for guests

KC Blues –
   state of ISKCON
   women's issue
full moon waning
   poison *acarya*

KC Blues no more master
sitting on the *vyasasana*

but 200 little guys
and 500 attacking them and 42
schisms with near gurus
and underground
and no fun allowed?
Blues means you get it out
get it out
    get it out
        you feel good with
unhappiness chased like
whistling in a round sound
They say he's okay I know
it.

Monk under eye of master
didn't try his exploration
tricks yet. Not yet –
he grew up even better
although always faithful to
the master. You can grow
on your own, not just
mimic or parrot and it's
not bad

but the old times when
he was in charge are
best or at least we
dig them
and they are the prototype.

pp. 16–17

Pleading His Offering

There is no way except the way
The catalogue from Shambala
in the garbage can
you ordered Issa's Year
Four Huts by Burton Watson on
virtues of the quiet life

dark dark sky you're not in the city
They play their own way

each one trying to learn his vocabulary
of past and speak in his own way
that improvising art

they have squeaks and belches and
caress and croons
and the truth of his own life.
Heart and soft

pushcarts.
I have not forgotten
New York City trumpet
me all alone now no
adventures. Play a slide show
of your protected trip to Europe
in a white Ford van

hot and twisted
He's always on your side trying
for the best in all
circumstances

hearing
chanting
remembering God – who can do it?

Fog horns. They leave you to
work on your own.
Find a tune

I repeat, I'm in the official camp
but seek authentic
title: He lived alone
The last month of Nov
The clever artist
Musing of what he can't do
The pee-pee pot,
The muser bruiser and the paintings
he didn't give up;
the year I...

tell how you sat and watched the
rowboats, you don't belong
to this nation or
to PA.
State and canoers and hunters and
new generations of devotees
on the farm called
Gita-nagari.

Tell of the pages in the gold-
covered book. They are good.
One said, Don't leave home
but always chant Hare Krishna.
So, he'd have to clean out
A room for a home temple
worship Deity nicely tell
his wife and kids from now on
we're gonna follow Lord Caitanya.
"You become a guru
He told me, and I'll never
leave you.
Save people of this land."

But Henry (Kurma) (Sats)
you're too shy you don't like
to disturb yourself or others
easygoing
how can you be like Arjuna
Aryan fighting preacher?

I can, he said and sighed and
Sat down realizing his own
voice was tired but
what he had to make songs
He hadn't asked Lord Caitanya
Can I write improvisations
to the music I hear?

He'd have said...
 If He said
use it while you can
 don't miss out
 on greatest jewel.

pp. 21-24

No Moonlight Drunks

(Could you, after this, just sit awhile, in here with sounds of
flies buzz and outdoor winds, just be – not even write right
away?)

It is really just okay we
are okay
They are friendly bears
 I want it that way

they say what they have

---

to say

now I asked if he would
like to be the man in
the moon
like Li Po down on earth
drunk in moon reflect?

He said No I'm a devotee
Vaisnava wannabe
We don't get drunk
    Sweet and Lovely
sometimes we are apt
to be allowed
sweet rice and honey and
get drunk on *kirtana*

but moon drops
and wine
Tao – no?

He said
    My thing is to remember
Govinda in the moonlight
and don't go home

but you can't do that
then *sadhana*
pradhana to *mahat-tattva*

clear note of anguish
bugle call on the hill
Don't bring danger home
on our heads

they went out and sold as
many books as they could

we lived a past
 Swami talking to Bhaktivedanta Institute
Scientist devotees
 "Is God within the jiva?"

Utter chaos
rubbing him down was
Hari Sauri
and I was around in
U.S., vans, doing a bit profile – read Srimad-
     Bhagavatam at least
cute stuff allowed.

pp. 24–26

You Don't Know What Love Is

(*Reading* Caitanya-caritamrta, *I admit I don't know prema-
vesa, but I read anyway, although not for long, every day.*)

It's a sad thing you're not knowing
you don't know unless you know
the meaning of the blues, sleepless
nights tears,
 worldly soulful
Well, the gopis' love is something else.
But it's that grief
they are singing of in reflection
perverted.

Be true to your way sing it
the sadness of this world and

ISKCON's failure to raise it to be the
boat on which all could come

but there is comfort in this.
Tell it wise man, foolish man
the only way you can.
Over and over.

Please give us
    devotional service in various ways
Be cheerful and grateful for what
you've been given

please excuse my pious
utterances and actions
    I tell them, People we are
a community.
    We know the truth, don't we?
We
and they
I walk the earth and I'm part of it although a
    stranger
oh man/how good it is
God is good/He gives the
rain/the pain reminds us not
to live here
But we dally and try to possess.
Work and do something to
pass it on.

They say Oh we want big results,
bring people, one person to Krishna consciousness
and Krishna will be pleased with you

by your actions, publish a
book that can be used
Krishna, Love is
    tears love is separation

from beloved Krishna
Radha, Visakha know
I know not

preachers who sacrifice for him
fearless
    in Russia and NYC
know
    love motivates them
sing of it
        you don't know
        you know it's the best thing
        pleases the Lord
        who is Love.

pp. 33–35

Say It (Over and Over Again)

Some things should be repeated like
I love it – love you
But they say it's better not to

oh, come here with me
hear this
Why ballads? For variety.

It's true I love You, say it
good man
go higher and low to tell
I love You/I love You
it can be said
people who don't talk say it's
foolishness.
Say it to myself, to the wind and air

I want to be a devotee
I'm not a good one
say a good thing that won't
hurt others the earth

say it I love I
write
    I Krishna's devotee
want to be

my saying is weak
    doesn't make the thing happen
but it's true
    to say it

Hare Krishna Hare Krishna, Krishna Krishna Hare Hare
Hare Rama Hare Rama, Rama Rama Hare Hare

say it over and over on beads
finger wearing down with saying it

"Distribute books, distribute books"
here comes death
in walked Bud
better be careful
mind the preacher
Swami's my Boss
Lord is nigh

say it – I'm afraid
    get headaches
    repeat it repeat
    be quiet
prove by actions
    Gita
forgive
the same thing – he

said iron rod in the fire
I say but
    to keep my mind fixed
I don't care what "they" say
Now Lord I'm gonna rest my
case and go to chant Your names Your
names
    Krishna Krishna Krishna Krishna Krishna
    he!
Say it again
    Please save me.

pp. 35–37

The Art of Saying in a Difficult World
(*Always threatened whether this is the best thing to do, this daring association, "They are non-devotees," etc*)

So, I write and write, people...
I want to be liked / I want
to be popular
    they want to make for good
in the world
 so, bring yourself
But concentrate one thing.
Make it good by practice
you are preaching to people

to be good
come listen to this music with me
I'm tired of rancor/I can't
just accept what comes in
    dreams
    discriminate,

know the good and bad

find the best
    the best and go with it
    some do and some just watch...

defend yourself

get work done
    Leave this place – But
they don't know
    you have to come back
with this knowledge we
preach to the world

heavy we carry that news –
do we believe it – or know it
ourselves –
    work to clean your mind
and attain Krishna consciousness

Lord this is my destiny.
I say if you can enjoy your
way, I can go my way.

The big sound
I want to be in love
in race, trace

oh, he's good / he wanted to be
liked
    he wants to tell the things
that can't be said
melancholic
troubled
excellent artist
telling life's secrets – what

we all know
why do we fight
let us gather and hear something
good together

can we please
He keeps trying and succeeding
He's got...
Please friend can I initiate
you in these mysteries
of someone so intense
    and good?

Oh yes, I accept it if you say
but then I may quit.

He's up and down trying but
what if he's wrong

Krishna what if I'm not
Approved?
    It was all a waste?
No, the attempt is in
your favor
    but you have to go
back and do over what's wrong

you hide a practice
that's questionable
    they want to find wrong in you
So, you are timid?
To hell with them, I'll do
what's right
    what's most
I need to
want to open my soul
    and reveal a music art
it's to remove veneer

and play all right

He's unhappy and saying it but
in such a way we feel
and know it and say that's true about life
and our lives could
be changed for the better

and if the world remains deaf
and heartless
and even kills us or
our master says, "The attempt was wrong."

- well if the world rejects I'll
still give
but we beg the master to
accept us.
    Please accept the humble attempt
to be like a musician
a pandita
a sweeper
a Crimean news reporter
of the imagination introducing us
into Krishna consciousness

Ramananda Raya thought himself fallen
and Lord Caitanya embraced him
give me a few drops of
your mercy to give to the world
here is a satisfied person
but working to please
guru and serve you
    do what he wants
    make the effort
    Lord Lord day,
Your day.

pp. 54_58

No Lark

Here you go slow meditation
the place that kills you

but there's a lark in Krishna consciousness
so, what if I have to meet a guy
I can always chant Hare Krishna
I can always be there
in the shed
Always?
Go to your own chanting
happy Krishna will accept me.

I'm not the only Krishna conscious writer
in the world

piano cortège. Rain sweeps
in here seeps in here.
Savage thrust
lonely aching

I say when you've got Krishna it's
not so bad

So, he turns to me and says,
"Where is your Krishna?"
I say...
Better not...yes preach it's
in Gita
it's in my master,
in me a little

you explained the tradition with no

certainty he'll understand –
that's preaching

the stark dark day is
light in your breast a hope
always

like to give it to others but
sometimes fear they may take
if from you, savage
demon atheists attack
on bhakti creeper

naw, you're all right I know
Krishna as the daring boy in *rasika*
text who's up all night but
I can't tell of that to
participate
    I think of Him as offering me
yat karosi
    and at the end-goal I
may see Him

for I now offering what I can
my earnest attempt
on a dark day
raining I am Krishna consciousness
trying

Lord Hare Hare Krishna *mantra*
24 hours
    4 hours at least

Krishna up all night?
In my breast.

pp. 68-70

Green Dolphin Street

You know where you want to go

I am striding in a beat
that's
words
go beyond jargon

say I don't care
    rain inside is not happening
there's no way no
railroad this God/in spare
time he's going to the street

the street alone
in Krishna consciousness
secret ville Land. He's the fellow in the
shaved head and sneakers
come on
leave behind
those fears
    you can say anything
for show and then come back
to this

Green Dolphin Street is code
for
password
    "Let him in"
he's okay
    he knows Balarama
who killed Romaharsana
he blesses us with

his writing
   he served Swami
   yeah I didn't do the
worst

he's going to have to
do more
but he's the Swami's
he's the person you can trust
the easy go
he's not against
hot *kirtana*s
But sees *kirtana*
in many words
ways

aggressive
you can say
stay and chant with us
don't go so fast
   I'm old
short of breath
But happy and can
Krishna Krishna

the way / is here
Krishna is in front
and middle
I play this way
with Krishna my Lord
and master
pass to Green Dolphin
you don't have to know
it's this way / trust
me / trust Alf and Joe
trust no one
just trust Krishna in your heart

and whatever your master told you

keep away from non-devotees
blues and fears
you'll die get new
body like Bhisma, etc.

right*pp. 70–72*

❋   ❋   ❋

Mood Indigo

An old favorite
 you can just feel
okay
it's "blue" You Irishmen
don't know blue?

You Bengalis?
You pure spirit
    it's when rain sprinkles
in through the shut window

and you think of no home
you can't reach the transcendental
you can't reach up
there to care enough

the ashram is cold so are
hearts it seems

it's a virtuoso stand by a
performer and professional blue
just a passing mood
    so be *nistha*

you wanted to see the sadhu
nothing seemed to go right
and you left wondering
why Krishna left you
in material straits

now as for transcendental blue
that I don't know

you can call that if
you want
    but it's totally different
what I heard
they are fixed in spiritual
fixed on blue boy
mood indigo means
Syama on the mind and that's a pure bliss for
pure souls

no intox of this world
I sure hope my friend won't die
but we all have to
that grief goes black

but blue blue
is this world and for us, reaching up
    we know we'll make
it somehow
    when I win I can't say

but I do love the chant
and won't give up. He is
the pilot,
and we'll get out of this
funk. I'll tell you about that
another time

me I don't know nuthin'
nuthin' at all
    except what I heard
in 26th Second Avenue
I'll tell you...

pp. 73–75

Revival

We're not in this for enjoy
but it is

join together against
hard times

big band sound – better get
it your soul before
blacks out
    it's good news

go to pray
bow
down and keep away
evils

I say you are in tune
with the good a man can
do / nobody's going to like
it so much
    "old-timers"
    "I don't understand."

train / violence / I afraid

I pray
they mock
I dream
    Christ on wall
black priest
no no again I remember
    religion came to me on
Lower East Side
And I hold on to it
in ancient chant

India I nod sideways and
roll on floor
    and sweat and jive
and sing I got off on
that *kirtana*

where is time, cult, where is
Lord Caitanya
where's guru? It's all
still there

oh yeah
oh yeah. It's there you
can call it down
his mercy even when
he's apart if you call – who
can say that's not him?
Mere sentiment
Cold heads don't
know
we embrace
yeah, He's the Lord
Krishna Krishna kind
bow down praise
prasadam and fast
oh

when you thought it was over
it was still going
it was bawling a good time
is a good *kirtana*
as a blues

polite Mass
ah ah here's
grand old dance
it's made up but
what can I do as long as
they are enthusiastic

but what about *sahajiyas*?
Yeah that's possible so slow
down and sit and here's a good
basic *Srimad-Bhagavatam* lecture
    yeah, it's okay

pp. 127–30

ABOUT THE AUTHORS

Satsvarupa dasa Goswami is a writer, poet, and artist. He is also the author of Srila Prabhupada's authorized biography, *Srila Prabhupada-lilamrta*. While previously traveling, lecturing and instructing disciples worldwide, he has published many books including poems, memoirs, essays and novels.

Rev. John F. Endler is a senior Baptist minister who serves a congregation in Hartford, Connecticut.